Becoming King

Becoming King

Martin Luther King Jr. and the Making of a National Leader

Troy Jackson

Introduction by
Clayborne Carson

The University Press of Kentucky

Scholarly publisher for the Commonwealth,
serving Bellarmine University, Berea College, Centre College of Kentucky,
Eastern Kentucky University, The Filson Historical Society, Georgetown College,
Kentucky Historical Society, Kentucky State University, Morehead State University,
Murray State University, Northern Kentucky University, Transylvania University,
University of Kentucky, University of Louisville, and Western Kentucky University.
All rights reserved.

Editorial and Sales Offices: The University Press of Kentucky
663 South Limestone Street, Lexington, Kentucky 40508-4008
www.kentuckypress.com

12 11 10 09 08   5 4 3 2

Library of Congress Cataloging-in-Publication Data

Jackson, Troy, 1968–
  Becoming King : Martin Luther King, Jr. and the making of a national leader /
Troy Jackson.
    p. cm. — (Civil rights and the struggle for Black equality in the twentieth
century)
  Includes bibliographical references and index.
  ISBN 978-0-8131-2520-6 (hardcover : alk. paper)
  1. King, Martin Luther, Jr., 1929–1968. 2. African American civil rights
workers—Biography. 3. Baptists—United States—Clergy—Biography. 4. African
Americans—Civil rights—Alabama—Montgomery—History—20th century. 5.
Montgomery (Ala.)—Race relations. 6. Segregation in transportation—Alabama—
Montgomery—History—20th century. I. Title.
  E185.97.K5J343 2008
  323.092—dc22
  [B]   2008025041

This book is printed on acid-free recycled paper meeting
the requirements of the American National Standard
for Permanence in Paper for Printed Library Materials.

∞ ✪

Manufactured in the United States of America.

 Member of the Association of
American University Presses

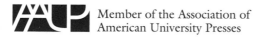

For Amanda, Jacob, Emma, and Ellie

Contents

Acknowledgments

This book reflects the valuable suggestions and recommendations of many scholars and readers. Dr. Gerald Smith's knowledge of the field helped me clearly define the scope of the work. Dr. Smith also provided detailed feedback on the entire manuscript at several points during the writing process. Many other professors from the University of Kentucky provided helpful reflections and raised important questions that helped enhance this work, including Dr. Kathi Kern, Dr. Ronald Eller, Dr. Philip Harling, Dr. Eric Christiansen, and Dr. Armando J. Prats. Lexington Theological Seminary's Dr. Jimmy L. Kirby also provided useful feedback.

Other scholars also contributed to this work, including Dr. Clayborne Carson, senior editor of the Martin Luther King Jr. Papers Project, who inspired me to take on a project that incorporated the work I had done as an editor with the King Papers Project. Dr. Carson and his wife, Susan Carson, also provided wonderful hospitality during research trips to Stanford University. Other editors with the project, including Dr. Kieran Taylor and Dr. Sue Englander, provided helpful suggestions. I am honored that the King scholar Dr. Keith Miller read the entire manuscript and offered helpful suggestions and encouragement. Theologian Dr. Curtis DeYoung of Bethel University also provided helpful feedback. Others who read and commented on the work include Brandie Atkins, Aaron Cowan, Rob Gioelli, Emily Gioelli, Les Stoneham, and Jeff Suess. Thanks to Susan Brady for her very diligent editorial work on this manuscript, and for her many helpful suggestions.

I am thankful for the support of University Christian Church, where I serve as pastor. The congregation has encouraged my academic pursuits and provided a sabbatical that allowed me to complete the bulk of my research.

My family has been supportive throughout. My wife, Amanda, has encouraged my educational pursuits throughout our marriage. This manuscript would not have been completed without Amanda's patience and perseverance. My children, Jacob, Emma, and Ellie, helped me keep my priorities in order during the writing process. My parents, Robert and Mary Jackson, encouraged my academic pursuits from an early age. Thank you to my entire family for your love and support through the years.

Introduction

What if Martin Luther King Jr. had never accepted the call to preach at Dexter Avenue Baptist Church in Montgomery? Would he have become a famed civil rights leader? Would the bus boycott movement have succeeded? How was the subsequent course of American history altered by the contingencies that brought together King and the Montgomery movement?

Although it may be difficult for those who see King as a Great Man and national icon to imagine contemporary America without taking into account his historical impact, Troy Jackson allows us to understand the evolution of King's leadership within a sustained protest movement initiated by others. Rather than diminishing King's historical significance, Jackson's revealing, insightful account of the Montgomery bus boycott invites a deeper understanding of the many unexpected and profound ways that movement transformed King as well as other participants. Jackson points out that King himself was aware of his limitations and the accidental nature of his sudden fame. Even as he rose to international prominence as spokesperson for the boycott, King often cautioned against the tendency of others to inflate his importance. "Help me, O God, to see that I'm just a symbol of a movement," he pleaded in a sermon delivered after the successful end of the boycott. "Help me to realize that I'm where I am because of the forces of history and because of the fifty thousand Negroes of Alabama who will never get their names in the papers and in the headline. O God, help me to see that where I stand today, I stand because others helped me to stand there and because the forces of history projected me there. And this moment would have come in history even if M. L. King had never been born." He added, "Because if I don't see that, I will become the biggest fool in America."[1]

Troy Jackson was a colleague of mine in the long-term effort to publish a definitive edition of *The Papers of Martin Luther King, Jr.,* and his

Becoming King builds on vast documentation that the King Papers Project has assembled since 1985, when Coretta Scott King named me to direct the project. The hundreds of thousands of documents that the project's staff examined in hundreds of archives and personal collections have illuminated not only King's life but also the lives of thousands of individuals who affected King's life and were affected by him. The third volume of *The Papers*[2] focused on the Montgomery bus boycott, but Jackson also makes effective use of the original research he contributed to volume 6, *Advocate of the Social Gospel, September 1958–March 1963*,[3] which traces the development of King's religious ideas. The latter volume brought together many of King's student papers from Crozer Theological Seminary and Boston University with a treasure trove of materials from the files that King used to prepare the sermons he delivered at Montgomery's Dexter Avenue Baptist Church, Atlanta's Ebenezer Baptist Church, and other places. These sermonic materials, which remained in the basement of King's Atlanta home for three decades after his death, provided a new window into the experiences that shaped King before his arrival in Montgomery. They also gave Jackson a sensitive understanding of how King's experiences during the boycott reshaped his identity as a social gospel minister. Jackson's years of immersion in King's papers, his background as a clergyman, and his years of in-depth research regarding the Montgomery boycott movement allow readers of *Becoming King* to comprehend the complexity and imaginative possibilities of religious biography converging with social history.

Although Jackson's study provides ample evidence to support the conviction of many of Montgomery's black residents that their movement "made" King into the leader capable of all he would later accomplish, the interaction of the man and the movement was by no means one-sided. King arrived in Montgomery with a wealth of experiences and intellectual exposure that served him well once Rosa Parks suddenly changed the course of his life. After Parks's arrest on December 1, 1955, for refusing to give up her bus seat to a white man, King was at first reluctant to assume a leading role in the boycott movement, having rejected previous entreaties to seek the presidency of the local NAACP branch. Yet Jackson shows that he was singularly well prepared to offer a kind of leadership that helped transform a local movement with limited goals—such as more polite enforcement of segregation rules—into a movement with far-reaching implications for race relations in the United States and throughout the world. The Montgomery Improvement Association (MIA) had numerous other leaders capable of mobilizing and sustaining a mass movement, and King was not being overly modest in asserting that the boycott would have happened even if he had never lived. But King's presence made a major difference in determining how the boycott would be seen by those who supported or opposed it and by those who would later contemplate its significance.

Although King was surprised when other black leaders chose him as MIA spokesperson, his hastily drafted remarks at the MIA's first mass meeting on December 5, 1955, were a remarkable example of his ability to convey the historical significance of events as they unfolded. Like his great speech at the 1963 March on Washington, King's speech at Montgomery's Holt Street Baptist Church was a compelling religious and political rationale for nonviolent resistance in pursuit of ultimate racial reconciliation. At a time when the one-day boycott had received little attention outside Montgomery and when few could have been certain that it could be continued for days or weeks (much less for 381 days!), King audaciously linked the boycott's modest initial goals to transcendent principles: "If we are wrong, the Supreme Court of this nation is wrong. If we are wrong, the Constitution of the United States is wrong. If we are wrong, God Almighty is wrong. If we are wrong, Jesus of Nazareth was merely a utopian dreamer that never came down to earth. If we are wrong, justice is a lie, love has no meaning. And we are determined here in Montgomery to work and fight until justice runs down like water and righteousness like a mighty stream."

While King assumed the crucial task of inspiring black residents, other MIA leaders were already beginning to establish the transportation alternatives that sustained the boycott. As Jackson points out, resourceful and experienced NAACP leaders such as Parks and E. D. Nixon had challenged the southern Jim Crow system years before King's arrival. Similarly, Jo Ann Robinson of Montgomery's Women's Political Council did not require King's guidance before drafting and duplicating thousands of leaflets urging residents to stay off buses. These individuals, along with others such as Ralph Abernathy, might well have gained more prominence if they had not been overshadowed by King. Still, although the boycott had already attracted overwhelming black support when he became head of the MIA, King's uplifting oratory on the first night of the boycott provided an unexpected stimulus to a mass movement already in progress. Using imagery that subtly linked the boycott to the struggle to end slavery, King's address concluded with a portentous passage that became an accurate prediction of the nascent movement's place in the long struggle for social justice: "Right here in Montgomery, when the history books are written in the future, somebody will have to say, 'There lived a race of people, a *black* people, fleecy locks and black complexion, people who had the moral courage to stand up for their rights. And thereby they injected a new meaning into the veins of history and of civilization.'"

King was neither a historian nor a civil rights lawyer, but his training and experiences as a Baptist minister gave him an inclusive, historical perspective that allowed him to understand the civil rights militancy spurred by the Supreme Court's 1954 *Brown v. Board of Education* as confirmation of his prophetic worldview. Although Jackson recognizes that King would sometimes find it difficult to translate his intellectual radicalism into civil disobedience, his sympathy for the oppressed was deeply rooted and enduring. One of King's earliest seminary papers, written when he was nineteen—seven years before the start of the Montgomery boycott—demonstrates that he was already committed to a ministry based on knowing "the problems of the people that I am pastoring." At this early stage of King's ministry, moreover, civil rights reform was only an aspect of his social gospel agenda. When King defined his pastoral mission—"I must be concerned about unemployment, slumms [*sic*], and economic insecurity"—racial segregation and discrimination were conspicuously absent from the list, which was a prescient suggestion of his antipoverty crusade two decades later.[4] Although he was undoubtedly concerned about civil rights, his basic identity as a social gospel minister was already firmly established before the *Brown* era of mass civil rights activism.

Growing up as the son of the Reverend Martin Luther King Sr., the younger King had absorbed the essentials of the social gospel at an early age. Daddy King was part of a well-established tradition of black ministers, particularly those in black-controlled churches, also providing political as well as spiritual leadership. As the younger King became aware of the dangers his father faced while advocating black voting rights and equal salaries for black schoolteachers, he came to admire his father's ability to stand up to whites—"they never attacked him physically, a fact that filled my brother and sister and me with wonder as we grew up in this tension-packed atmosphere." Such formative experiences as well as his own encounters with southern racism infused the younger King with an abhorrence of segregation, which he found "rationally inexplicable and morally unjustifiable."[5] Although as a teenager King would reject his father's biblical literalism, he would retain his admiration for a father who "set forth a noble example I didn't mind following" and whose "moral and ethical ideals" remained precious to him "even in moments of theological doubt."[6] When King accepted his call to Dexter, he cited the same social gospel credo (Luke 4:18–19) that his father had used in 1940 while advising fellow ministers regarding "the true mission of the church": "The spirit of the Lord is upon me, because he hath anointed me to preach the Gospel to the poor; he hath sent me to heal the broken-hearted, to preach deliverance to the captives, and the recovering of sight to the blind, to set at liberty them that are bruised."[7] King's conception of his social gospel mission would evolve during his years at Crozer, due in part to the considerable impact of Reinhold Niebuhr's neo-orthodox critique of liberal Christianity. He continued to seek a middle ground between Walter Rauschenbusch's social gospel optimism and Niebuhr's skepticism about human perfectibility by eclectically synthesizing "the best in liberal theology with the best in neo-orthodox theology."[8] King's underlying commitment to his social gospel ministry did not waver. Indeed, it may have been the unyielding nature of King's basic theological convictions that limited his prospects as a theologian. A scholarly synthesizer rather than an original scholar, he drew upon the ideas of more creative theologians—sometimes without attribution, and without adding many new insights of his own. He graduated from Crozer highly adept at explaining and defending his basic religious beliefs. Modern notions of historical exegesis assuaged the religious doubts of his teenage years and answered his need for religion that was "intellectually respectable as well as emotionally satisfying."[9] Similarly, his graduate studies in systematic theology at Boston University provided opportunities to incorporate the personalist theology of his mentors into his belief system. King's dissertation predictably rejected the views of theologians Paul Tillich and Henry

Nelson Wieman, who, in King's view, reduced God to an abstraction. "In God there is feeling and will, responsive to the deepest yearnings of the human heart; this God both evokes and answers prayers," King concluded.[10]

Although King's academic writings would provide a scholarly gloss for his oratory in Montgomery, it was in King's personal correspondence and his early sermons that he first expressed forcefully the social gospel vision that distinguished his leadership during the bus boycott and afterward. In particular, King's correspondence with Coretta Scott during their courtship in Boston reveals that he expected a major social transformation extending beyond civil rights reform. Because King was attracted to Scott partly because of her political involvement—she had been a Progressive Party activist during the 1948 election and involved in pacifist causes at Antioch College—he was able to confide to her his own radical leanings. "I imagine you already know that I am much more socialistic in my economic theory than capitalistic," he wrote in a July 1952 letter prompted by Scott's gift of Edward Bellamy's socialistic fantasy *Looking Backward 2000–1887* (originally published in 1888). King asserted confidently that capitalism had "outlived its usefulness," having "brought about a system that takes necessities from the masses to give luxuries to the classes." King added that the change "would be evolutionary rather than revolutionary. This, it seems to me, is the most sane and ethical way for social change to take place." Although the public expression of such thoughts would have been political heresy, King informed his future wife that both capitalism and communism were inconsistent with true Christian values. Even Bellamy was faulted for failing "to see that man is a sinner . . . and will still be a sinner until he submits to his life to the Grace of God. Ultimately our problem is [a?] theological one." Cautioning Scott against excessive optimism, King observed: "It is probably true that capitalism is on its death bed, but social systems have a way of developing a long and powerful death bed breathing capacity. Remember it took feudalism more than 500 years to pass out from its death bed. Capitalism will be in America quite a few more years my dear."

King was not quite so candid in his sermons as in his letters to Scott, but the sermons he delivered while assisting his father at Ebenezer during the summer of 1953 (soon after his marriage in June) viewed racial segregation and discrimination in the context of a wide-ranging critique of the modern world and as aspects of a global struggle for peace with social justice. Several of these sermons focused criticism on modernity's "false Gods"—science, nationalism, and materialism. Sharply criticizing American chauvinism and anticommunism, King offered blunt advice: "One cannot worship this false god of nationalism and the God of Christianity at the same time."[11] In another sermon King prepared that summer, he insisted international peace was the "cry that is ringing in the ears of the peoples of the world," but such peace could be achieved only when Christians "place righteousness first. So long as we place our selfish economic gains first we will never have peace. So long as the nations of the world are contesting to see which can be the most [imperialistic] we will [never] have peace. Indeed the deep rumbling of discontent in our world today on the part of the masses is [actually] a revolt against imperialism, economic exploitation, and colonialism that has been perpetuated by western civilization for all these many years."[12]

King's comprehensive Christian worldview was perhaps most evident in the sermon "Communism's Challenge to Christianity," which he delivered in August 1953 and, in various forms, later in his life. While rejecting communism as secularistic and materialistic, King nonetheless insisted that communism was "Christianity's most formidable competitor and only serious rival." Marxian thought, King argued, should challenge Christians to express their own "passionate concern for social justice." Returning to the passage in the book of Luke that his father had used thirteen years earlier, King argued, "The Christian ought always to begin with a bias in favor of a movement which protests against the unfair treatment of the poor, for surely Christianity is itself such a protest." Karl Marx could hardly be blamed for calling religion an opiate of the masses, King lamented. "When religion becomes [so] involved in a future good 'over yonder' that it forgets the present evils 'over here' it is a dry as dust religion and needs to be condemned."[13]

Less than a year after King delivered his sermon on communism, he accepted the call to become the pastor of the Dexter congregation and began to refine his unique leadership style. Jackson assesses the strengths and the limitations of this leadership, noting, for example, that King's global prophetic vision ensured his prominence but sometimes obscured the pressing, prosaic concerns of the working-class MIA members who had regularly ridden buses and thus sacrificed the most on a daily basis during the boycott. Vernon Johns, King's sometimes abrasive predecessor at Dexter, actually focused his ministry more than did King on the economic issues that were central to Christian social gospel. King, for his part, pushed gently yet consistently against complacency after becoming pastor of a congregation known to be difficult to control. Wary of the power of the church's deacons, King used his acceptance address as an occasion to assert his spiritual authority and to suggest the immensity of the task ahead. Only twenty-five, he challenged his mostly older congregation to expand their vision: "It is a significant fact that I come to the pastorate of Dexter at the most crucial hour of our world's history; at a time when the flame of war might arise at any time to redden the skies of our dark and dreary world; at a time when men know all [too] well that without the proper guidance the whole of civilization can be plunged across the abyss of destruction. . . . Dexter, like all other churches, must somehow lead men and women of a decadent generation to the high mountain of peace and salvation."

That some Dexter members welcomed King's ambitious agenda would become evident during the bus boycott, but it is nonetheless worth noting that King not only encouraged church members to become registered voters and NAACP leaders but also to see the southern Jim Crow system as part of a passing global order of colonialism and imperialism. In the aftermath of the Supreme Court's *Brown* decision of May 1954, King became even more convinced that segregation was doomed, unless, as he warned in an address the following year to Montgomery's NAACP branch, black Americans became "victims to the cult of inevitable progress." King also warned against becoming "so complacent that we forget the struggles of other minorities. We must unite with oppressed minorities throughout the world."[14] As Rosa Parks listened to King's address, she might well have been encouraged to take her own stand against complacency less than six months later. King's words undoubtedly inspired black leaders who shared his sense that the southern Jim Crow system was a vulnerable anachronism. Soon after King spoke, he was invited to join the branch's executive committee.

Thus, the decision to elect King to head the MIA was unexpected, but the qualities of mind that King demonstrated in his early ministry were well suited to the role of being the principal spokesperson of the boycott movement. His subsequent decade of civil rights leadership was, in some respects, a departure from his original social gospel mission, but only to the extent that he necessarily narrowed his focus to the southern issues of segregation and racial barriers to voting. Seen from the perspective of his entire ministry, the years from Montgomery to the signing of the Voting Rights Act of 1965 were a time during which he felt compelled to play down the radicalism of his social gospel Christianity. To be sure, during his entire public life, he would often describe the African American freedom struggle in the context of African and Asian anticolonial struggles, and he would often draw attention to the issue of international peace. But only toward the end of this decade of civil rights reform did these broader concerns become a central part of his message, as it was in his rarely heard Nobel lecture following his acceptance of the Nobel Peace Prize in December 1964. Only after the Voting Rights bill had been enacted did King make clear that even this landmark reform did not fulfill his dream. Only then would he return to his social gospel mission of achieving economic justice, bringing his ministry to Chicago and then Memphis as part of the Poor People's Campaign. Only then, to the consternation of those who saw him merely as a civil rights leader, would he speak out unambiguously against war, imperialism, and militarism.

It is worthwhile to speculate regarding what would have happened to King if he had not accepted the call to Dexter or if he had not been selected to head the MIA. If not for Rosa Parks, he might not have become the preeminent African American of his era or a Nobel laureate or have his birth commemorated with a national holiday. It is also likely that, if not for King's role in the Montgomery bus boycott, the contributions of grassroots activists in Montgomery and other protest centers would be remembered differently. Jackson suggests, moreover, that King's oratorical brilliance may have fostered his rise to international prominence while also diminishing his ability to sustain a mass movement. Not until the Birmingham campaign of 1963 would King experience a similar degree of success in mobilizing an entire black community. By acknowledging that the bus boycott had only a limited impact on the lives of Montgomery's black working class, *Becoming King* is a necessary corrective to romanticized versions of civil rights progress and Great Man historical myths.

Yet Jackson also reminds us that historic social movements provide opportunities for some men and women of all classes and backgrounds to rise unexpectedly to greatness.

Having acknowledged the importance of contingency in King's emergence as a leader, he demonstrates that King's prophetic vision encouraged others to see their resistance to injustice as more historically significant than would otherwise have been the case. Because of King, the African American freedom struggle gained a historical significance it would otherwise have lacked. The Montgomery bus boycott would have happened without King, but King's oratory helped to ensure that the boycott became one of those exceptional local movements for justice that would send ripples of inspiration to oppressed people elsewhere.

Clayborne Carson

Notes

1. King, "Conquering Self-Centeredness," August 11, 1957.

2. *Birth of a New Age, December 1955–December 1956,* ed. Clayborne Carson, Stewart Burns, Susan Carson, Peter Holloran, and Dana L. H. Powell (Berkeley and Los Angeles: University of California Press, 1997).

3. Ed. Clayborne Carson, Susan Carson, Susan Englander, Troy Jackson, and Gerald L. Smith (Berkeley and Los Angeles: University of California Press, 2007).

4. King, "Preaching Ministry" [September 14–November 24, 1948], in *Papers of Martin Luther King, Jr.,* 6: 72.

5. Clayborne Carson, ed., *The Autobiography of Martin Luther King, Jr.* (New York: Warner Books, 1998), 5.

6. Ibid., 16.

7. Quote in introduction to *Papers of Martin Luther King, Jr.,* vol. 1, *Called to Serve, January 1929–June 1951,* ed. Clayborne Carson, Ralph E. Luker, and Penny A. Russell (Berkeley and Los Angeles: University of California Press, 1992), 33–34.

8. King, "How Modern Christians Should Think of Man," November 29, 1949–February 15, 1950, in *Papers,* 1: 274.

9. Carson, ed., *Autobiography,* 15.

10. King, "A Comparison of the Conceptions of God in the Thinking of Paul Tillich and Henry Nelson Wieman," April 15, 1955, in *Papers,* 2: 512.

11. King, "The False God of Nationalism," July 12, 1953, in *Papers,* 6: 132.

12. King, "First Things First," August 2, 1953, in *Papers,* 6: 144–45.

13. King, "Communism's Challenge to Christianity," August 9, 1953, in *Papers,* 6: 148–49.

14. King, "The Peril of Superficial Optimism in the Area of Race Relations," June 19, 1955, in *Papers,* 6: 215.

Prologue

> The history books may write it Rev. King was born in Atlanta, and then came to Montgomery, but we feel that he was born in Montgomery in the struggle here, and now he is moving to Atlanta for bigger responsibilities.
> —Member of Dexter Avenue Baptist Church, November 1959

Every year in elementary school classrooms throughout the United States, teachers share heroic stories that took place in Montgomery, Alabama, during the 1950s. Young children learn about the arrest of Rosa Parks, the boycott of Montgomery city buses, and the emergence of a young Baptist preacher named Martin Luther King Jr. One doesn't have to be a historian to know the significant role the Montgomery movement played in the emergence of a broader civil rights struggle during the 1950s and 1960s. Although historians have written countless books covering the life and career of Martin Luther King, while others have contributed dozens of studies that cover aspects of the civil rights movement in Montgomery, a narrative recounting the important influence of this community on King's career and civil rights leadership has yet to be written.[1]

Brave white and black activists of Montgomery had a significant impact on King's leadership. Not only did a handful of courageous men and women in Montgomery spearhead a protest movement; they also nurtured, influenced, and helped launch King's public ministry. A closer examination of the Montgomery movement reveals how a young English professor at Alabama State University (Jo Ann Robinson) and a middle-aged Pullman porter (E. D. Nixon) played a larger role in King's civil rights leadership than a white theologian like Reinhold Niebuhr or a global leader like Mahatma Gandhi. This book demonstrates how Montgomery and her people provided the true birthplace of Martin Luther King's civil rights leadership.[2]

In an essay published over a decade ago, Charles Payne argued that the story of the Montgomery movement needed to be retold. Contrary to the top-down, King-centered narrative of the boycott, Payne suggested that "Montgomery was largely a willed phenomenon, a history made by everyday people who were willing to do their spadework, not one shaped entirely by impersonal social forces or great individual leadership." Asserting that many studies were "more theatrical than instructive," he charged that "the popular conception of Montgomery—a tired woman refused to give up her seat and a prophet rose up to lead the grateful masses—is a good story but useless history." This book attempts to be both a good story and useful history by emphasizing the contributions of many men and women, black and white, to Montgomery's local struggle.[3]

A more in-depth analysis of Montgomery in the 1950s demands a significant examination of the very real class differences in the African American community. Most local black leaders prior to the boycott believed the masses were passive and unwilling to get involved in any significant effort to bring change to their city. The rapid and nearly unanimous response by the working class to the call for a bus boycott contradicts this assessment. In reality, most blacks who organized to dismantle segregation were professionals who did not really know much about the daily lives or the thoughts of their town's working-class blacks. By contrast, E. D. Nixon was a local leader who knew the so-called "black masses" in his city. Nixon worked for decades to improve the conditions facing African American laborers in Montgomery. He coupled a passion for overcoming segregation with a zeal for economic justice. He was not simply seeking an end to racial discrimination; he also sought justice in the courtrooms and economic opportunities that would extend to all of the black community.

Conditions on city buses galvanized African American leaders and professionals along with the working class, resulting in an incredibly effective thirteen-month protest. Black professionals were ready to organize in an effort to win an ideological battle against white supremacy by insisting whites treat their race with dignity. Working-class people who actually rode the buses each day were tired of the abuse and mistreatment they experienced directly. The people were ready to act, and their protest captured the attention of the nation and the world. A year later, they celebrated the end of segregated buses in Montgomery.

Most studies of Montgomery and the broader civil rights movement tend to leave the city's struggle behind after the conclusion of the boycott and the launching of the Southern Christian Leadership Conference. Even works that take very seriously the contributions of many local men and women years before the boycott do not explore what happened in the city between 1957 and the end of the decade. This book, however, examines the lack of a sustained movement and the absence of economic gains after the dawn of integrated buses. Although King gained a great deal from his experiences in Montgomery, the city itself remained segregated and racially repressive long after King returned to Atlanta. King friend and Alabama State College professor Lawrence Reddick claimed a year after the boycott that the true test of success for Montgomery was not "found in what it has done for the Negro community in this city" but rather through its "positive national and international effect." The Montgomery movement provided a stepping-stone for a growing national civil rights movement, but its sustained local impact on the daily lives of black citizens from all socioeconomic classes was minimal.[4]

King's role, influence, and development remain an important part of the Montgomery story and the broader civil rights movement. While many more studies of local struggles are essential, there is also a need for the leaders and institutions of the movement to be understood through the lens of local communities. Glenn Eskew, in his work on the freedom struggle in Birmingham, includes a reexamination of King from the perspective of the people who participated in perhaps the most significant campaign of the era. In this book, instead of viewing Montgomery through the lens of King's leadership, his leadership is explored through the lens of the civil rights struggle in Montgomery. Such an approach underscores King's ability to connect with the educated and the unlettered, professionals and the working class. This also allows for a sharper critique of the shortcomings of King's leadership following the bus protest, limitations he would not address until the last few years of his life. As the boycott came to an end, King's inner circle began to be dominated by clergy and a few college professors who turned their focus to voter registration efforts and better recreation facilities. E. D. Nixon's concern for sustained economic development and job creation was left behind, as was the original boycott demand for black bus drivers. Although King maintained an ability to listen to and speak the language of the working class, following the boycott his approach to the freedom struggle was defined more by professionals and clergy than by working-class activists.[5]

By examining King's activities after the boycott through the lens of Montgomery, one sees how he slowly disengaged from the local struggle. While maintaining symbolic leadership as the president of the Montgomery Improvement Association, King's energies drifted more and more to the broader regional struggle. Elevated to national prominence by the success of the boycott, King used his impressive resume, oratorical gifts, and tactical skills to contribute to other local movements. He would never again be as intimately connected to local activists as he was in Montgomery. His elevated status led to criticisms of his leadership, with members of the Student Nonviolent Coordinating Committee referring to King derisively as "de Lawd" by 1962. Five years earlier, King had already begun to disengage from the only local movement to which he had a true grassroots connection. The strong pull of the regional and national platform eclipsed his efforts in Montgomery, where due to white intransigence and violence as well as reemerging divisions within the black community, moving forward proved tedious and tiring. By understanding the more complete story of Montgomery, one gains a better understanding of the strengths and limitations of King's civil rights leadership.[6]

The local movement also demonstrates the indispensable contributions of women in the struggle for civil rights. Many early histories of the civil rights era emphasized the significance of male leaders while failing to recognize the efforts of female leaders. Jo Ann Robinson's memoir on the Montgomery movement helped correct this omission. *Women in the Civil Rights Movement,* a volume of essays published in the early 1990s, furthered the effort to emphasize the critical contributions of women like Robinson, Rosa Parks, Fannie Lou Hamer, Mary Fair Burks, and Ella Baker. A close look at Montgomery from 1948 to 1960 continues this important effort by demonstrating not only the significance of white and black women to the local struggle, but also the influence they had on King's development.[7]

Scholars have recognized the church-based and religious roots of the civil rights movement for decades. Many of the leaders were black clergy; mass meetings tended to take place in local congregations; and one of the leading organizations pushing for social change in the South was the Southern Christian Leadership Conference. Recent studies have explored in greater depth the way religion, theology, and the church helped inspire and define the struggle. By examining the earliest sermons and religious writings of King before, during, and after the boycott, this work highlights the significant and sustained theological underpinnings that help explain why King had the influence and following that he did. King's optimistic, hope-filled message rooted in the power of God inspired men and women to remain in and sacrifice for the struggle. His consistent emphasis on the love ethic found in the life and teachings of Jesus provided the theological undergirding for the strategy of nonviolence. King's growing faith in God also fueled his conviction that the civil rights movement could become a vehicle for redemption in Montgomery, the South, and throughout the nation.[8]

As a Baptist minister, King delivered sermons that provide an excellent window into his thought and development as a leader. Through the Martin Luther King Jr. Papers Project, hundreds of King's early homiletic manuscripts, outlines, and recorded sermons are now available to researchers through the publication of their latest volume. These religious writings demonstrate more clearly the theological commitments King brought to Montgomery. King's oratorical skills coupled with a passionate commitment to the power of love and the centrality of the social gospel allowed him to be the ideal spokesperson and leader for the Montgomery movement. Years before the boycott, King was already regularly addressing issues of race, segregation, peace, and economic injustice from the pulpit. The core of King's message stayed consistent throughout his adult life. By 1954, King and Montgomery were ready for each other.[9]

Montgomery demonstrates that King's sermons and speeches became most poignant when accompanied by direct action, something he was willing to participate in, but not something he ever initiated. Taylor Branch, in his three-part series on King's public career, concludes that King's inclination was to inspire social change through oratory. Following the bus boycott, he was unsure where the movement should go next, and "under these conditions, oratory grew upon him like a narcotic." Unable to effectively transfer the model of the bus boycott to address other local challenges or broader regional injustice, King replaced nonviolent direct action with public speaking. Branch concludes that "this conversion approach had brought King the orator's nectar—applause, admiration, and credit for quite a few tearful if temporary changes of heart—but in everyday life Negroes remained a segregated people, invisible or menial specimens except for celebrity aberrations such as King himself." Following the boycott, it was not until the advent of the sit-in movement, the formation of the Student Nonviolent Coordinating Committee (SNCC), and the demonstration of courage by the Freedom Riders that the civil rights movement became a national phenomenon. These and subsequent local movements, buttressed by King's oratory and symbolic leadership, transformed the civil rights struggle into a regional civil rights movement that changed a nation. Without the courage and sacrifice of countless men and women from Montgomery to Greensboro and from Nashville to Birmingham, King's "I have a dream" speech would have fallen on deaf ears. King's oratory had its full potency only when accompanied by concrete engagement.[10]

The March on Washington was not the first time King learned both the limits and possibilities of the spoken word. King's first oratorical triumph, his Holt Street address delivered on the first day of the boycott, emerged only because of the fifty thousand African Americans who did not ride Montgomery's buses that day. In the speech, King claimed that the people gathered at Holt Street Baptist Church "because of our deep-seated belief that democracy transformed from thin paper to thick action is the greatest form of government on earth." King experienced the power of oratory coupled with "thick action" first in Montgomery.[11]

When King's sermons at Dexter Avenue Baptist Church between 1954 and 1960 are put in conversation with historical events chronicled through numerous oral histories, newspaper articles, and archival material, they reveal a growing passion, urgency, and faith forged in the midst of struggle. The fortitude of Montgomery activists such as E. D. Nixon, Jo Ann Robinson, Rufus Lewis, Mary Fair Burks, and Rosa Parks had a significant impact on King's early public ministry. Local grassroots leaders helped refine King's early experiences as they joined together in a prolonged struggle against white supremacy.

This study is structured chronologically. Chapter 1 examines the story of Montgomery from 1948 to 1953, demonstrating that years before King arrived in the Alabama capital, several black and white men and women were challenging segregation and white supremacy in their city. Chapter 2 explores King's ministry and theological development before he became pastor of Dexter Avenue Baptist Church. By the time he preached his first sermon at Dexter, King had already crafted a socially engaged understanding of Christianity that would form the heart of the social gospel he would preach throughout his public ministry. Chapter 3 reviews King's tenure in Montgomery prior to the bus boycott. He joined many in the city who, as Rosa Parks put it, were "hoping to make a contribution to the fulfillment of complete freedom for all people." Through involvement in the NAACP and his activities as pastor of Dexter, King supported the local movement before the boycott began.[12]

The fourth chapter concerns the first two months of the boycott, concluding with the bombing of King's home on January 30, 1956. Chapter 5 explores how King and the broader community responded to threats, violence, and legal maneuvers over the last ten months of the boycott. The sixth chapter examines how King gradually turned his attention away from Montgomery during his last three years at Dexter. By the time King departed the city, his focus had shifted to the national stage, to a struggle bigger than Montgomery.

Many of those who predated King in Montgomery faced difficult days as the local movement faltered. In the final analysis, the bus boycott did more for King and the emerging national civil rights movement than it did for the broader African American community in Montgomery. King took the lessons of Montgomery with him, as their courage, activism, and sacrifice prepared him for the many battles that awaited him. In the crucible of Montgomery, Martin Luther King Jr. was becoming King the civil rights leader.

1 "The Stirring of the Water"

I think the Negroes are stirring and they won't be held down much
longer.
                                            —Virginia Durr, 1951

Racially integrated events rarely occurred in Montgomery, but for several years both whites and blacks gathered together at the city's spacious
Cramton Bowl for an Easter sunrise celebration. Segregated seating applied at the municipal arena, but the all-white planning committee worked
to include African American preachers in the program as they developed
the service. Typically a black minister delivered a prayer and an African
American choral group from a local school led the audience in a few traditional spirituals while whites presented the balance of the program, including the sermon. The 1952 gathering proved to be the last, however.
Despite steady rainfall, city bus drivers found it more convenient to drop
off their black passengers several blocks from the entrance to the event.
Even if the weather had not dampened spirits, the discourteous treatment
they experienced at the hands of the bus drivers certainly did. Some did
not stay for the service, and many more lobbied their ministers to put
together all-black sunrise services in the future. Portia Trenholm, the wife
of the president of Alabama State College, claimed this was "the very first
spontaneous protest as a result of discourteous treatment on the buses."
The following year the black clergy bowed out of the planning process,
and African Americans attended a separate sunrise service on the Alabama
State College campus.[1]
    This act of protest on the part of the black citizenry of Montgomery
reveals their willingness to act collectively to resist mistreatment at the
hands of white bus drivers. While this action may have seemed inconsequential at the time, it demonstrates a discernible spirit of resistance
among African Americans in the city by the middle of the twentieth cen-

tury. Years before Martin Luther King Jr. arrived in Montgomery, a handful of whites and many blacks shared a growing dissatisfaction with the
racial status quo. Several were already hard at work testing strategies of
resistance to segregation.

The ranks of those questioning and even challenging Montgomery's
racial mores near the middle of the twentieth century were diverse. While
demeaning experiences due to segregation concerned the entire African
American community, leaders broadened their civil rights agenda to include broader economic concerns. Specifically, Dexter Avenue pastor Vernon Johns, Pullman porter E. D. Nixon, and seamstress Rosa Parks not
only challenged the physical markers of white supremacy evidenced by
segregation, but also questioned the more insidious and diffuse economic
oppression that gravely influenced the lives of poor and working-class
African Americans. While their agendas were not uniform, several men
and women had already decided their days of quiet submission under
segregation were over years before King ever set foot in the city. Though
their methods and philosophies differed, several were actively stirring the
waters in Montgomery.[2]

Montgomery sits on the Alabama River in the heart of the Black
Belt, a land with rich soil, a heritage of bountiful cotton crops, and a
legacy of slavery. In addition to its role as a major marketplace for the sale
and distribution of cotton, the city also serves as the state capital. The
community's investment in the institution of slavery made it a hotbed of
southern political maneuvering following the election of Abraham Lincoln. When southern voices arguing for secession from the United States
prevailed, Montgomery was chosen to host a convention of slave states.
Following the Civil War, the city continued to depend upon cotton from
hinterland plantations to fuel the economy. Many former slaves transi-
tioned to either tenant farming or sharecropping, and as a result cotton
production remained the economic bellwether for the region. Thanks
to a combination of state government jobs and the region's rich agri-
cultural land, Montgomery did not aggressively pursue industrialization.
The city's economy during the twentieth century was shaped more by
advances in aviation than in industrialization.[3]

A few years after their first flight, Wilbur and Orville Wright searched
for a place to train prospective pilots during the colder winter months.

They selected a site on the outskirts of Montgomery, which became known as Maxwell Field. While the training school was relatively short-lived, aviation remained a permanent feature of the city's economy. Over the coming decades, Montgomery became home to two air force bases, introducing a reliance on the federal government into the local economy.[4]

The increase in military personnel reshaped the city's job market and demographics. Following the Civil War, African Americans outnumbered whites until around 1910, by which time whites had pulled even with blacks. The white population continued to grow more rapidly over the next forty years, resulting in a 1950 population of more than 110,000, with roughly 60 percent white. This increase can be attributed to an influx of working-class whites who greatly reshaped municipal politics as the old political machine slowly lost control of the city. The military employed hundreds of Montgomery's new residents, who had no ties to historically elite families that had monopolized local political power. The city leaders' failure to attract and develop major manufacturing further weakened their hold. The populist Dave Birmingham capitalized on this growing distrust of political leaders in his 1953 campaign for a seat on the city commission. He went so far as to accuse politicians and city fathers of poisoning the city water supply, a claim that resonated with the suspicions of some of the town's newer residents. With the support of an effective alliance of a few registered African Americans and the white working class, Birmingham shocked the establishment with his election to the city commission. New political realities were but one indication that the city was undergoing significant social change.[5]

The economy and social structure of Montgomery depended upon the affordable service labor of the region's African American men and women. In the late 1950s, Baptist minister Ralph Abernathy estimated that service-oriented occupations accounted for 75–80 percent of the African American workforce. Approximately two-thirds of the black women in the area found employment as domestic workers. The lack of alternative industrial jobs significantly limited their earning potential. According to the 1950 U.S. Census, the median family income for African Americans in Montgomery in 1949 was $908, while in Birmingham, where the availability of industrial jobs bolstered the earning power of black residents, the median income was $1,609. While a small percentage of the city's black population held professional jobs, primarily in the education field or the military, the lack of industrial jobs made the gap between the classes in Montgomery's African American community particularly acute. The limited economy contributed to the stifling experience of life under white control for many of the city's African Americans.[6]

Kathy Dunn Jackson, who grew up in Montgomery during the 1940s and 1950s, still remembers the dehumanizing treatment she received when she had to have her tonsils and adenoids removed as a young child. Since there were no African American ear, nose, and throat doctors in the city, she had to have her surgery at St. Margaret's Hospital, which did not allow blacks to have a room in the main building following their surgery. Instead, hospital orderlies moved Jackson to a room shared with all the hospital's black patients in a small house behind the hospital. In follow-up visits with her doctor, she had to wait in a "colored" waiting room that doubled as a janitorial closet. Jackson's memories are indicative of the dehumanizing events that were all too common in Montgomery during the decade following World War II.[7]

Given the insidious nature of Montgomery's racism and segregation, it appeared that white supremacy was firmly in place. Further examination, however, reveals the presence of subtle changes in racial mores. A front-page article in the *Alabama Tribune* indicated "race plates" (a practice whereby a letter *C* was placed next to names of African Americans) would be dropped from the Montgomery phone directory. The rationale for the change, according to a company representative, was "to avoid discrimination against Negro people." He indicated that all married women, regardless of race, would be given the title "MRS." before their names. In addition to this symbolic change, significant services for African Americans also expanded. Montgomery established two black high schools: Booker T. Washington and George Washington Carver High. St. Jude's Hospital opened, marking the first hospital for blacks in the city. Local white leaders provided these expanding services for African Americans within the framework of white supremacy and segregation. While easier access to quality medical care and education directly enhanced the daily lives of Montgomery's African American citizens, these services did not ameliorate the dehumanizing pall of segregation and economic marginalization they continued to face. Even though President Harry S. Truman's

1948 Executive Order integrating the armed forces provided an oasis of growing inclusion at Maxwell Air Force Base, African Americans who worked there returned each evening to a segregated southern city.[8]

As Montgomery's African Americans gained access to additional community services and institutions, their challenges to overt racism expanded. Protests following incidents of police brutality even led a few whites to question unwarranted violence by police against African Americans. When Montgomery police mercilessly beat an African American, Robert Felder, so severely that he was hospitalized for several weeks, his white employer took the unusual step of reporting the incident to the press. Police chief Ralph B. King dismissed the officers involved, but he paid a price for his diligence. Bowing to public pressure, the city commissioners forced Chief King to retire. A few years later, the police arrested Gertrude Perkins on a charge of public drunkenness. Rather than transporting her to the police station, the arresting officers took her to a remote location where they raped her. When the incident came to light, police chief Carlisle E. Johnstone vigorously pursued harsh reprimands and even the prosecution of the officers involved. Once again, the city commission did not back their police chief. The mayor accused the NAACP of fabricating the whole story, and police records were altered to protect the identities of the accused rapists. When city authorities ignored his recommendations, Chief Johnstone began searching for a job in another community and soon left the city.[9]

Police brutality against African Americans went even further one hot August afternoon, when an intoxicated World War II veteran named Hilliard Brooks attempted to ride a Montgomery bus. Driver C. L. Hood would not allow him to board, but Brooks refused to back down and unleashed a string of obscenities. When the police officer M. E. Mills arrived on the scene, he pushed Brooks to the ground and fired a fatal shot when Brooks scrambled to get back up. Alabama State professor Jo Ann Robinson recalled that Brooks simply got "out of place" with the bus driver and paid the ultimate price. Following a protest by friends of Brooks, a police review board found the officer's actions justified, an assessment endorsed by the mayor. While a few whites and many African Americans questioned the violence and abuse visited upon African Americans, city officials continued to sanction excessive force by police officers.

Those rare local white leaders willing to voice concerns and challenge the racial status quo did not last long in Montgomery. African American acts of resistance seemed to be making little headway. Still, the challenges themselves demonstrate the willingness of some to take risks to challenge white supremacy.[10]

Despite the persistence of racial repression, black institutions of higher learning remained a vibrant force in the region. Tuskegee Institute, a black normal school just thirty miles east of Montgomery, was founded by Booker T. Washington in 1881. Under his leadership, the school focused on industrial education while attempting to accommodate the wishes of southern white authorities to maintain a segregated society. The faculty of the school became part of a small but growing black middle class in the region. By the 1930s, the advent of the automobile had dramatically reduced the travel time between Tuskegee and the state capital, allowing the school's faculty to become regular visitors to Montgomery for shopping and cultural events.[11]

Alabama State College (ASC), which sat right in the heart of Montgomery, had an even greater influence on the city. Originally a normal school located in Marian, Alabama, the institution moved to Montgomery in 1886. By the middle of the twentieth century, the college had nearly two thousand students and employed two hundred faculty and staff members. ASC's president was H. Councill Trenholm, who at the age of twenty-five succeeded his father in 1925. Under his leadership through 1961, the school grew from a junior college to a four-year institution, and began to bestow graduate degrees in 1940. Trenholm worked to carefully balance fidelity to the concerns of African Americans with the expectations of the white government officials who helped fund the school. On the twenty-fifth anniversary of his presidency, Professor Jo Ann Robinson penned a letter of congratulations to Trenholm: "It is my belief that true greatness can be measured only in terms of services one renders to humanity. If this is any criterion, you are one of the few *truly great* and I respect and admire you for it."[12]

Careful to avoid controversy, Trenholm earned the admiration of blacks and whites. His stewardship of ASC provided a haven for educated African American leaders in Montgomery. Many of the employees at ASC knew their jobs were tied to state government subsidies of their school.

Most followed Trenholm's lead in cautiously interacting with white leaders, as they sought to better their lives and social standing through compromise. ASC employees and graduates helped provide Montgomery with a growing black middle-class community.

In addition to black colleges, the NAACP had been active since the institution of a local chapter in 1918. The following year, the state chapter met in the basement of Dexter Avenue Baptist Church in an effort to get state authorities to take a strong stand against lynching and to improve educational opportunities for blacks. The NAACP was also active in voter registration efforts, and the organization served to bring together many seeking racial justice in the Montgomery area, including a Pullman porter named E. D. Nixon. As a member of the Brotherhood of Sleeping Car Porters under the leadership of A. Philip Randolph, Nixon earned a reputation as a tireless fighter for justice and social change. He also became the person to whom working-class blacks went when they had significant issues with the courts or local government officials. The Montgomery chapter of the NAACP, however, was more often than not dominated by moderate professional blacks who preferred a cautious approach to racial advancement. As one local resident noted, the organization was actively involved in the community, "but not very much really to get down to the masses of the people—just the top layer of the Negroes." Many ASC faculty and a few local clergy participated in the local chapter, resulting in an organization that relied on a deliberate legal strategy that was largely nonconfrontational.[13]

During the mid 1940s, the local NAACP elections proved to be a battlefield as segments of the African American community competed with one another for control of this significant civil rights organization. In December 1944, Nixon decided to run for president of the local chapter, facing Robert Matthews, who worked for Pilgrim Insurance Company. Matthews won the election by just a few votes, prompting Nixon to compose a letter of protest to Walter White in the NAACP national office. According to Nixon, Matthews triumphed through illegal means, stuffing the ballot box with the ballots of fellow employees of Pilgrim Insurance who only showed up once a year for the election. Although indignant over how the election was conducted, Nixon claimed his true concern was for the people of Montgomery, as Matthews was not "qualified for the office" and "is afraid to oppose white people when he knows that they are wrong." Unlike Matthews, others in the city were laboring to bring change and reform: "all the work that has been done in Montgomery for the pass [*sic*] year was done by Mr. W. G. Porter [NAACP vice president], Mrs. Rosa L. Parks, and myself." In a handwritten postscript to the typed letter, Nixon shared what his platform would have included had he been elected, emphasizing that under his leadership the NAACP would be "a branch for the people."[14]

Apparently many of Nixon's concerns regarding Mr. Matthews's leadership had merit. Donald Jones, a NAACP national representative, visited the city in May 1945. Following his visit, Jones composed a letter to Ella Baker, who was serving as the director of branches for the NAACP. Jones concluded that "the Branch is in a bad way due to a lack of competent leadership not only in the Branch, but apparently in the community as a whole. Usually in a Branch there is at least one individual who stands out, sometimes in the Branch setup and sometimes in opposition; but in Montgomery I found nobody who seemed to have the capacity to do a job." Jones called Matthews "hopeless" and observed that "besides being incompetent he's disinterested. The main reason for his being president, it seems, is because he works for the Pilgrim Insurance Company there which has had one of its personal [*sic*] always as president for the last several terms, obviously for prestige purposes." The leadership of the NAACP in Montgomery had been reduced to part of a patronage system controlled by a particularly powerful African American–owned business. Nixon's concerns about the effectiveness of the branch were warranted.[15]

Nixon was determined to win the next election for the presidency of the NAACP, and began appealing to potential new members to support his candidacy. He attempted to persuade potential members by calling for "a more militant N.A.A.C.P. in Montgomery, because we need a program to offer the people, because we need to return the N.A.A.C.P. to the people as their organization." Nixon planned an organizational meeting for October 11, nearly two months before the election, to plan strategy. In a handwritten note at the bottom of one of his form letters, he asked NAACP vice president W. G. Porter to ask Ella Baker for five hundred new membership envelopes as he expected to "need these in my campaign."

In what was described as the best turnout for an election in many years, Nixon was elected as the new president. For a few years, the local chapter of the NAACP was under leadership that represented the working-class African Americans in the city. During his tenure as president, Nixon relied on a member of the working class as his secretary, a local seamstress named Rosa Parks.[16]

Born and raised near Montgomery, Parks attended a NAACP meeting after seeing a picture of her former schoolmate, Mrs. Johnnie Carr, next to a story about the NAACP in a local paper. When Parks arrived at the meeting, not only was her old friend absent, but Parks was the only woman in attendance. The men soon nominated and elected her secretary of the chapter. Parks later recalled: "I was too timid to say no. I just started taking minutes." She began working with Nixon, and supported his leadership of the local and state chapters of the NAACP. She also helped establish and lead the local NAACP Youth Council. When Nixon lost the presidency of the chapter, she took a two-year break from the organization, although she continued to volunteer her time to assist Nixon. After long days working as a seamstress at Crittenden's Tailor Shop in Montgomery, she would spend the early evening completing essential office tasks for Nixon, who had begun to focus on other activities after his tenure as NAACP president in the late 1940s. Parks was a respectable member of the African American community who worked hard to support her family financially while at the same time laboring tirelessly, often in tandem with Nixon, to bring substantive change to the racial climate in her city.[17]

E. D. Nixon led several local organizations over the years, including the Citizens Overall Committee, an attempt to unite Montgomery's African Americans to address community challenges. He traced his drive to fight for civil rights to a meeting with the mayor of Montgomery during the 1920s, in which Nixon raised concerns about the safety of a drainage ditch in the city that had recently claimed the lives of two young African American boys. The mayor was not pleased that Nixon had come to city hall with the grievance, and even threatened to throw him in jail. Nixon remembered: "After that incident, I knew there would not be any recreation or any form of civil rights for black people unless they were ready and willing to get out and fight for it." He put this philosophy into action over the following decades.[18]

In addition to the Citizens Overall Committee, Nixon founded the Montgomery Welfare League and also led the Progressive Democratic Action Committee, which Jo Ann Robinson described as "an old, well-established organization of black leaders, men and women. Some of the best political minds in Montgomery were in this group." Vigilant in his attempts to highlight injustice, Nixon charged in the *Alabama Tribune* that some counties in Alabama had instituted "quota style racial restrictions" on African Americans following the 1952 general election, while others had prevented blacks from voting altogether. He further alleged that "5,000 Negroes have been denied the right to register and vote for no other reason than that they are Negroes." Nixon threatened legal action to secure the ballot for black citizens in Alabama. He was never afraid to publicly challenge white leaders to ensure full citizenship for himself and all blacks in Alabama.[19]

Few African American men in Montgomery displayed the public courage embodied in Nixon's rhetoric and actions. His union membership and associated job security as a Pullman porter ensured his job was secure from the retribution of local whites. Having grown up in poverty and poorly educated, Nixon made a special point to connect with the city's working-class blacks. He understood the significant socioeconomic needs that plagued many of his friends and neighbors. Through his association with Randolph and the Brotherhood of Sleeping Car Porters, Nixon had learned the power of ordinary people joining together for a common cause. He became their advocate, and worked not only to stir the people to action but to alert professional blacks to the dire financial and social conditions facing many in Montgomery.

Most middle-class African Americans elected to keep their distance from Nixon, however. While he had some degree of economic independence, most of them did not. When Nixon walked the streets of downtown Montgomery, he remembered "some of your so-called big people who are close to the white folks" crossing the street to avoid being seen with him. Donald Jones, in his 1945 assessment of the local NAACP chapter, characterized Nixon as "the strongest man in the community in civic affairs, pretty influential among the rank and file," but he also had reservations about Nixon. Jones thought that Nixon "fancies himself an amateur detective" who was always trying to demonstrate some injustice

in the courts toward local African Americans. The letters of correspondence between the local branch and the national office of the NAACP
during the 1940s help paint a picture of Nixon as a passionate and aggressive leader who would not let the slightest injustice or insult go un-
challenged. While Nixon's tenacity was vital for change to happen in the
Jim Crow South, his concern over the minutiae of local branch affairs
and concerns could prove wearisome for even the most ardent activists.
Even Ella Baker seemed to grow weary of Nixon's detailed appeals to
the national office for rulings to solve local disputes. Baker ended one
letter to Nixon concerning the use of branch monies for a USO party
for returning World War II veterans: "Nevertheless, I do not believe that
the money spent for the veterans' social should be made a major issue."
Although Nixon's intensity could prove controversial and threatening
and even exhausting to those around him, the local pastor Solomon Seay
recognized in him "an entwined combination of courage and wisdom.
He was well qualified to be standing at the threshold of a change in the
course of history."[20]

Despite his bold public stands, Nixon developed a few connections
with whites in Montgomery. As early as 1945, he was part of clandestine
interracial gatherings at Dexter Avenue Methodist Church, a white congregation led by Reverend Andrew Turnipseed. The group met in the
middle of the night to avoid reprisals. Many of those who gathered—a
group that included ASC professor J. E. Pierce, Tuskegee professor Dean
Gomillion, and *Southern Farmer* editor Gould Beech—played a role in
the 1946 populist-inspired gubernatorial campaign of Jim Folsom, who
served as Alabama governor from 1947 to 1951 and again from 1955
to 1959. While Turnipseed was not the only white challenging segregation in Montgomery, he claimed no other Methodist ministers publicly
supported his efforts: "The other Methodist preachers here that I could
count on was none. They had never been in the stirring of the water of
this kind of matter." While fellow clergy did not support his efforts, a
handful of former New Deal Democrats in Montgomery brought a vibrant, if small, white contingent advocating for racial change.[21]

Following the death of Franklin Roosevelt in 1945, many connected
to his administration began to depart the capital, including Aubrey Williams, who had served as the executive director of the National Youth

Administration. Williams returned to his native Alabama to purchase and run, with the financial backing of Chicago department store mogul Marshall Field, the struggling *Southern Farmer* magazine. He enlisted fellow New Dealer Gould Beech to serve as editor of the monthly paper, which they retooled to espouse populist and racially inclusive positions from its headquarters just outside Montgomery.[22]

Given their proximity to the state capital, Williams and Gould could not resist the temptation to get involved in local and state affairs. During one election season, they even worked to find an alternative candidate for the state legislature, which they perceived to be controlled by a racial demagogue. They nominated Steven Busby, an energetic if naïve young candidate. Their goal was for Busby to garner at least 25 percent of the vote, demonstrating the presence of a significant minority of Montgomery residents who were eager for change. In the buildup to the election, Beech spoke with Nixon, who agreed to mobilize the grand total of sixty registered black voters behind their candidate. Beech and Williams rallied the liberals in town, including local labor, and surprisingly Busby won the seat. This small victory demonstrated the latent radicalism in Montgomery that could effect small changes and have an impact, provided reactionaries were unaware of the possible ramifications. Jim Folsom's two nonconsecutive terms as governor (1947–51, 1955–59) also reveal the appeal of populist candidates in Alabama. Known as a friend of the working class, Folsom reached out to the small number of black voters in the state and refused to engage in racial demagoguery.[23]

Former New Deal Democrats Clifford and Virginia Foster Durr soon joined Williams in Montgomery. Clifford had served as the first director of the Federal Communications Commission (FCC) under Roosevelt, while Virginia had been very active in the Southern Conference for Human Welfare (SCHW) and the movement to abolish the poll tax. Following a brief stint in Denver, the couple returned to their native Alabama. Clifford established a law practice that counted the *Southern Farmer* among its clients. Virginia invested some of her time connecting with other like-minded people in the city, including Nixon and Aubrey Williams.

The racial mores of Virginia Durr's home state shocked her after spending nearly two decades away. In a letter penned shortly after her return, she described her response to the "steady and continuous" oppression of African Americans: "It is like seeing a great stone lying on them—but it lies just as heavily on the white people too—and I feel so continually guilty that I am not doing anything about it." Despite experiencing "constant pain" regarding the racial situation, she believed African Americans were "stirring and they won't be held down much longer." As New Deal Democrats who had forged friendships with southern progressives like Myles Horton, James Dombrowski, and Myles Horton, Williams and the Durrs found common ground with Nixon's agenda to challenge both Jim Crow segregation and economic injustice.[24]

Although she felt guilty for not being involved in efforts to challenge segregation, Virginia Durr did develop friendships with a few women, both white and black. An organization called the United Church Women, which held regular interracial prayer meetings in the city, became an important connection point for Durr. Through these meetings, Durr met women like Juliette Morgan, Olive Andrews, and Clara Rutledge.[25]

Juliette Morgan was a local white librarian and one of the more outspoken advocates for a more racially inclusive city and state. In an editorial published in the *Montgomery Advertiser,* Morgan voiced support for federal action to combat "discrimination against minority groups." Noting her opinion was in the minority, she added that "Ministers, some editors, social workers, and educators, and other thinking people are speaking out against the savage old mores of the South, otherwise referred to as 'our Southern traditions.'" She argued that the Democratic Party slogan "White Supremacy" was "an insult to the colored races" and "a disgrace to the white," adding that "those who insist that the states can handle civil rights are, for the most part, more concerned with maintaining the status quo than they are in securing civil rights for any minority." While Montgomery tolerated the few who did not support white supremacy as long as they did not become too vocal, Morgan foreshadowed sentiments that would later be seen as threatening by those committed to segregation.[26]

Morgan's letter drew the attention of James Dombrowski, the president of the Southern Conference Education Fund. He wrote Morgan to inquire about her editorial, asking how she developed such radical views. In her response, Morgan claimed that her opinions were widely shared in Montgomery, but most were "afraid of speaking out." To support her claim, she noted that a few of her white friends who worked to educate African Americans told her they could no longer vote under the "white supremacy" banner of the state Democratic Party. Morgan pointed to "two perfectly splendid Episcopal ministers here who are working steadily against prejudice" and "a very fine Methodist minister who never misses a chance." She was also inspired by Jane Addams's questions: "Who if not you? When if not now?" Morgan did not simply write about the need for racial changes in Alabama; she got involved. A committed Episcopalian, she participated in the Council on Human Relations organization headed up by her friend and local priest Thomas Thrasher. She also participated in an interracial prayer group organized in part by Olive Andrews.[27]

Like Morgan, Andrews became active in challenging the southern way of life by working for integration. While not as outspoken as Morgan, she was very involved in efforts to organize women in the city. Andrews was one of the leaders in the effort to integrate Montgomery's United Church Women, a program of the National Council of Churches. During the 1940s and 1950s, she was an active member of Trinity Presbyterian Church. Because of her church involvement and thanks to her reputation as a Bible teacher, Andrews received an invitation from Stillman College, a Presbyterian school for African Americans in Tuscaloosa, to teach summer classes. She later recalled her first trip to Stillman: "I went up that year and had just one little part on the program. It was the first time that I had ever been the minority. It was sort of a scary feeling when I got up to make my little presentation—to look out over all these black faces, I had never been there, in a situation like that before." After a few years as a teacher at Stillman, Andrews was put in charge of the summer program, which in her mind was originally "very paternalistic." Over time, things changed: "Gradually we integrated the staff. Where they formerly used to have me up in the cafeteria at different times, the staff would have a private dining room. We integrated that. We just went on and ate with all the delegates."[28]

Andrews soon began wrestling with the incongruity between her integrated experiences at Stillman and her segregated hometown: "I would come back to Montgomery, to the situation here, and it was very difficult. You just had to change your personality altogether almost to get back into Montgomery. That's where I just found out that all people are just people. So we started then from that, having this little group meet for Bible Study." The local group was all black except for Andrews until she met with Mrs. Dorothy Rogers Tilly of the Southern Regional Conference. Tilly connected Andrews with a national organization and helped her begin to network with other like-minded white women in Montgomery. The prayer group met monthly in black churches since most white congregations proved hesitant to permit an integrated meeting in their facilities. Andrews planned the agenda, arranged for speakers, and secured locations for this rare interracial gathering in the city. Virginia Durr recognized the contribution Andrews made to the community, claiming she "built the first bridge that was built in Montgomery. She put her whole soul and heart into it and she was the foundation. She really began the process of interchange between the two races on an equal basis."[29]

When Virginia Durr moved to Montgomery, it was Clara Rutledge who invited her to a meeting of Andrews's prayer group, which was also called the Fellowship of the Concerned. The wife of I. B. Rutledge, who served as the chief of the local Bureau of County Aid, Clara found creative ways to join the local struggle for racial justice. She mobilized a group of white southern churchwomen who attended court hearings in Montgomery when a possible miscarriage of justice against an African American was before the court. When E. D. Nixon suspected a black defendant was not guilty in an upcoming case, he would often call Clara Rutledge, who "would fill that left hand side when you go into the old police court with white women on the front seats, on the first two or three front seats. And it was mighty hard for a judge to go too far wrong with all those white women standing there listening." Rutledge, Andrews, and Morgan joined with Nixon and other African Americans in the early 1950s as part of a vibrant group willing to challenge racial mores in Montgomery.[30]

Long before the NAACP or New Deal Democrats arrived on the scene, the black church was already an integral part of the lives of many of the city's African Americans. The city's first African American Baptist church emerged out of the white-controlled First Baptist Church in 1867 as a logical outgrowth of their desire for greater autonomy following the end of slavery. Originally called Columbus Street Baptist Church, it was later renamed the First Baptist Church by the congregation. Ten years after its founding, a small group left to form the Second Colored Baptist

Church. While the exact reasons for the church split are sketchy, later explanations emphasize the role of class, suggesting that those departing Columbus Street Baptist objected to the congregation's emotive styles of worship and the muddy entrance to the building following heavy rains. The Second Colored Baptist Church soon purchased an old slave-trader's pen a short block from the State Capitol on the corner of Dexter and Decatur avenues. With the construction of their building on the site, the church changed its name to Dexter Avenue Baptist Church.[31]

The class distinctions between First Baptist and Dexter Avenue persisted. While First Baptist remained a largely working-class congregation, many black professionals filled the pews at Dexter. Ralph David Abernathy, a graduate of Alabama State College, became the pastor of First Baptist in 1951. Abernathy regularly delineated the distinctions between the two congregations, noting that, at First Baptist, "you may preach about Jesus from the pulpit. But at Dexter, they would prefer that you not mention his name. They would prefer you talk about Plato or Socrates or somebody like that. And if you just have to mention Jesus, they would like you to do it just as quietly and briefly as possible." Abernathy's comments refer to the refined, educated nature of Dexter, leading outsiders to view her congregants as more concerned with projecting an educated and refined image than with striving to assist poor African Americans in Montgomery.[32]

Dexter had a history of community involvement, however. Under the leadership of Robert Chapman Judkins, who served as pastor from 1905 to 1916, the congregation embraced the activism common during the Progressive Era. He founded a weekly newspaper for blacks in the area and established an annual lecture series that featured many high-profile speakers, including Booker T. Washington and Nannie Helen Burroughs. Under Judkins's leadership, the congregation spoke out on issues of racial violence and lynching, suffrage for blacks and women, and Prohibition. During his tenure, women in the congregation were particularly active through the women's missionary society, which urged women to pursue racial uplift through accommodationist strategies while also addressing significant health, education, and suffrage issues that affected all of Montgomery's African American citizens. Challenged by two world wars, the Great Depression, a financial crunch, and some poor choices of pastors,

Dexter struggled for over thirty years after the end of Judkins's ministry. They had high hopes, however, when they named Vernon Johns to fill their pulpit in 1948.[33]

Considered one of the most skilled black preachers in the nation, Johns impressed the people of Dexter immediately. His legendary reputation and renowned preaching ability thrilled the status-conscious congregation. Dexter deacon Robert D. Nesbitt Sr. called Johns "one of the greatest orators I have ever heard." Johns was also known for his intelligence, evidenced by his ability to quote the great poets and Scripture from memory. Nesbitt, who had led the committee to hire Johns, claimed he "never once saw Dr. Johns read from the bible. He never needed to open a bible. He knew it from cover to cover. He could quote scripture unendingly." When Dexter members traveled beyond Montgomery, they could proudly claim to have Vernon Johns as their pastor.[34]

Johns was more than a brilliant man or an accomplished orator. His pursuit of justice and his courageous acts of defiance in the face of the white elite helped unearth a passion for social action and protest in Montgomery. He was unafraid to couple tough rhetoric with confrontation. One day Johns decided to take a trip on a city bus. He paid his fare at the front of the bus and prepared to find a seat. The unwritten rule on Montgomery buses was that while blacks could board in front to pay their fare, they had to get back off and reenter through the rear door to find a seat. When the driver ordered Johns to follow this practice, the pastor balked. He demanded his money back and prepared to exit, preferring to walk instead. Before leaving, he called for everybody to exit the bus in protest of such dehumanizing treatment. The rest of the riders remained silent in their seats as Johns departed alone. This lack of action frustrated Johns, but it did not cause him to shrink from confrontations with white authorities.[35]

Johns shocked the entire city with his response to a report that police had nearly beaten a black man to death for a speeding violation. On the Dexter church billboard, located just a block from the State Capitol, Johns posted the title of his next sermon: "It's Safe to Murder Negroes in Alabama." Johns never shied away from proclaiming the obvious but unspoken truth regarding racial mores in Montgomery, and though many of Dexter's black professionals feared repercussions, some also took pride in their pastor's bold stands.[36]

Years later, many remembered the significant role Johns's activism played in preparing the community for the coming civil rights movement. Although the recollections of Dexter members give Johns too much credit for the community's later activism, they accurately emphasize his boldness. According to J. E. Pierce, a professor of political science at ASC and member of Dexter, Johns was "a very militant person, and he did not stand back." Prior to Johns's ministry, Pierce contended that the African American community was paralyzed by fear. While not all African Americans in Montgomery were afraid, those with the courage of Johns were few and far between. Pierce believed Johns planted seeds of resistance that bore fruit years later through the courageous days of the bus boycott. Dexter member Rufus Lewis concurred, noting that Johns "was a militant man in that anything that happened in the community, he would talk about it in the church in regards to denying Negroes their rights. He would preach about it." Eugene Ligon, who was the owner and operator of a Montgomery diner called the Regal Café, claimed that Johns "was the focal point of things that concerned the black community. He had the power of speaking and persuasion to get people to listen to him; and they did." A published history of Dexter described Johns's tenure in glowing terms: "His dramatic teachings aroused not only the Dexter family, but thousands of citizens of Montgomery to the social transition which was taking place in the Southern way of life. Of him it was said 'he kindled the flame of thought in the citizens of Montgomery.' His sermons were relevant to social and contemporary problems but were highlighted by a spiritual base." Although in retrospect the people of Dexter admired Johns, his willingness to rock the boat both within the church and in the broader community frightened many. A growing number of Dexter members began to view Johns as a threat to their dignity and even their livelihood.[37]

Dexter's reputation was well established throughout the community. Fred Gray, who attended ASC from 1947 to 1951 and returned to Montgomery in 1954 as the city's second black attorney, developed some strong impressions of the congregation. He believed Dexter "was not known as a church that would get involved in real community projects. It was more or less a church of the black middle class and had not been very active in any community activities that I can recall, and certainly nothing that could be interpreted as being controversial because you had a lot of persons there who were in the education field." Gray's reflections correctly identified at least one of the factors influencing many in the congregation to evade controversy: their employment as educators. Not only were the city's primary and secondary public schools under the authority of white officials, but Alabama State was largely funded through the State of Alabama, making its teachers vulnerable to white reprisals. Simply put, if they wanted to remain secure in their positions, teachers and professors knew to steer clear of controversial actions in the community.[38]

Though some feared possible repercussions under Johns's leadership, he inspired others with his boldness. Among those influenced by Johns's challenges was Dexter member Mary Fair Burks. In the early 1950s, Burks founded the most significant African American group working for social change in Montgomery during that time: the Women's Political Council (WPC). Burks later claimed the WPC was "the outgrowth of scars I suffered as a result of racism as well as my desire to arouse black middle-class women to do something about the things they could change in segregated Montgomery." One day while driving through Montgomery, Burks narrowly missed a white woman who darted into a crosswalk after the light had turned green. A police officer witnessed the close call and promptly arrested Burks. Following a brief time in jail, she "resolved to do something more about segregation besides waging my own personal war. My arrest convinced me that defiance alone would do little or nothing to remedy such situations. Only organized effort could do that." The following Sunday, Johns's sermon included one of his usual attacks on the complacency of the congregation's members. Burks heeded the reproach by directly challenging black women in Montgomery to get involved, noting that their "outward indifference was a mask to protect their psyche and their sanity."[39]

Burks immediately got to work developing the new organization. She personally contacted fifty women for an initial meeting, with the hope that a new group could address some of Montgomery's most pressing racial problems. The WPC was not Montgomery's first significant gathering of African American women seeking change in the city. In addition to very active women's ministries at Dexter, the city had various black women's clubs, including the Ten Times One Is Ten Club, an organization founded in 1888 to support racial uplift and philanthropy. Anna Duncan established another prominent black women's club in 1897. The Twentieth Century Club, which was later renamed the Anna M. Duncan Club, focused on supporting African American culture and engaging in philanthropic efforts. Soon after its founding, the group became a significant organizing force for the National Association of Colored Women. The organization's club song includes the following lyrics: "Our race must be enlightened, we must earn our daily bread, we must give our time and talent and the hungry must be fed." The song's closing solidifies the uplift ideology that fueled the club in its early years: "Lifting others is our motto, We're lifting as we climb." The Women's Political Council hoped to build on the rich history of the more established black women's clubs in the community by adopting a more politically engaged approach.[40]

Burks's vision for a new women's organization struck a chord in the community, particularly given the refusal of Montgomery's League of Women Voters to accept African American members. Forty women attended the inaugural meeting and most backed the idea with great enthusiasm. The newly formed organization settled on a three-pronged approach. First, they would pursue political action, including voter registration and evaluating candidates. Second, they would seek to remedy abuses on city buses and segregation in the city park system. Third, they would set their sights on education, including helping high school students better understand democracy and teaching literacy to adults so their language would be proficient enough to be able to register to vote.[41]

The formation of the WPC reveals that not all ASC professors cowered in fear. The organization's most influential base was near the Alabama State campus, which served as the location for the group's original chapter. The charter member Thelma Glass confirmed that it was "made up of persons like me who were in at the University and school teachers and others in the city and what not—and some outstanding religious leaders—women who had always shown interest in making things better." Another early member was Mrs. Irene West, who was a graduate of Alabama State Normal School and the widow of a dentist. One of the older women involved in the organization, West brought them instant credibility with many in the city's African American community. Local pastor Solomon Seay described West as "a fearless woman who was involved in every movement that had as its goal the freedom of her race." With the support of many of the city's most prominent black women, the WPC was primed to play a critical role in local politics.[42]

No member of the WPC was more active than Jo Ann Robinson. She came to Montgomery to teach English at ASC, and her willingness to seek justice for blacks in the segregated South crystallized soon after. Following her first semester at ASC, Robinson prepared to visit her family in Ohio for Christmas. Although she owned a car, she elected to take a bus to the airport to avoid the hassle of long-term parking. Not used to riding public transportation, Robinson boarded the bus, paid her fare, and took an available seat near the front. The driver began instructing her to move almost at once, but she was so surprised by his words that she froze. Soon the driver was standing above her shouting, "Get up from there." Unaware of the Jim Crow laws governing buses in the city and humiliated by the treatment she received from the driver, Robinson quickly exited and found other transportation to the airport. As she reflected on this dehumanizing episode, Robinson's resolve to get involved in changing the climate in Montgomery grew. Her most significant role in the local struggle was as president of the WPC.[43]

When Robinson replaced Burks as head of the WPC, she brought a more activist and confrontational spirit to the organization. Although Robinson did not completely overhaul the WPC when she assumed the presidency, she did lead the organization into addressing the mistreatment of African American passengers on city buses and to confront the city commission. Robinson herself admits that by the early 1950s the WPC had become the "go-to" organization for Montgomery blacks who had issues or grievances they wanted the city to address. In 1953 alone, they received well over thirty citizen complaints against the bus company.[44]

As early as 1952, the WPC began raising concerns about the treatment of black passengers on city buses to the city commission. Their complaints included a seating arrangement that reserved the front ten seats for whites, whether the bus had any white riders or not. If whites boarded the bus and there were no available seats in the first ten rows, the black passengers in the seats closest to the front were frequently ordered by the driver to relinquish their seats. Adding to the frustration was the lack of courtesy displayed by drivers, who were granted police powers while on duty. In a public hearing held by the city commission on the possibility of raising fares on the city bus lines, the WPC made their concerns known. Led by Mrs. Zolena J. Pierce (wife of the political science professor J. E. Pierce) and Mrs. Sadie Brooks (wife of Joseph Brooks, Trenholm's assistant), they pleaded for the city to make immediate changes, but the only response they received was an agreement by the commission to take the WPC proposal under advisement. Leaders of the WPC met directly with city commissioners in November and December 1953. Again they raised concerns shared by many in the African American community, including frustrations with the buses, but to no avail. Despite a lack of early success, the WPC demonstrated a tireless commitment to challenge the racial status quo that would become more evident in the coming years. They were not alone.[45]

Among the more committed African American activists in Montgomery was another Dexter member: Rufus Lewis. A graduate of Fisk University and the former coach of the ASC football team, Lewis labored to provide educational opportunities to black veterans returning from World War II. He was also a very successful businessman who oversaw the largest black funeral home business in the city. According to Montgomery pastor Solomon Seay, Lewis applied his business acumen to the local struggle. The primary focus of his activities was to help blacks register to vote, a task he organized through his leadership of an organization called the Citizens Steering Committee. Thelma Glass called Lewis "one of the hardest workers in voter registration that I've ever met in my life."[46]

In a climate of poll taxes, literacy tests, and comprehension tests, many blacks had to attempt to register several times before they were finally put on the voting rolls. One of the greatest challenges was keeping local African Americans motivated enough to try to register. Lewis claimed that he dedicated his life to helping people overcome all barriers that would prevent them from participating in the electoral process: "My labors in this area commenced years before the bus boycott or the protest movement commenced. I used to go around to the homes of adults and business establishments owned by Black people and encourage them to go to the courthouse and register to vote." To provide a greater incentive for his fellow citizens to register, Lewis opened a nightclub called the

Citizens Club that was open only to registered voters. Partially inspired by Vernon Johns, Dexter congregants like Burks, Robinson, and Lewis began to work tirelessly to advance the cause of African Americans in Montgomery.[47]

Johns was not only seeking political and educational advancement, however. He also campaigned tirelessly for greater black economic development to benefit the working class. Dexter parishioner Thelma Rice remembers a warm afternoon when she was approached by Johns, who was busy selling eggs to passersby. What began as an attempt to peddle eggs became a discussion regarding what blacks in Montgomery needed most, with each settling on economic advances. In Rice's view, Johns was so convinced of the need for a viable economic base among African Americans that "he lived it and practiced it." One of the ways he demonstrated his concern for economic community development was to establish an African American food cooperative known as the Farm and City Enterprises. He hoped the dollar would begin to turn over several times within the black community, creating jobs while providing greater economic independence from white Montgomery.[48]

For many in the congregation, Johns's practice of selling vegetables, fruits, and occasionally honey-cured hams from the church basement on Sunday afternoons was cause for embarrassment. Johns's lack of decorum, his impatience, and his bad temper led many of Dexter's leaders to seek a change in pastoral leadership. Dexter member Warren Brown later referred to Johns as "a hot-tempered individual." Johns's militancy limited how much impact he could have within the walls of Dexter and in the broader community. Nesbitt shared this assessment: "Dr. Johns had a vision and the depth needed to lead, but he was too violent. His philosophy was 'I want it and I want it now.'"[49]

The congregation's deacon board had a long history of controlling the church's pastors, but Johns had his own agenda. During his five years at Dexter, Johns and the church leaders were in a perpetual power struggle. One area of disagreement was the church's refusal to use black spirituals in their worship services. While Johns agreed with Dexter's general disdain for emotionalism, he was very fond of traditional spirituals, believing they represented a part of their history they ought to embrace and celebrate. The church's embarrassment of their own heritage irritated

Johns. Occasionally he would attempt to add an unplanned spiritual to the service. From the pulpit he would interrupt the planned service and demand that the organist play "I Got Shoes" or "Go Down, Moses," but never successfully. Johns's decision to go to the campus of ASC to sell watermelons marked the beginning of the end for his tenure at Dexter. For many of the ASC faculty, this was the last straw, especially when Johns embarrassed them on their home turf of the college campus. Another battle with the deacons ensued, leading Johns to announce that he would be preaching his farewell sermon on May 3, 1953. The board saw their chance and acted quickly, accepting Johns's announcement that he had preached his farewell sermon and declaring the pulpit vacant. Although Johns refused to vacate the parsonage until the church had the city turn off the home's utilities, his days as Dexter's pastor were over.[50]

In the end, the benefits of retaining Vernon Johns could not outweigh the difficulties his ministry imposed on the congregation. The majority of congregation members were simply too embarrassed by Johns's undignified peddling of fruit and too fearful of white reprisal for his boldness. Dexter Avenue Baptist Church had a pastoral vacancy that would not be filled for nearly a year. Johns's dismissal reveals the reticence of many African Americans in Montgomery to publicly challenge the white power structure, even vicariously, as through a pastor or community leader. They knew that violating any of the South's racial mores could have tragic results, as the story of Jeremiah Reeves demonstrates.

In late 1952, authorities arrested Reeves, a seventeen-year-old African American, for allegedly robbing, assaulting, and raping forty-six-year-old Mrs. Frances Prescott. While rumors persisted that Reeves and his supposed victim were actually having an affair, his trial proved to be an opportunity to reinforce the threat of the black male to the southern way of life. A few days after the jury found Reeves guilty and sentenced him to death, the story of a nineteen-year-old African American named John Smith made the local papers. According to an editorial on the incident, Smith "was chased 20 miles, fired at by a would-be captor, and scared half to death—all out of 'mistake.'" Calling the situation "a graphic illustration of the way mob hysteria develops," they quoted a local farmer who said he "wanted to kill the Negro but couldn't get close enough. Another pursuer shot at him." Citing the Reeves case, they claimed that "the hysteria which threatened Smith is partly understandable." In the minds of many whites in Montgomery, the threat of black males harming or even raping white women made the most unjust actions "partly understandable." There is no indication in the newspaper that the authorities charged the man who shot at Smith with any crime.[51]

The Reeves trial and conviction reminded white men how important it was to publicly fight for segregation lest they put white women at risk. Black men took note of how quickly an all-white jury sentenced Reeves to death and undoubtedly heard about the twenty-mile chase of John Smith. African American males who transgressed the racial code, or were even suspected of doing so, put their lives at risk. White women were reminded that their reputations were at stake should they cross racial lines. Black women, however, continued to operate below the surface. Not viewed as a threat and barely noticed by white society, black women had the freedom to challenge racism by stealth. Even when they negotiated with the mayor in his office, the community barely noticed. While black women were not alone in fighting white supremacy in Montgomery at midcentury, their voices were some of the most consistent. Though many black men in the city were just as frustrated with the racial status quo, they had more to lose by being outspoken. Whites believed they had much more to fear from black men, and therefore they responded more quickly, and often violently, to any who got out of line. As whites fixed their attention on black men, several black women were stirring the waters of racial change in Montgomery.

In December 1953, Alabama's capital city appeared calm. On the surface, blacks and whites alike seemed fully acclimated to the mores of southern race relations. Most whites in the city felt they lived in a city of racial harmony. With the departure of the fearless Vernon Johns, some whites breathed a sigh of relief. Still there was a stirring of the waters in Montgomery as people from both races worked to unleash an assault on segregation. Nixon and Parks had not lost their concern for a movement to secure changes that would benefit the tens of thousands of working-class African Americans in and around Montgomery. Beneath the surface, the waters were stirring. Dexter member Thelma Rice remembered: "African-Americans in Montgomery were not as soft and idle in the late 1940s and early 1950s as the public has been led to believe. Years before the bus boycott numerous organizations composed of and headed by African Americans were working to secure civil rights for the race locally." A few hours' drive east of Montgomery, a young doctoral student named Martin Luther King Jr. was ready for a place to put his pastoral training into action. Within a few months, King would join those in Montgomery eager to challenge white supremacy.[52]

2 "The Gospel I Will Preach"

> Let us continue to hope, work, and pray that in the future we will live
> to see a warless world, a better distribution of wealth, and a broth-
> erhood that transcends race or color. This is the gospel that I will
> preach to the world.
> —Martin Luther King Jr., July 18, 1952

Before Martin Luther King Jr. celebrated his twenty-fifth birthday, he had
already devoted several years to preparing for the pastorate. Although he
was the son and grandson of black Baptist preachers, he was not interested in simply following in their footsteps. King was unwilling to pastor
in a tradition that, as he saw it, had all too often valued the heart above
the head, the future above the present, and the spiritual above the physical. He was determined to chart a new course by creatively appropriating
the thoughts, methods, and language of the leading preachers and theologians of the day. He sought out role models, such as Morehouse College president Benjamin Mays, who embodied aspects of an intellectually
engaged ministry. This is not to suggest that King somehow eschewed his
religious heritage. Only because he was so thoroughly grounded and well
versed in the black Baptist tradition did he have the freedom to refashion
his role and objectives as a pastor. Knowing the terrain so well, he was
able to blaze new trails while remaining familiar to his congregation and
community.

In a letter composed while in graduate school, King laid out a vision
for his ministry, which he called "the gospel I will preach to the world":
"Let us continue to hope, work, and pray that in the future we will live
to see a warless world, a better distribution of wealth, and a brotherhood
that transcends race or color." King came to Montgomery with a heartfelt
hope that, with his diligent and faithful effort, God could use his church
to assist in racial uplift while he and his congregation labored for social

change. King's earliest religious writings demonstrate that he had worked hard to prepare for this opportunity, crafting a language, a ministry philosophy, and a persona that could inspire thoughtful and purposeful engagement and the transformation of culture. Years before he arrived in Montgomery, King believed in the revolutionary and redemptive power of love. The transforming potency of love was the gospel King would preach to the world.[1]

Michael King Jr. was born on Auburn Avenue in Atlanta on January 15, 1929. Known to close friends and family as "M. L.," his name was officially changed to Martin several years later. The African American community around Auburn Avenue served as an incubator for his development throughout his childhood. Just a few blocks from King's house sat his "second home," Ebenezer Baptist Church, a congregation under the leadership of his grandfather and father. Atlanta also housed Morehouse College, where King earned his bachelor's degree in 1948. King's upbringing in a southern city greatly shaped his life and ministry.[2]

During King's childhood, the African American community in Atlanta had a higher percentage of college graduates than any other southern city. With several black colleges, including Atlanta University, Spelman College, and Morehouse College, the city's educated black elite assumed roles as spokespeople for their race. Following the devastating 1906 race riot, which resulted in dozens of African American fatalities and the devastation of many black neighborhoods in Atlanta, community leaders adopted a strategy of racial progress rooted in black respectability, or an attempt to achieve racial advancement through embodying the most sublime values of white America. With the onslaught of the Great Depression and the subsequent New Deal, many educated African Americans had the opportunity to become a part of government programs designed to assist those marginalized in their communities. This resulted in an entrenched black professional leadership class in Atlanta and an increasing gulf between the classes and the masses.[3]

Atlanta provided King with many models of successful, well-educated African Americans who were able to become part of the system and deliver greater services for their community. He also witnessed the emerging gap between the working and professional classes, a chasm he never embraced. On a smaller scale, Montgomery exhibited similar dynamics between the professional and working classes, easing King's later transition into the ministry in Alabama's capital city. Had King remained in Atlanta, his emergence into leadership would have happened at a much slower rate, given the number of pastors and community leaders already established as community power brokers as well as the long shadow of his prominent father. Although Atlanta played a major role in fostering King's development, he became King the civil rights leader in Montgomery.

King brought much of Atlanta with him to Montgomery, however, including the influence of his immediate family. When King's maternal grandfather, Reverend A. D. Williams, took the helm of Ebenezer Baptist Church in 1894, the struggling Atlanta congregation numbered only thirteen members. Under Williams's leadership, Ebenezer grew to several hundred, began an ambitious building program, and became one of the leading African American congregations in the city. King's grandfather was also active in the broader community, serving for a time as the branch president of the NAACP during the organization's early years in the South. Although Williams died while Martin Luther King Jr. was only two, Williams had a significant influence on the development of King's father. Martin Luther King Sr., later known simply as "Daddy King," took over Ebenezer after his father-in-law's death and helped the church grow from six hundred members in 1931 to several thousand by the late 1940s. He made a name for himself not only in Atlanta but also on the national stage as an active participant in the country's largest African American organization, the National Baptist Convention. His congregation sat on "Sweet Auburn," one of the most significant black business districts in the nation. Segregated housing ensured that black professionals and the working class lived in relatively close proximity, but Ebenezer was primarily populated by working-class congregants. The Great Depression struck Atlanta's African American community early and hard, and Daddy King's congregation was no exception. Faced with possible foreclosure on their building, the young pastor rallied his church both financially and numerically. Following in the tradition of Williams, Daddy King served as a local leader of the NAACP, led a massive voter registration drive in 1939, and worked for the equalization of black teachers' salaries with those of their white counterparts in Atlanta's public schools.[4]

In one of his few extant early speeches, Daddy King called for a church that would "touch every phase of community life," including politics. Citing Jesus' commitment to proclaiming good news to the poor, brokenhearted, and captive, King Sr. articulated the necessity of embodying a "social gospel" that combined a concern for people's souls with a dedication to meeting their physical needs: "How can people be happy without jobs, food, shelter and clothes? . . . God hasten the time when every minister will become a registered voter and a part of every movement for the betterment of our people." In his acceptance speech as the new pastor of Dexter Avenue Baptist Church, King Jr. turned to the same text his father had used, citing Jesus' words in his hometown synagogue in Nazareth, found in Luke 4: "I have felt with Jesus that the Spirit of the Lord is upon me, because he hath anointed me to preach the gospel to the poor, to heal the brokenhearted, to preach deliverance to the captives, and to set at liberty them that are bruised." However much King would seek to construct a unique identity as a pastor, the Gospel he would preach remained rooted in the language and tradition of his father and grandfather.[5]

King's mother, Alberta Williams King, also played a significant role in shaping her eldest son. King described the daughter of Reverend A. D. Williams as one "behind the scene setting forth those motherly cares, the lack of which leaves a missing link in life." Historian Lewis Baldwin directly connects King's concern for the poor and his early disdain for capitalism with the influence of his mother. While Daddy King tended to have a more positive view of capitalism as a means for possible racial uplift, King's mother saw the desperation of the Great Depression as evidence of the tragic flaws of America's economic system. Young King grew up witnessing long bread lines and other consequences of the "tragic poverty" of his neighborhood. King also observed how socially engaged his father and mother were, which planted in him a passionate concern for social transformation that would mark his public ministry.[6]

As the son of a preacher, King's family extended to Ebenezer Baptist. He joined the church the same day as his older sister, Christine, determined "not to let her get ahead of me." For King, conversion was much more of a process or journey than the result of some "crisis moment." Ebenezer exposed him to a vast network of black Baptist preachers from throughout the nation. Some of the most renowned preachers of the day stayed in his home during revivals. Many scholars have mined the influence of the black church tradition on King, including a recent work by Mervyn Warren, who aptly calls the black church King's "conscious ancestral home, continually feeding and flavoring his religious and educational development as well as his clerical activities." His religious heritage greatly influenced King's worldview, preaching, and ministry. Literally hundreds of times a year he observed and participated in the rituals and practices of his church. He listened to countless sermons, learning not only the language of the pulpit, but also how to move and lead a congregation. The lessons King internalized during his formative years at Ebenezer provided the roots for much of what he would endeavor to accomplish as a pastor and civil rights leader. His church would continue to shape King even as he took advantage of a wartime early admission program to matriculate at Morehouse.[7]

King began studies at Morehouse in the fall of 1944 at the age of fifteen. According to his own accounts, he entered college as a religious skeptic, more interested in a career in law than in pursuing a life of ministry. Through exposure to religion professor George Kelsey and college president Benjamin Mays, King found models for a socially active and intellectually rigorous ministry. Captivated by their examples and influenced by his roots in his father's church, King decided to become a preacher. Although he had begun to consider the ministry while in high school, at the time he still grappled with skepticism. While a senior at Morehouse, his urge to enter the ministry "appeared again with an inescapable drive." King's later reflections on his call emphasized his desire to serve humanity while minimizing the "miraculous or supernatural."[8]

King's descriptions of his call to ministry demonstrate his desire to fashion a new kind of pastorate that maintained its roots in the African American tradition. For black Baptists, the story of one's call to preach was extremely important and tended to have formulaic features. Such narratives typically focused on supernatural and emotional elements that included initial resistance and disobedience to the call, followed by a later decision to fully obey God's voice by entering the ministry. King's story included a period of resistance, but the battle was not centered on whether to obey God or not. His struggle was intellectual as he wrestled with personal doubts and ecclesiological shortcomings. King eventually embraced his calling not due to an emotionally charged event or supernatural intervention, but as a rational destination at the end of a rigorous intellectual journey. King credited not only the example of traditional pastors such as his father but also the influence of faculty members at Morehouse with serving as inspirations for the new type of minister he hoped to become. In explaining his decision, King highlighted a "desire to serve God and humanity" and the contention that he could best contribute to society through the pastorate. He sought to couch his ministry service in terms that would be readily applauded by the more rationalistic white liberal church tradition while not completely dismissing the significance of a call to preach. Morehouse College was the place where King began to flesh out the type of ministry he hoped to embody.[9]

King benefited significantly from his interaction with Benjamin Mays. In contrast to the Alabama State College president H. Councill Trenholm, Mays was willing to speak publicly against segregation. While King was a student at Morehouse, Mays began writing a weekly column for the *Pittsburgh Courier*, a nationally syndicated and widely read African American newspaper. Mays later acknowledged that the themes of his newspaper articles often corresponded with his weekly Tuesday morning chapel service sermons. Chapel services were compulsory in the 1940s, and Mays spoke nearly every Tuesday to the entire student body. King's interaction with Mays extended beyond the chapel, as they developed what Mays later called "a real friendship which was strengthened by visits in his home and by fairly frequent informal chats on the campus and in my office." These conversations often included analysis of some of the points of Mays's sermons, occasionally resulting in King's disagreement with some of Mays's arguments. Morehouse provided an atmosphere of intellectual curiosity that appealed to young King, leading him to pastor and preach in a fashion that would foster questioning and debate. Perhaps as an attempt to validate his educational pedigree for largely white audiences, King's later writings often minimized the influence of his time at Morehouse. The limited mention of Mays's influence in King's later publications should not minimize the very significant role he played in shaping King's leadership style and his early homiletic themes. A comparison of Mays's *Pittsburgh Courier* articles with King's early sermons provides firm evidence for what scholars have long suspected: Benjamin Mays had a major impact on the language and themes that became staples of King's preaching and thought.[10]

One of the criticisms King often leveled against the traditional black church was its tendency to deal almost exclusively with spiritual matters while not consistently addressing social challenges. In a Crozer Seminary assignment, King argued that modern preaching must "deal with great social problems," adding that sermons should help people "adjust to the complexities of modern society." During Tuesday chapel services, Mays modeled precisely this type of engagement with the great issues of the day. He regularly addressed topics that were pertinent to the black community and thus should be on the minds and hearts of any Morehouse graduate.[11]

Mays regularly considered issues of concern to the African American community, including efforts to gain voting rights. In his first article for the *Pittsburgh Courier*, published in June 1946, Mays hailed a recent victory in an effort to secure the ballot for blacks in Georgia. He also issued a challenge to his readers, calling southern blacks to pay the necessary price required for substantive racial change in the region. While some expected justice to be a given, Mays prescribed long-term commitment and struggle as prerequisites for African Americans' achievement of full voting rights. Part of Mays's mission was to develop "Morehouse Men" who would become the vanguard of the new black leadership. Through hard work, discipline, and sacrifice, these emerging leaders would usher in a new day for African Americans. After four years under Mays's tutelage, King understood that substantive social change would require vigorous effort. This was a lesson Mays wanted every Morehouse graduate to not only understand but embody.[12]

Mays combined his admonition for commitment and sacrifice with a broad value-based critique of racist politicians. He was quite willing to chastise reactionary white leaders by name, suggesting that their fight to "keep the Negro a third-rate citizen" was a battle against the ideals of the United States and the teachings of Jesus. Mays's strategy was to challenge the supposed authority of racist government officials by appealing to a higher law found in the Constitution and the Bible. He consistently appealed to timeless moral principles to suggest that "evil carries within its structure its own self-destruction." African Americans had embodied such hope in the face of overwhelming oppression since the early days of slavery. The theme was not new, but Mays articulated this hope in educated language, something King would adopt for himself. In numerous school papers and sermons, King emphasized the ultimate death and destruction of evil by articulating a hope-filled faith in the face of violence, unjust laws, and oppressive economic institutions. He even developed a quotation-laden refrain that he used countless times in sermons and speeches to justify hope: "There is something in the universe that justifies Carlyle in saying, 'No lie can live forever.' There is something in this universe which justifies William Cullen Bryant saying, 'Truth crushed to earth will rise again.' There is something which justifies James Russell Lowell in saying, 'Truth forever on the scaffold, wrong forever on the throne, yet the scaffold sways the future.' There is something in the universe that justifies the Biblical writer in saying, 'You shall reap what you sow.'" True to his religious heritage, King clung to hope even in unfriendly circumstances. Throughout his ministry, King preached a Gospel grounded in an optimistic hope for the ultimate triumph of God in the face of any challenge.[13]

Mays's hope did not prevent him from seeing some of the damage that racism had caused. He mined the psychological implications of discrimination, recognizing that one of the greatest challenges facing blacks was their deeply rooted sense of inadequacy, leading him to call segregation "a badge of inferiority." He cited the devastating consequences of slavery, segregation, and discrimination to explain the particular challenge to self-esteem that blacks often faced. Like Mays, King also explored the detrimental psychological effects experienced by many African Americans, noting, "it's so easy for us to feel inferior because we have lived so long amid the tragic midnight of injustice and oppression." Both Mays and King recognized that feelings of inferiority often led to passivity and fear.[14]

Over and over again, Mays challenged his readers to overcome their trepidation, calling fear "the greatest enemy of mankind." He believed that as long as black southerners were under the influence of fear, they would lack the necessary boldness and resolve to sustain a movement for change. When fear rules, progress becomes stunted, justice is deferred, and equality proves evasive. The courage that is so essential to significant social advancement can easily fall prey to crippling cowardice. King took this message to heart, claiming fear was the root cause of warfare and racism. As Vernon Johns, E. D. Nixon, Rosa Parks, and Mary Fair Burks were calling on the people of Montgomery to take courageous stands for justice, Mays emphasized to King and anybody who would listen that fear was one of the greatest enemies that could retard the racial progress society so desperately needed.[15]

Following a tradition of racial uplift, Mays prescribed hard work and responsibility in the face of strong and destructive social mores and preju- dices. His hope for every Morehouse graduate was that they would cause all of society to take notice of their achievements and diligence. Mays continually preached the importance of doing any job "as if God sent you into the world at this precise moment in history to do this work." King massaged and crafted this theme into one of his set rhetorical pieces that he repeated regularly in sermons and public speeches. King joined Mays in believing that a strong work ethic could help blacks overcome inferior- ity and fear, reshape distorted white perceptions, and thus enable them to chart a course of bold action necessary for the challenges ahead. King's preaching and ministry sought to affirm the God-given dignity of African Americans while also calling on them to live up to high expectations and greater responsibility.[16]

In Mays's view, the battle for civil rights would be waged in the South. He also realized that many of the best and brightest African Americans preferred the more polite racism of the North, Northeast, and West. To counteract this pull, Mays directly challenged all who would listen with his argument that the ultimate commitment to the cause of justice and equality could only be lived out in the South. He went so far as to call southern blacks "the most courageous" on the American scene. Mays believed that circumstances demanded that people of courage live in the South, proving their ability to overcome fear and oppression. Not only did King call for courage in the face of fear, but he also heeded Mays's challenge to return to the South.[17] When King began to ponder where to live and serve following graduate school, perhaps he remembered the challenge of Mays years earlier. Despite the difficulties of being a pastor in the heart of Dixie, King decided to return to the South, setting his life on a trajectory that would place him on the front lines of one of the most significant social movements in human history.[18]

Mays saw the leadership and social philosophy of India's Gandhi as a possible model for the direction in which African Americans should move to secure greater equality in the United States. During King's junior year at Morehouse, Mays traveled to India, where he met Gandhi. Following the Indian leader's death in early 1948, Mays wrote an article fondly recalling the ninety minutes they had spent together a year earlier. The primary topic of their discussion had been the use of nonviolence as a method for bringing about social change. Mays credited "the moral and spiritual power of non-violence" as the turning point in the struggle for Indian independence from Great Britain. While not a novel assessment, Mays's articulation of this belief must have made an impression on young King. When looking for models and examples to hold up before his students at Morehouse, Mays found none more powerful than Gandhi's independence movement in India.[19]

Over his last eighteen months at Morehouse, King was in regular contact with a man who had met with and been inspired by Gandhi. Although King rarely mentioned Gandhi in his early religious writings and sermons, Mays's enthusiastic articulation of his precepts planted seeds that would fully blossom years later as King entered into the heart of the struggle for civil rights in Montgomery. In one extant assignment submitted for a course at Crozer, King did include a reference to the Indian leader as an example of one whose life demonstrated "the working of the Spirit of God." While it would be many years before King would intensely study Gandhi's life and strategies, part of the resonance of the Indian movement with him can be linked to his exposure to Benjamin Mays.[20]

Although King may not have adopted nonviolence as a way of life until he found himself on the front lines of the struggle in Montgomery, he did subscribe to the Gandhian belief that the welfare of the oppressor must be taken into account in social struggle. Mays stressed this same theme in his speeches and articles, noting that discrimination "scars not only the soul of the segregated but the soul of the segregator as well." From his student days onward, King consistently articulated that oppressors have value and are worthy of redemption. His hope was that by appealing to the hearts of these churchgoing, God-worshiping southerners, not only would laws be transformed, but the spirits of white southerners would be redeemed. Even in his earliest sermons and religious writings,

King already embraced the transforming power of the love ethic found in the teachings and life of Jesus.[21]

Years before he arrived in Montgomery, King believed in the redemptive power of love. As his public ministry and civil rights leadership took flight, he articulated a vision of African Americans carrying out a noble mission to both overcome segregation and save the soul of America. Mays had sounded a similar note while King was a student at Morehouse, arguing that the fight for justice and equality is part of "a battle to save the soul of the South and the soul of America." For King, the ultimate weapon against evil and the best hope for redemption was found in one's capacity to love. Appealing not only to Gandhi and Mays but also to the words of Jesus, King preached incessantly about the need to love and forgive as "love has within [it] a redemptive power." King called forgiveness "the Christian weapon of social redemption" and the "Christian weapon against social evil," believing that it represented "the solution to the race problem." While King would develop a greater depth of understanding and conviction regarding nonviolence, many of his root convictions regarding the redemptive power of love were established long before he came to Montgomery.[22]

King changed and matured during his four years at Morehouse. Many scholars have emphasized the significance of the black Baptist roots in shaping the young King's preaching and leadership, while others have noted how the white northern academy influenced his thought and convictions. The pivotal importance of Morehouse and Benjamin Mays are often downplayed. This oversight needs to be corrected. Were it not for King's time at Morehouse and his exposure to a role model like Mays, one may justifiably ask whether King would have entered the ministry at all. During his time at Morehouse, King acquired the academic tools and language to navigate the educational landscape of Crozer Seminary and Boston University. He was able to engage the ideas that formed the curriculum of the white academy. King was prepared to set out on a task of synthesizing the vibrant black church tradition with the language and ideas of white theologians.

After his son's four years at Morehouse, Daddy King offered King Jr. the opportunity to be the assistant pastor at Ebenezer. Convinced of the pressing need for a more educated pastorate, and desiring to move out of the shadow of his imposing father, the young King declined. Instead he chose to head north to Crozer Theological Seminary. Located in a suburb of Philadelphia, Crozer was one of the leading seminaries of the day. The institution had also made a commitment to expand its diversity by accepting several African American students in the fall of 1948, including King as well as fellow Morehouse graduate and King's close friend Walter McCall. Unlike many of his classmates, when nineteen-year-old Martin King searched for a seat in his first preaching course at Crozer, he did so as a licensed preacher, well-schooled in the African American church tradition. Although as a graduate of Morehouse he had all the educational credentials he would need to serve as a pastor in an African American Baptist church, King was not interested in merely following in the footsteps of his father or fulfilling the expectations placed on African American pastors. He was determined to break the mold, and three years at an elite white seminary would allow him to incorporate the best ideas and practices of the white liberal church into his pastorate.

King's time at Crozer was a season of development and growth rather than one of activism. However, when a restaurant in New Jersey refused service to King and some of his friends, they refused to leave quietly. The owner finally threatened them with a gun and forcibly removed them. King and his companions tried to take the matter to the courts based on New Jersey's civil rights laws, but they had to drop their case when none of the white witnesses would agree to testify. For the most part, however, King chose to avoid confrontation during this season of his life. This was far from King's only negative experience during his time at Crozer. At one point, a fellow student pointed a gun at him, believing King had played a prank on him. King earned respect from fellow students with his calm response to this incident and for not holding a grudge against the gun-waving classmate. King preferred to respond to the scorn of a few students and professors with affability, forbearance, and forgiveness.[23]

As King completed his education at Crozer, some in Montgomery were already in the midst of a struggle for justice. Robinson had joined Burks as part of the Women's Political Council (WPC). Vernon Johns was boldly challenging segregation and white violence in the pulpit and on the streets of Alabama's capital. Although no longer an officer with the local NAACP, E. D. Nixon continued to agitate for change. King's direct involvement in the southern struggle would have to wait, however. He wanted to further his education before returning South, leading him to Boston University, where he pursued a Ph.D. in theology.

King intended to study a school of philosophy known as "personalism" with Edgar Brightman, one of Boston University's many renowned professors. The core principle of personalism when applied to theology is that human beings in a community provide the best approximation of the character of God. Personalism supports having faith in a personal God who is in relationship with creation. This view meshed well with the tradition of many black churches, which tended to emphasize God's accessibility and involvement in the world. Always interested in being a well-educated pastor, King was excited to embrace a theological system and language that validated many of his deepest religious convictions.[24]

In later years, King paid homage to the influence of significant white theologians, philosophers, and social theorists when recounting his intellectual development. In an essay titled "Pilgrimage to Nonviolence" penned for inclusion in *Stride toward Freedom,* King emphasized his exposure to Walter Rauschenbusch, Karl Marx, Friedrich Nietzsche, and Reinhold Niebuhr. Many scholars disagree with the weight the essay grants to these thinkers, noting that they merely provided systems and language for deeply held beliefs King had developed years earlier from the African American Baptist church. For example, while King credited Niebuhr's *Moral Man and Moral Society* for providing a necessary corrective to the unbridled optimism found in liberalism, many historians have rightly tempered the significance of Niebuhr's influence, noting that living under segregation and white supremacy would check anyone's unbridled optimism. During King's first months at seminary, he was already questioning the significance of "high-minded" liberalism, suggesting it failed to address the daily challenges and struggles people face.[25]

By the time King reached Crozer, he was already familiar with the published sermons of the more renowned preachers of the day. Keith Miller has helpfully examined the extensive use of these homilies in King's preaching, showing how he regularly borrowed titles, themes, images, and even paragraphs as building blocks for his own sermons. In an exercise for a preaching course during his first year at Crozer, Robert Keighton asked the class to write five brief sermon introductions. For one of these, King copied the title and a two-sentence introduction from Fulton Sheen's "The Effects of Conversion." King continued to use the words and ideas of others in the pulpit, as evidenced in a sermon delivered at Ebenezer titled "The False God of Science," which began with a paraphrase of the introduction from Harry Emerson Fosdick's "Why Worship?" The very next week, King again reworked portions of a Fosdick sermon in his introduction and as arguments to bolster a few of the sermon's main points. In the same summer, King borrowed significant portions of Fosdick's "Righteousness First" sermon for a message he retitled "First Things First." He also leaned heavily on a Robert J. McCracken homily to compose "Communism's Challenge to Christianity." As many scholars have noted, King clearly used and failed to cite the work of other preachers for many of his homilies.[26]

Although King benefited significantly from his studies and his exposure to the sermon collections of prominent white preachers, his wife, Coretta Scott, greatly influenced him as well. She was more of an activist than King when they met during his first year in Boston. A native of Alabama, Scott had attended the integrated Antioch College in Ohio before enrolling at the New England Conservatory of Music. She was interested in politics and had actively supported the presidential candidacy of Progressive Party candidate Henry Wallace in 1948, attending the party's convention as a youth delegate. There is significant evidence that Scott and King shared many convictions regarding the necessity for economic and political change.[27]

Shortly after they began dating, Scott gave King a copy of Edward Bellamy's utopian look at the future, *Looking Backward: 2000–1887*. The book celebrates the emergence of a classless society achieved through the demise of capitalism. Scott wrote a brief note to King inside the book: "Dear Martin, I should be interested to know your reaction to Bellamy's predictions about our society. In some ways it is rather encouraging to see how our social order has changed since Bellamy's time. There is still hope for the future. . . . Lest we become too impatient." After reading the book, King wrote Scott a letter that included his thoughts on Bellamy's work. Calling the author "a social prophet," King added, "I imagine you already know that I am much more socialistic in my economic theory than capitalistic." Perhaps seeking to impress his activist-minded girlfriend, King included words he had used in a prayer at the conclusion of a sermon three years earlier: "Let us continue to hope, work, and pray that in the future we will live to see a warless world, a better distribution of wealth, and a brotherhood that transcends race or color." This time King added, "This is the gospel that I will preach to the world." With their engagement and subsequent marriage in 1953, King found a wife who would stimulate him intellectually and urge him to be more of an activist for the ideals to which they both subscribed.[28]

When considering King's time in Philadelphia and Boston, it is easy to forget that he spent every summer back home in Atlanta working as an assistant pastor for his father at Ebenezer. In addition to filling pulpits in the northern church, including Twelfth Avenue Baptist Church in Boston, King remained grounded in the southern African American church. King preached regularly at Ebenezer during summer breaks as his father traveled or tended to other pastoral and denominational duties. This time at Ebenezer helped keep King connected to the concerns and challenges facing working-class African Americans in the segregated South. As he prepared to preach each Sunday, the composition of his audience demanded that he bridge the gap between the academy and the people as he attempted to share about the power and love of God. Many of King's early Ebenezer sermon manuscripts remain, and their content demonstrates his efforts to remain connected to his home community in Atlanta.

During King's graduate student years, he directly addressed racial issues from the pulpit. In an early sermon at Ebenezer, King noted: "The average white southerner is not bad. He goes to church every Sunday. He worships the same God we worship. He will send thousands of dollars to Africa and China for the missionary effort. Yet at the same time he will spend thousands of dollars in an attempt to keep the Negro segregated and discriminated." A few weeks later, King challenged the United States to observe their faults rather than constantly pointing out the flaws in the Soviet Union: "While we see the splinters in Russia's eye we fail to see the great plank of racial segregation and discrimination which is blocking the progress of America." King did not let his audience off too easily, however, proceeding to chastise African Americans for discriminating against one another and seeing "the splinters in the white man's eye" while failing to recognize "the planks in their own eye." Even as a young theology student, King was ready and willing to challenge injustice while also calling on his parishioners to examine themselves first so that true social transformation could occur. Years before King assumed the pastorate at Dexter, his sermons already included bold challenges to America and the church on issues of race, international affairs, and economic justice.[29]

During summer breaks, King used his opportunities to preach at Ebenezer to further refine themes that bridged his emerging theology with the expectations of a congregation. In "Loving Your Enemies," King called his listeners to examine themselves, to "see the good points in your enemy," and not to seek their adversary's demise even when the opportunity presented itself. King argued that one should love one's enemy "because the process of hate for hate brings disaster to all involved," "because hate distorts the whole personality," and "because love has within it a redemptive power." This sermon contains many of the essential elements of the social ethic King would one day preach to the world. Eighteen months before he first ascended to the pulpit at Dexter, King's vision for social change had already taken shape, and at its core was the revolutionary power of love found in the teachings of Jesus.[30]

Despite King's core commitment to ideas of social and economic change, he was far from the front lines of the struggle already emerging in the South. He was a radical scholar and preacher, but not yet an activist. In Montgomery, Alabama, however, radical activists like E. D. Nixon, Rosa Parks, and Jo Ann Robinson were already hard at work. Six weeks after King's sermon on love at Ebenezer, Jo Ann Robinson penned a letter to the editor of the *Montgomery Advertiser*. Noting that a local five-and-dime store had recently added two separate lunch counters for blacks and whites, she offered praise for the store's manager, noting he "deserves much credit for realizing that Negro people, too, must eat. Human frailty makes it utterly impossible for men, irrespective of color, to deny pangs of hunger or thirst." Complaining that in many stores "even ice water is not available for Negroes," she marveled at a water fountain at a local store "where all kinds of people drink: Sick people, well people, clean people, dirty people. The fountain has been so scientifically constructed that germs cannot get to the flow of water—that is from white faces anyway. Seemingly, only black faces can contaminate and make the water unfit for human consumption." While King preached a Gospel of love and justice, Robinson used humor as she publicly lobbied for opportunities she knew African Americans deserved. Robert D. Nesbitt Jr., the chairperson of the search committee at Montgomery's Dexter Avenue Baptist Church, would help connect King with Robinson and other civil rights activists in Montgomery.[31]

Deacon Nesbitt was in Atlanta on a business trip when a friend told him he ought to visit with young King. Nesbitt felt a great deal of pressure as he searched for his congregation's next pastor. He had led previous search teams that had resulted in two controversial pastors, each of whom had left under duress. The Dexter deacon decided to follow up on the lead and ended up in the home of one of Atlanta's most prominent Baptist ministers, Martin Luther King Sr. Nesbitt liked what he saw in Daddy King's eldest son, the promising Martin Luther King Jr. As the child of a pastor, young King knew the expectations and challenges of the pastorate. He was also a candidate for a doctoral degree, a feature that was sure to impress the many educators who regularly attended Dexter. Despite King Sr.'s misgivings about the strong deacon board and the "silk-stocking" reputation of Dexter, Nesbitt prevailed upon King Jr. to preach a sermon at the Montgomery church. For his part, King considered Dexter a promising opportunity and a suitable proving ground for the intellectually and socially engaged pastorate he had laboriously crafted, and he agreed to preach at the church in early January. In Montgomery, King's Gospel would intersect with the public activism of Robinson, Nixon, Burks, and Parks. They were ready for each other. Nesbitt's visit to the King home provided just the opportunity Martin Luther King Jr. needed to set him on a path that would propel him to the forefront of the civil rights movement.[32]

3   "Making a Contribution"

> The Highlander Folk School seems like a wonderful place. I am look-
> ing forward with eager anticipation to attending the workshop, hop-
> ing to make a contribution to the fulfillment of complete freedom
> for all people.
>
> —Rosa Parks, July 6, 1955

As 1954 dawned, Martin Luther King Jr. was aggressively pursuing various job opportunities. He had just completed his coursework and examination requirements for his doctorate at Boston University and hoped
to find a teaching or pastoral position to support both himself and his
wife while finishing his dissertation. Although tempted by academic opportunities, he preferred to begin his career as a pastor. Through Dexter
Avenue Baptist Church deacon Robert Nesbitt, King received an invitation to preach a sermon at the historic Montgomery church, which was
without a pastor following the departure of Vernon Johns. The day before he was scheduled to preach, he traveled from Atlanta to Montgomery
with an unexpected passenger: Vernon Johns. The former Dexter pastor
was preaching at Ralph Abernathy's First Baptist Church the following
morning.[1]

As the men drove, they passed within a few miles of the campus of
Tuskegee Institute, where that very day NAACP attorney Thurgood
Marshall was delivering a keynote address for the National Newspaper
Publishers Association. Attendees packed the chapel to hear the lawyer
who had argued the pending *Brown v. Board of Education* case before the
U.S. Supreme Court. Marshall asserted that segregation was coming to
an end, while also admitting that many southerners were willing to go to
great lengths to impede any challenge to white supremacy, as evidenced
by those "talking about calling out the militia and using other drastic
measures." He challenged his audience to "overcome the stigma of sec-

53

ond class citizenship in our own minds. There must be a willingness on the part of those who have college training and those who have money to help those who have neither." Although King did not hear Marshall's challenge, Montgomery was the type of place where he could demonstrate a willingness to make a contribution by going to the front line of the civil rights struggle.[2]

Several men and women in Alabama's capital city were already pushing for substantive change. Some were even considering a boycott of city buses should white authorities not ensure better treatment for the African Americans who depended on public transit. Although King was not yet sure where he would serve, he was ready to do his part. In Montgomery, King would have the opportunity to rub shoulders with men and women who had been making a contribution to the freedom struggle for years. He would learn a great deal from them, and he would be emboldened by their courage and commitment. King would also provide a message of hope and become a much-needed bridge between the black economic classes in Montgomery. Before King could speak words that could move a nation, he had to first learn to use the spoken word to move a congregation and a community.

King decided to deliver one of his tested sermons, "The Dimensions of a Complete Life," for the Dexter congregation. Knowing he would be evaluated on how well he preached, he was nervous: "That Saturday evening as I began going over my sermon, I was aware of a certain anxiety. Although I had preached many times before—having served as associate pastor of my father's church in Atlanta for four years, and having done all of the preaching there for three successive summers—I was very conscious this time that I was on trial." King knew the reputation of the Dexter congregation: relatively wealthy, educated, discriminating. Despite all of his experience behind the pulpit, he found himself wondering, "How could I best impress the congregation?" King's sermon called on the congregation to make positive contributions in the lives of others: "The prayer that every man should learn to pray is, 'Lord teach me to unselfishly serve humanity.' No man should become so involved in his personal ambitions that he forgets that other people exist in the world. Indeed if my life's work is not developed for the good of humanity, it is meaningless and Godless." Should King become the pastor of Dexter, he served notice that he would insist that the congregation resist the temptation to focus inwardly. As was the case in most southern cities during the 1950s, African American professionals faced the temptation to put caution first. King challenged them to elevate their commitment to the needs of others no matter what the cost.[3]

Following King's trip to Montgomery, Dexter's pulpit committee recommended that the congregation call King to serve as their next pastor, and the members unanimously supported the selection. The committee asked him to return so they could discuss the details of their offer. He made his way back to the racially divided city of Montgomery still unsure if he and his wife, Coretta, were ready to return to the South. The circumstances surrounding Miss Ophelia Hill's funeral demonstrate the racial climate the Kings would encounter should they answer Dexter's call. Hill, who served for over a quarter century as the supervisor of Montgomery's African American schools, was a member of St. Peter's Episcopal Church. When she died, her largely white church refused to hold her funeral services, so her white rector officiated at the funeral service in a local Colored Methodist Episcopal church. Some of the pews in the church were labeled with signs reading, "Reserved for white friends." Such incidents led Alabama native Virginia Durr, who had recently returned to the state after over a decade in Washington, D.C., to describe Montgomery as a place of "death, decay, corruption, frustration, bitterness and sorrow. The Lost Cause is right." White supremacy was the dominant reality that affected the daily lives of black and white alike. Following nearly six years studying in the North, the King family had to assess the cost of reentering the heart of Dixie.[4]

A few days before King's return trip, an article appeared in the town's African American newspaper that further demonstrated racial tension in Montgomery. African American pastor and Alabama State College student Uriah J. Fields wrote to denounce the unequal treatment blacks continually received on city buses. He noted overcrowding on routes that serviced African American sections of town and lamented the way fares were collected from black riders. He also complained that African Americans often had "to stand up on buses when there are vacant seats in the front." Fields challenged drivers to treat black female riders with dignity and kindness. After calling for immediate organization against those who perpetuate degrading treatment on the buses, Fields laid out the following five recommendations:

1. Provide buses on any given route in proportion to the population of bus riders in that area.
2. Apply the rule "first come, first served" in seating passengers. Especially on buses serving in predominantly Negro areas.
3. Forbid bus drivers from insisting or even requesting that Negroes enter the bus through the back door.
4. Hire qualified Negroes for the position of bus driver.
5. It is further recommended that a course or a period of orientation be given each bus driver on chivalry.[5]

Fields's sentiments were not new, and they were not his alone. Members of the Women's Political Council (WPC) and Pullman porter E. D. Nixon shared Fields's frustrations. WPC president Jo Ann Robinson, wrote a letter to Montgomery mayor W. A. Gayle, offering her reflections on a recent meeting with city commissioners. The WPC had made three specific requests regarding city buses: that blacks fill seats from the back, and whites from the front, until all seats are taken; that blacks not have to exit and reenter in the back after paying; and that buses stop at every block in residential African American neighborhoods, as was the case in white sections of town. While Robinson reported progress on the number of stops many buses were making, the city had failed to address their seating and boarding concerns. Robinson then added: "More and more of our people are already arranging with neighbors and friends to ride to keep from being insulted and humiliated by bus drivers. There has even been talk from twenty-five or more organizations of planning a city-wide boycott of buses."[6]

The letters by Fields and Robinson reveal not only the level of frustration over inequities in Montgomery, but also a willingness to speak up about the problems and to engage the city in seeking solutions. They also demonstrate different priorities among those seeking racial justice in the city. Although Fields's letter included as an important demand the hiring of black bus drivers, Robinson's letter failed to mention a desire for the bus company to employ African American drivers. This seemingly minor divergence in priorities would remain a source of contention over the coming years, as leaders never unified around clear economic initiatives that would benefit the working class. Nevertheless, local activists were already contemplating bold tactics to challenge white supremacy as King returned to the city to negotiate the terms of his employment at Dexter.

The pulpit committee asked King to preach again during his second visit to Dexter. In his sermon titled "Going Forward by Going Backward," he offered a harsh critique of society, which had pursued knowledge and materialism while neglecting timeless moral principles and a devotion to God that could transform the world into a "brotherhood." Despite the destructive impulses of humanity, King urged the people of Dexter to cling to hope based on a firm belief in the ultimate triumph of justice and righteousness. Should King answer the call to Dexter, he intended to contribute to the local struggle by reminding his congregation to place their trust in God as they moved forward. King's belief in the limitless power of God led him to articulate a message of hope even amidst Montgomery's dehumanizing conditions.[7]

The possibilities at Dexter had piqued King's interest, leading him to accept the offer to become the church's pastor. He returned to Montgomery on May 2, 1954, and preached a version of "Accepting Responsibility for Your Actions." King encouraged his listeners to not allow the excuses of heredity or environment to determine their lives, but instead to focus on their own responses to life's challenges. Among his examples of those who had achieved despite hindrances were African American singers Marian Anderson and Roland Hayes as well as Abraham Lincoln. King tempered his previous emphasis on the individual and put his new congregation on notice regarding the type of leadership he would provide: "I happen to be a firm believer in what is called the 'social gospel.'" King's written manuscript does not flesh out his definition of the term, but he did emphasize the necessity of pursuing "social reform." While King's theological and social views broadened and sharpened during his years in seminary and graduate school, his basic concern for the goals of social change remained consistent. His commitment to the social gospel would move from theory to practice in the years ahead.[8]

After the sermon, King delivered an acceptance address to his new congregation, noting, "I come to the pastorate of Dexter at a most crucial hour of our world's history." The challenges of war and the anxieties of the modern industrialized world had led many to turn to the church. To be ready for those seeking direction and hope in a time of uncertainty, King prescribed an agenda of moral uplift, calling his parishioners to "lead men and women of a decadent generation to the high mountain of peace and salvation." He also evidenced a self-effacing quality, claiming he was neither a "great preacher" nor a "profound scholar" and came with "nothing so special to offer." Nevertheless, he closed the address with confidence: "I come with a feeling that I've been called to preach and to lead God's people." Just as Jesus had began his public ministry as recorded in the Gospel of Luke, King called upon the words of Isaiah 61 to conclude his address: "I have felt with Jesus that the spirit of the Lord is upon me, because he hath anointed me to preach the gospel to the poor, to heal the brokenhearted, to preach deliverance to the captives, and to set at liberty them that are bruised." King's first few sermons and acceptance address reveal the Gospel he would preach at Dexter. He proclaimed an optimistic message of hope rooted in the power of God that ought to inspire people to boldly challenge injustice and tirelessly serve those in greatest need.[9]

King came to Montgomery during a time of social change and polarization on both the local and national scene. One day after King's acceptance address, city police added African American officers to the force for the first time. The proposal had been considered for over a year, and the impetus for the policy came out of a political deal brokered by E. D. Nixon and Montgomery public safety commissioner Dave Birmingham prior to his 1953 election. Birmingham, whose appeal was primarily to the newer, white working-class citizens of Montgomery, recognized the need to court the black vote in his election against his old-guard opponent. Nixon agreed he would deliver the African American vote for Birmingham if the city commission candidate promised to hire black police officers. True to his word, a few weeks after the election, Birmingham brought the issue before the city commissioners for the first time.[10]

In December 1953, following a meeting with black leaders and Mayor Gayle, Birmingham explained the delay in securing African American officers: "We've been talking about the idea in Montgomery for two years, but the Grand Jury recommended the project only about six or eight weeks ago, and of course no provision was made for it in the 1954 budget. As soon as physically and financially possible, we will entertain the idea of putting on Negro policemen in Negro districts." Aware of the potential political ramifications of his lobbying on this issue, Birmingham also sought to ameliorate the concerns of Montgomery's white citizens, stating, "If Negroes are added to the force they will not make arrests except in those areas to which they are specifically assigned."[11]

A few months later, Mayor Gayle finally announced the city's decision to employ four black police officers. He was quick to qualify the new policy: "I would like to emphasize that the colored policemen will be screened very carefully by the City Commission. They will be hired on a trial basis. The Negro officers will be used only in the Negro sections of Montgomery and will arrest colored people. White people will be arrested by colored police only under the most extreme, emergency circumstances." Given the caveats offered by Mayor Gayle and Commissioner Birmingham, the only response published on the *Montgomery Advertiser* editorial page was positive. A few weeks later, the city swore in its first four black officers. In the fall of 1954, the number of African American police officers grew to seven when three black women joined the force.[12]

Soon after King's acceptance address, the U.S. Supreme Court issued its first *Brown v. Board of Education* decision, declaring school segregation unconstitutional. During a time when this ruling was fresh in the minds and hearts of blacks throughout the South, King commuted from Boston to Montgomery a few times a month throughout the summer as he continued to work on his dissertation. When he preached, King urged his new congregation to take courageous stands for justice, while criticizing the cowardice and hypocrisy of whites regarding issues of race. In a sermon titled "Mental and Spiritual Slavery," King explored the biblical story of the Roman ruler Pilate, who chose to conform to the wishes of the crowd by handing Jesus over to be crucified. King compared Pilate's silence to that of most whites in the South. It could not have escaped King, however, that his congregation included many who felt daily pressure to conform to white southern mores. They believed that their jobs, the well-being of their families, and even their lives depended on acquiescing to the status quo. King also knew that his predecessor at Dexter had consistently challenged the congregation to display greater courage in challenging racism. While King lacked some of Johns's rougher edges, he echoed Johns's challenge: "Most people today are in Pilate's shoes i.e. conformist. Most people would take stands on their ideas but they are afraid of being non-conformist." King later added, "Take the minister choosing between truth and keeping in with their members and being popular with the brethren." He called his parishioners to not allow their timidity to derail progress at this critical hour, noting that "the great progressive moves of history have been ruined by the perpetuity of 'Pilateness.'" For a congregation filled with African American teachers and professors whose jobs were in the hands of white government officials, nonconformity came with a price. King let his congregation know early on that he expected them to be willing to pay the price necessary to not hold back a "great progressive move of history."[13]

During his first summer at Dexter, King did not shy away from attacking segregation. He made it clear that he intended the congregation to be a socially engaged church that was not afraid to directly challenge white racism. He called into question the validity of a Christianity that includes those "who lynch Negroes," noting the "strongest advocators of segregation in America also worship Christ." The following week King shifted his focus to the responsibility his congregation must take in bringing substantive change to Montgomery: "Man is body as well as soul, and any religion that pretends to care for the souls of people but is not interested in the slums that damn them, the city government that corrupts them, and the economic order that cripples them, is a dry, passive do nothing religion in need of new blood." King envisioned a socially engaged congregation that would meet challenges and obstacles head on, suggesting that "unless we preach the social gospel our evangelistic gospel will be meaningless." As he became more comfortable with his new congregation, King would continue to lobby for community transformation as part of God's call on the people of Dexter. Even before he took up residence in Montgomery, King was already making a contribution through powerful homilies intended to inspire his new congregation to courageously join their race's struggle for freedom.[14]

In September 1954, Martin and Coretta Scott King relocated from Boston to Montgomery, setting up residence in the church's parsonage several blocks from the church. With the move, King assumed his role as the full-time pastor of Dexter. Meanwhile, the first school year following the *Brown* decision began. Although the Supreme Court would not issue implementation orders on their ruling until 1955, a few were determined to test the decision much sooner. At the dawn of the 1954–1955 academic year, E. D. Nixon and *Southern Farmer* editor Aubrey Williams attempted to enroll twenty-three African American children in an all-white school, filing a lawsuit on their behalf. Nixon later claimed he "was the first man anywhere in the United States to lead a group of black children into an all-white school. That was at the William Harrison School—ain't ten minutes' drive from here—out on the bypass. They wouldn't let them stay, but I carried them there." The local African American paper also credited Aubrey Williams for displaying "Christian courage and the finest sense of democratic responsibility" in his attempt to assist parents in enrolling their children in the nearest and best public schools that fall. During King's first week in town, Williams and Nixon proved willing to take action by directly challenging Jim Crow segregation.[15]

In his first sermon following the move, King preached on one of his favorite subjects: love. In examining the nature of God's love, he noted that it is "too broad to be limited to a particular race. It is too big to be wrapped in a particularlistic [*sic*] garment. It is too great to be encompassed by any single nation. God is a universal God. This fact has been a ray of hope and has given a sense of belonging to hundreds of disinherited people." To display the encouragement that God's love can bring, King cited "the illustration of the old slave preacher," a story found in a tape-recorded version of this sermon years later: "This is what the old slave preacher used to say. He didn't have his grammar right but he knew God, and he would stand before the people caught in the dark night of slavery with nothing to look forward to the next morning but the long row of cotton ahead, the sizzling heat, and the rawhide whip of the overseer. He would stand up before them after they had worked from camp to cane. He said now, 'You ain't no slave. You ain't no nigger. But you're God's child.'" Following this illustration, King told his Dexter congregation, "All of the hate in the world cannot destroy the universal effect of God's love." In the face of the absurd hatred and exclusion blacks experienced every day in Montgomery, King pointed to the power of God's love as the source of sanity and dignity for "God's love is redemptive." King's enduring faith in the transforming and redemptive possibilities of love proved to be an unwavering conviction of his public ministry.[16]

A few days after moving to Montgomery, King attended the National Baptist Convention in St. Louis, where he delivered an address before the women's auxiliary. Despite the unsuccessful effort to integrate Montgomery's public schools, King offered an optimistic speech trumpeting the inevitability of racial progress, desegregation, and social change: "Ultimately history brings into being the new order to blot out the tragic reign of the old order." During his first year at Dexter, King continued to believe that "the tide has turned" and "segregation is passing away." On the ground in Montgomery, however, dissatisfaction with the degrading effects of segregation grew. Whether inspired by optimism in the wake of the *Brown* decision or simply fed up with the racial status quo, several people in the city were ready to stand up and be counted in the fight for true freedom.[17]

At the front of the line, as had been the case for several decades, was E. D. Nixon. In addition to his attempt to register black students in white schools, he also became the first African American since the beginning of the twentieth century to run for public office in a Montgomery County Democratic primary. Although he lost the race, he continued to set a bold example for blacks by challenging any so-called restrictions imposed by white society. During the summer of 1954, Nixon was named the chairperson of a voter registration effort for the 2nd Congressional District in Alabama. In his remarks at the organization's meeting, Nixon vowed to "lead the fight to open the way for Negro voting." In homage to Nixon's efforts in 1954, the "colored section" of the *Montgomery Advertiser* named him Montgomery's "Man of the Year."[18]

Despite Nixon's activism, most African American men avoided overt challenges to Montgomery's racist laws and mores. As a member of the Brotherhood of Sleeping Car Porters whose job was not tied to the local community, Nixon was less vulnerable to economic retribution by local whites. Those whose service jobs depended on the goodwill of local white businessmen could not afford to share Nixon's boldness. According to Jo Ann Robinson, many black men stopped riding the city buses during this period, fearing the abuse and humiliation they so often received from bus drivers. They also were tired of feeling powerless while drivers disrespected and mistreated African American women. According to Robinson, "at no time did a single man ever stand up in defense of the women." Men were more vulnerable to economic and physical reprisals if they stepped out of their place, as often families depended on income from their jobs to make ends meet. Any overt protest, if discovered, could easily lead to the loss of a job, a price that was simply too high for most to pay. So, "if they were on the bus when trouble started, they merely got up and got off." Confronted with perpetual repression, many working-class black males chose to avoid confrontations altogether.[19]

King never had to ride the buses in Montgomery. Although he undoubtedly heard about the community's concerns over the bus situation, his earliest impressions of the city were from a broader perspective. He noticed the heavy influence of the Maxwell and Gunter Air Force bases, which employed roughly 7 percent of the city's workforce and, according to chamber of commerce reports, pumped over $50 million into the city's economy each year. King could not help but notice that while these bases had such a significant economic impact on the region, they operated under different social rules than the city did: "the bases, which contributed so much to the economic life of the community, were fully integrated," but "the city around them adhered to a rigorous pattern of racial segregation." King also encountered a divided black community, particularly among the leadership. He became aware of the many subgroups, programs, organizations, and competing personalities that stifled any significant efforts to bring about change. King admired the individual leaders but surmised, "While the heads of each of these organizations were able and dedicated leaders with common aims, their separate allegiances made it difficult for them to come together on the basis of a higher unity."[20]

Although King did not have an answer to the divisions that beset Montgomery's black community, he was determined that both he and his congregants would make a contribution to the local struggle. King's series of recommendations for Dexter, written during his first week as a resident of Montgomery, emphasized the central role of the pastor in church polity. Claiming that a pastor's authority flows both from God and from the people, he asserted that a call to serve as pastor affirms "the unconditional willingness of the people to accept the pastor's leadership," which means "leadership never ascends from the pew to the pulpit, but it invariably descends from the pulpit to the pew." In King's view, a pastor should "never be considered a mere puppet for the whimsical and capricious mistreatment of those who wish to show their independence, and 'use their liberty for a cloak of maliciousness.'"[21]

These early statements by King have been cited by some to argue that King was not interested in the voices of the average people, but instead operated from a "top-down" understanding of leadership. Many of these assessments of King's leadership drawn from this particular speech fail to account for the larger context that King was entering. In general, new ministers often find themselves in precarious positions. Church boards are filled with volunteers who are not easily replaced. Particularly in the Baptist church polity, deacon boards held a tremendous amount of sway, especially during the first few years of a pastor's tenure, before the minister could develop loyalty and strong relationships with the people. In this speech, King was attempting to emphasize the trust they placed in him by voting him in as pastor, and to underscore his authority through an appeal to a divine sanction of his position.[22]

King also believed his bold statements regarding his authority were warranted given the reputation Dexter had earned over the years. Known as a "deacons' church," many ministers in the National Baptist Convention believed Dexter's board was heavy-handed when dealing with their pastors. When one of Daddy King's friends found out that King Jr. was considering assuming the pastorate at Dexter, the friend said: "Mike, there's one man on the board at Dexter to watch out for. He may be dead by now, but if he is still alive, don't you go there, because he'll give you hell." When King learned that Deacon Thomas H. Randall was not only very much alive, but served as chair of the deacons, he came to the church expecting difficulties. The level of trust was so low between pastors and deacons at Dexter that, during King's first year, Deacon Randall is said to have kept a notebook on King in which he recorded any misdeeds, shortcomings, and complaints from the people. King's proposals represented a strategic attempt to wrest some control of the congregation from the deacon board.[23]

King made thirty-four recommendations to his new congregation, among which was the creation of a social and political action committee.

Arguing that "the gospel of Jesus is a social gospel as well as a personal gospel seeking to save the whole man," King developed this new group to keep "the congregation intelligently informed concerning the social, political and economic situation." King gave the new committee the responsibility of highlighting the work of the local NAACP and helping make sure that "every member of Dexter" would become "a registered voter." The roster of those appointed to serve the congregation through this new vessel included Mary Fair Burks as chair, Jo Ann Robinson as co-chair, and Rufus Lewis as a committee member. Rather than inspire new social activism in the lives of committee members, this new group provided a platform in the church to trumpet the causes about which committee members were already passionate. In later reflections regarding the formation of the Social and Political Action Committee, King admitted: "I sought members for this committee who had already evinced an interest in social problems, and who had some prior experience in this area. Fortunately this was not a difficult task, for Dexter had several members who were deeply concerned about community problems, and who accepted with alacrity."[24]

King's decision to launch a social and political action committee demonstrates his desire to move beyond rhetoric to launch specific actions in the struggle for civil rights. King also knew he had ready allies in those who would serve on this nascent committee. He provided space and a platform within Dexter for those who were already very much involved in the struggle in the broader community. He would also learn from the boldness of his parishioners, who were already outspoken leaders. Inspired by their courage, he hoped others at Dexter would share in his admiration of Lewis, Robinson, and Burks by getting more involved in the freedom struggle.

From all indications, the Social and Political Action Committee went to work immediately. Their second report consisted of a voting survey issued to the congregation. Coretta Scott King filled out one of the forms, indicating that she was not a registered voter because she had "not been living in the state for the last nine years." She did express a desire to become a registered voter, and when asked how the committee could help her in this process, she wrote: "Would like to know when I can register. Also I would like a copy of State laws." A few weeks later, the committee produced a third report for the church in an attempt to update the congregation on voting issues on the eve of the November gubernatorial elections. The document emphasized the importance of paying one's poll tax and also warned those who registered before 1950 that they needed to fill out a reidentification form. Intended to help inform voters on key issues on the ballot, the committee urged "every qualified voter to go to the polls on election day, no matter how seemingly insignificant the election may be. Your vote may mean the difference between the defeat or victory of some issue that might vitally affect your welfare. Go to the polls November 2, take a neighbor along with you, and friends as well!"[25]

King knew one of the best ways to inspire his congregation to get involved in the community was through his sermons. After his move from Boston, King finally had the opportunity to get comfortable with preaching weekly. He took the task seriously, often spending well over fifteen hours a week in preparation. He described his routine as follows: "I usually began an outline on Tuesday. On Wednesday I did the necessary research and thought of illustrative material and life situations that would give the sermon practical content. On Friday I began writing and usually finished the writing on Saturday night." King's first year and a half at Dexter marked the only time in his pastoral career that his schedule allowed him to focus significant attention to the development and delivery of his weekly sermons.[26]

Many Dexter members had vivid memories of King's preaching. Thelma Rice recognized the high quality of both the content and presentation of his sermons: "I was impressed with the command that he had over what he wanted to say and the way he said it, with conviction." Another parishioner, Mrs. O. B. Underwood, called young King "an outstanding preacher." She remembered resistance to his messages as well, however: "Many people didn't like his way of delivering Sunday morning messages. But most of the younger people and certainly most of his friends were very much in accord with his thoughts." She admired his directness: "the way he was able to deliver a message, it always hit, and it probably hit too hard. We used to laugh about many of the messages because you could sit in the back of the church and point out certain people that you knew said, 'looks like this message was aimed at that particular person.'" Underwood summarized King's early sermons as having strong religious and social content, while also being "easily understood by all." She was also impressed with King's delivery: "His voice was soothing; he could gain your attention almost immediately; you didn't wander when he was speaking; you listened when he was speaking, whether it was a mass meeting or a church service or a social gathering, feeling extremely elated." Dexter member Alfreida Dean Thomas concurred, noting: "I was closest to him, I would say, if you were speaking in a spiritual sense, during the sermons in church. I just always felt that everything that he said was directly related to me, as well as the other people, but very, very directly related to me and very much an influence on my life."[27]

During the fall of 1954, King's sermons continued to touch on social and political topics. As a new pastor, he also had an ambitious agenda for church growth. One of his conditions for accepting the position was that his compensation would increase as the church grew, and increased numbers would certainly bolster his worth in the eyes of his new congregation. In one early sermon, King challenged his listeners to actively proselytize others in the community if they truly believed "Christianity has the power to give new meaning to life." As they shared Jesus' good news, King encouraged them to be prepared to "defend the Church where necessary." His recommendations to the church included programs that would attract a larger membership, and he intentionally espoused greater evangelistic fervor from the pulpit.[28]

King also pushed his congregation to engage their community in new and daring ways. Believing the timeliness of movements was a critical element in their success, King lamented those who had struggled and come up short in the past, citing the "vision of racial equality" of the former vice president and 1948 presidential candidate Henry Wallace as an example of a movement that was ahead of its time. "On the other hand," King noted, "there are times when history is ready to accept a new event." In King's view, the people of Montgomery were living in such a time. The question for the congregation and its new pastor was whether they would passionately commit themselves to the task at hand.[29]

As King began to settle into his role as Dexter's pastor, he was making a favorable impression on the broader African American community in Montgomery. Early in 1955, the local NAACP met at the Metropolitan Methodist Episcopal Church in Montgomery. In opening comments,

W. C. Patton, the state conference president, updated the members on the status of the Jeremiah Reeves case, including a proposal for the Montgomery branch to pay attorney fees for the death-row inmate. The group also voted to vigorously oppose a segregated inaugural ball for Governor-elect Folsom to be held at Alabama State College. King delivered the address for the event, in which he encouraged newly installed officers to recognize that, "while we have come a long way," there is still "a long way to go." He also applauded the chapter's condemnation of the segregated inaugural ball. Years later, E. D. Nixon recalled hearing King speak for the first time: "King spoke to the NAACP in the Metropolitan Church. Me and [Alabama State University professor J. E.] Pierce was sitting back in the back of the church, and when King got through talking I said to Pierce, I said, 'Pierce, that guy makes a heck of a good speech.' He said, 'He sure did.' I said, 'Pierce, I don't know how I'm going to do it, but some day I'm going to hang him to the stars.'" King also impressed future Montgomery Improvement Association leader Johnnie Carr: "He just got up and made a few remarks after he had been introduced by Mr. Robert Nesbitt. Rosa [Parks] and I were there and I just turned around and said, 'Listen to that. He's something, isn't he?' The flow of his words and the way that he expressed them while talking about ordinary things. We discovered something in him that just made him seem a little bit different from others."[30]

The decision to have segregated balls to celebrate Governor-elect Folsom's inauguration prompted Uriah J. Fields to write a letter to the editor in which he called such segregation "undemocratic and unjustified." Fields noted that "many Negroes cast their votes for him, standing in the same lines with their white friends and using the same voting machines." A delegate to the 1952 Republican Convention in Chicago, he appealed to his experiences there as a model for Alabama: "I had the privilege of attending that ball along with other American citizens. Why can't I and other Negroes do the same for our incoming governor in this great state of Alabama?" Although Fields's attempt to persuade white southern Democrats by appealing to the practices of the Republican Party was ill-conceived at best, his letter does demonstrate a growing willingness by many African Americans to let whites know how they felt about racial discrimination.[31]

At Dexter, the Social and Political Action Committee continued to educate the congregation regarding voting requirements, regulations, and important dates. Sixteen church members attended registration clinics sponsored by the committee, and through a newsletter they highlighted the upcoming city commission election. An editorial in the newsletter championed the cause of a newly formed African American organization in the city, the Citizens Coordinating Committee. The article celebrated the new organization, noting that it was "composed of all the organizations of the city of Montgomery, whether civic, political, cultural, social or religious," and that the group formed "to provide a medium for cooperative efforts among all groups" with specific attention "placed on economic cooperation." King, who believed African Americans in Montgomery were too divided, later reflected on the promise of this new venture: "I can remember the anticipation with which I attended the first meeting of this group, feeling here the Negro community had an answer to a problem that had stood too long as a stumbling block to social progress." The organization did not last long, however, as personality conflicts and turf wars prevented any substantive coordination. King remembered: "Due to a lack of tenacity on the part of the leaders and of active interest on the part of the citizens in general, the Citizens Coordinating Committee finally dissolved. With the breakdown of this promising undertaking, it appeared that the tragic division in the Negro community could be cured only by some divine miracle." Even as the battle lines were forming in Montgomery, the African American community was unable to join together to speak and act with one voice in order to achieve social change.[32]

A lack of cohesiveness did not slow down the leaders of the Women's Political Council. During January 1955, they met with the city commissioners, seeking to broker additional gains following the hiring of black police officers the previous year. The group requested spots on the city's Parks and Recreation Board, as they hoped to eventually integrate the city's park system. While the commissioners did not provide the desired response to their demands, Mayor Gayle did take this opportunity to praise the work of the city's African American police officers. If they could not secure action from current elected officials, many blacks in Montgomery were ready to invest significant energy into electing the next city commissioners at the polls in March.[33]

Nixon, who had run for public office the previous year, helped lead the charge for a more politically engaged African American populace. In a letter penned in early February, Virginia Durr took note of Nixon's bold leadership, calling him "the most effective and bravest fighter for equal rights" in the city. She emphasized the external support he received from his union (the Brotherhood of Sleeping Car Porters) and the NAACP that allowed him to persevere despite perpetual resistance by those in power. Durr concluded that Nixon had "more support on a national basis than any man in Montgomery, and is more effective politically than any other Negro here." Nixon joined forces with the WPC in an attempt to further engage the broader African American community in the upcoming local elections. They also hoped prospective office holders would hear and respond to the concerns of Montgomery's black population.[34]

On February 23, some of the city's African American leaders invited the city commission candidates to a forum hosted at the Ben Moore Hotel. When the candidates arrived, forum organizers presented them with a list of eight "urgent needs" that demanded "immediate attention." The black community asked the politicians to offer a response to each issue, beginning with "the present bus situation." Other concerns included a request for black representation on the Parks and Recreation Board, the need for a new subdivision for African American housing, jobs for qualified blacks in the community (concerning which they noted "everybody can not teach"), black representation on all boards affecting black citizens, a need for fire hydrants in congested areas, a dearth of sewage disposals in black neighborhoods, and the prevalence of narrow streets without curbing or pavement in many African American sections of Montgomery. The sheet concluded: "What will you do to improve these undemocratic practices? Your stand on these issues will enable us to better decide on whom we shall cast our ballot in the March election. Very truly yours, Montgomery Negroes."[35]

Amazingly, all of the candidates attended the meeting. Mayor William "Tacky" Gayle was noncommittal on the issues the African American community raised, as was candidate George Cleere. Dave Birmingham, Frank Parks, and the mayoral candidate Harold McGlynn did agree to appoint a black representative to the Parks and Recreation Board. Clyde C. Sellers, a candidate for public safety commissioner, gave a general speech but avoided addressing specifics. None of the candidates dealt with the bus situation, which was the number-one concern on the list. Nor did any engage any of the economic problems or quality of life issues that affected the daily lives of working-class and poor blacks in Montgomery.[36]

A few weeks later, Sellers took out a large advertisement in the *Montgomery Advertiser* in which he offered his answers to the concerns raised in the meeting. Regarding the bus situation, Sellers wrote: "There is a state law which requires segregation of passengers on public conveyances. I feel that there should ALWAYS be seats available for BOTH races on our buses." Unwilling to offer seats on any city board to African Americans, Sellers offered to "gladly work with their representatives in an attempt to establish a negro park and expanded recreational facilities in Montgomery." He flatly rejected the suggestion that a new black housing development be located in the rapidly expanding Lincoln Heights community. While not opposed to new homes for blacks, he worried that the lack of adequate African American schools in the Lincoln Heights area "would lead to dissatisfaction and dissention," leading him to conclude "NEVER in Lincoln Heights." Regarding the request that blacks be eligible for any civil service job for which they were qualified, the candidate proclaimed: "There ARE places in this nation where civil service jobs for negroes in cities are available, but not in Montgomery. I will expand [*sic*] every effort to keep it that way." Sellers ended his advertisement with these words: "I have answered these questions exactly the way I feel. I have many friends among the negroes of Montgomery and I will be fair and honest with them in all our contacts, yet *I will not* compromise my principles nor violate my Southern birthright to promise something I do not intend to do. *I will not be intimidated for the sake of a block of negro votes.* I come to you *not* seeking your votes with wild promises, but with positive and constructive program, based on my training and experience in the fields of business and law enforcement." Sellers coupled this advertisement with what one historian described as "the most blatantly and insistently racist addresses heard in Montgomery since the days of J. Johnston Moore, the Ku Klux Klan's candidate against Mayor Gunter in the 1920s." Sellers's commitment to a "no-compromise" approach with the city's African Americans led him to a victory in the commission elections, as he outpaced the incumbent Dave Birmingham 43 percent to 37 percent.[37]

During March, the election took a back seat in the minds and hearts of many black citizens when word spread that police had arrested a teenage girl for violating the segregation statutes on city buses. Claudette Colvin, a student at Booker T. Washington High School, refused to stand when ordered to get up from her seat to accommodate a white passenger. When an officer came to forcibly remove Colvin from the bus, she resisted. Women's Political Council member A. W. West remembered: "she fought like a little tigress. The policeman had scars all over his face." Clifford Durr supported the local black attorney Fred Gray as defense attorneys for Colvin. In the middle of the legal fight, Virginia Durr described the teenager in glowing terms, noting that she was willing to "stand her ground in the face of the big burly white bus driver, two big white policemen and one big white motor cop. They dragged her off the bus, handcuffed her, and put her in jail and the most marvelous thing about her was that the two other young Negro girls moved back, the woman by her moved back, and she was left entirely alone and still she would not move." When Durr asked Colvin why she did not move, the girl replied, "I done paid my dime, they didn't have no RIGHT to move me."[38]

Over the next few months, Durr wrote several letters seeking support for legal expenses, as many hoped the arrest and conviction might become a test case that would go all the way to the U.S. Supreme Court. When Durr pleaded for financial support for the Colvin case from friends around the country, she asked that checks be sent to Mrs. Rosa Parks. When the case went before the circuit court in early May, the authorities elected to try Colvin on assault and battery, dropping any charges of breaking segregation laws, thus preventing the emergence of any constitutional challenge from the case. Authorities tried and convicted Colvin, placing her on a year's probation. Summarizing the impact of the Colvin incident, Virginia Durr reflected, "this has created tremendous interest in the Negro community and made them all fighting mad and may help give them the courage to put up a real fight on the bus segregation issue."[39]

According to Ralph Abernathy, the teen's arrest added to the feeling of discontent in the African American community. In response, he was part of a group that had several meetings with city and bus officials in which they sought to "change the seating policy to a first come, first served basis; that is, with reserved seats for either group. Wherever the two races met, this would constitute the dividing line." When city leaders claimed the suggestion could not be done according to Alabama law, black leaders asked "that they clarify the seating policy and publish it in the paper so that each person would know where his section was, so that once a Negro got on the bus and was properly seated in the Negro section he would not have to worry about getting up, giving his seat to a white passenger. After several conferences, bus officials refused to clarify this policy." The lack of concrete action by city leaders further angered many African Americans.[40]

Meanwhile, as King completed his first year preaching at Dexter, he had several opportunities to speak to a broader community increasingly agitated by white leaders' lack of concern. In sermons and speeches, he consistently encouraged his audiences not to allow anger to give rise to bitterness. In May, he accepted an invitation from Alabama State College president and Dexter Avenue Baptist Church member H. Councill Trenholm to serve as the school's baccalaureate speaker at graduation. In the speech, King challenged the new graduates to not be prisoners of "rugged individualism and national isolationism." He encouraged them not to settle for mediocrity in "various fields of endeavor" or to give into "hate and bitterness." Despite the frustrations the graduates were sure to face as they entered the workforce, King called for a loving approach in the face of repression. As King heard stories of blatant racism and experienced the sting of segregation on a daily basis, he had to regularly remind Montgomery's African American community, including himself, of the need to overcome the temptation to hate.[41]

In mid-June, King delivered a speech for the Montgomery chapter of the NAACP titled "The Peril of Superficial Optimism in the Area of Race Relations." Dexter clerk and former search committee chair Robert D. Nesbitt introduced King: "He is a great asset to Montgomery by his activity in everything for the betterment of the community. He has launched an intensive campaign in the church for NAACP membership and voters." King began his address by recognizing the amazing progress that made optimism in the area of race relations much more tenable than it would have been a few years earlier. He even suggested that "segregation is dying. He is dying hard, but there is no doubt that his corpse awaits him." King warned against complacency, noting the persistence of prejudice in the hearts of some whites and the struggles of other minorities throughout the world: "We must be concerned because we are a part of humanity. Whatever affects one affects all." Despite the intransigence of racism, King claimed that God acted through the 1954 *Brown* decision, leading him to conclude "that segregation is just as dead as a doornail and the only thing I am uncertain about is how costly the segregationist will make the funeral." King espoused this same optimism when addressing his own congregation. In a sermon titled "Discerning the Signs of History," King claimed that "evil carries the seed of its own destruction. God spoke through nine men in 1954, on May 17. They examined the legal body of segregation and pronounced it constitutionally dead and ever since then things have been changing. We can go to places all over the South that we could not go last year."[42]

Later in the summer, King delivered "The Death of Evil upon the Seashore" to his Dexter congregation. Basing his comments on Phillips Brooks's nineteenth-century sermon "The Egyptians Dead upon the Seashore," King admitted: "We have seen evil. We have seen it walk the streets of Montgomery." He surmised that human history "is the history of a struggle between good and evil. In the midst of the upward climb of goodness there is the down pull of evil." Citing the Exodus story of the parting of the Red Sea and the subsequent death of the Egyptian army, King declared: "It was a joyous daybreak that had come to end the long night of their captivity. But even more, it was the death of evil; it was the death of inhuman oppression and crushing exploitation. The death of the Egyptians upon the seashore is a glaring symbol of the ultimate doom of evil in its struggle against good." King applied his interpretation of the Exodus story to the challenges facing his congregation:

> Many years ago we were thrown into the Egypt of segregation, and our great challenge has been to free ourselves from the crippling restrictions and paralyzing effects of this vicious system. For years it looked like we would never get out of this Egypt. The Red Sea always stood before us with discouraging dimensions. But one day through a worldshaking decree by the Supreme Court of America and an awakened moral conscience of many white people, backed up by the Providence of God, the Red Sea

was opened, and freedom and justice marched through to the other side. As we look back we see segregation and discrimination caught in the mighty rushing waters of historical fate.

King tempered his triumphant pronouncement, however, warning that the drowning Egyptians must have "struggled hard to survive in the Red Sea. They probably saw a log here and even a straw there, and I can imagine them reaching desperately for something as light as straw trying to survive. This is what is happening to segregation today. It is caught in the mighty Red Sea, and its advocators are reaching out for every little straw in an attempt to survive." This desperation accounted for the flurry of absurd obstructionist laws by southern legislatures. These actions simply reinforced that "the advocators of segregation have their backs against the wall. Segregation is drowning today in the rushing waters of historical necessity." Although the ultimate outcome was clear to King, the struggle in Montgomery was far from over.[43]

During the summer of 1955, a young white pastor who would prove an important ally in the ongoing struggle moved to Montgomery as the new pastor of Trinity Lutheran Church. Most whites in the city viewed Robert S. Graetz, a Caucasian pastor of an African American congregation, with suspicion. Considered outsiders by white southerners, Graetz and his family were not fully a part of the African American culture, either. As his family sought support, they "discovered quite early that there was an underground network of so-called 'liberals' who maintained close contact with each other." They became friends with I. B. and Clara Rutledge, Clifford and Virginia Durr, and other whites in the area. Graetz marveled at the activism of white women: "While white *men* were shouting 'Segregation forever!' and working hard to preserve their cherished traditions, white *women* all over the South were working just as hard to eliminate racial prejudice and segregation. Some were quite outspoken. Mrs. Rutledge was one of the finest, a remarkable, fearless woman, who lived into her nineties." Immediately Graetz realized that they were outsiders and intruders who posed a threat to "the societal fabric of the time. We knew that. But plenty of people around us, Negro and white, reinforced our conviction that the fabric not only needed to be changed but to be torn apart."[44]

Graetz developed a relationship with Robert Hughes, who served as the state director of the integrated Alabama Council on Human Relations. The organization's local chapter was one of the city's few groups that brought blacks and whites together. As Graetz put it, "In the 1950s a white person taking part in an integrated organization, especially in the South, defied all social mores and jeopardized the principles that controlled every aspect of lives." The countercultural nature of the Montgomery Council on Human Relations meant that businesspeople were reluctant to be identified with the group even if they agreed with its principles. Graetz remembers: "A few of them supported us, but they rarely came to our meetings. More commonly, wives became actively involved in *our* councils, while husbands took part in White Citizens Councils and other organizations working to preserve segregation."[45]

A few white women did continue to work behind the scenes to challenge the racial mores of Montgomery. In a letter to Mayor Gayle, Juliette Morgan expressed her "shock and horror" regarding Police Chief Reppenthal's recent remarks concerning black police officers: "They are just niggers doing a nigger's job." While Morgan recognized that her protests amount to "so much whistling at the whirlwind," she was unwilling to "stand by and not appeal to your sense of common decency in such a case as this. If I did, I would feel like those 'good Germans' who stood by and did nothing all during the 1930's." In an addendum at the bottom of her letter to Gayle, she added, "I have long felt that there are great inconsistencies in our professions of Christianity and democracy—and our way of life."[46]

As a handful of whites spoke out against Montgomery's racism, several African Americans sought to apply direct pressure on the city regarding the integration of public schools. At a midsummer executive meeting of the NAACP, members worked on developing a petition to present to the school board in an attempt to inspire some action by the fall. Attorney Fred Gray encouraged only those parents "whose jobs will not be in jeopardy" to sign the petition. The NAACP also continued to work through the courts, filing motions for new trials in both the Jeremiah Reeves and the Claudette Colvin cases. The minutes from the July meeting also indicate that the organization's local president, Robert L. Matthews (whom Nixon had replaced as NAACP president in 1946), nominated Martin

Luther King Jr. as a candidate to serve on the executive committee, noting he had "made a great contribution to the branch, bringing in memberships and contributions." Taking minutes at the NAACP meeting was Rosa Parks, who served as the organization's secretary. A few weeks later, she left the city for a pivotal two-week trip to the Highlander Folk School in Tennessee.[47]

Earlier that summer, Virginia Durr had recommended Parks, who did seamstress work for the Durr family, as an ideal delegate for a workshop on segregation that Myles Horton and the staff at Highlander had assembled. Unable to afford the workshop's cost, Parks was granted a scholarship, prompting her to write a letter of thanks to the school's executive secretary. In the note, she expressed her excitement regarding this opportunity: "I am looking forward with eager expectation to attending the workshop, hoping to make a contribution to the fulfillment of complete freedom for all people." Parks had a wonderful experience at the school: "I was forty-two years old, and it was one of the few times in my life up to that point when I did not feel any hostility from white people. I experienced people of different races and backgrounds meeting together in workshops and living together in peace and harmony. I felt that I could express myself honestly." She recalled wishing, as her time in Tennessee came to an end, that she could have stayed longer: "It was hard to leave, knowing what I was going back to."[48]

Upon her return from Highlander, Parks resumed her role as secretary for the next NAACP branch meeting. At the gathering hosted by the Metropolitan Methodist Episcopal Church, the chapter officially approved King as a new board member. They also publicized an upcoming Women's Day Program during which the featured speaker was to be introduced by Autherine Lucy, to whom the courts had recently granted the right to be admitted to the University of Alabama after being denied three years earlier. The group also continued to discuss the need for blacks to register to vote.[49]

Despite the efforts of Nixon, the WPC, and the NAACP, the entire African American community had not come together as a unified front in their fight against white supremacy. A large part of the problem was the gulf between black professionals and the black working class in and around Montgomery. Earlier in the year, Virginia Durr had noted the class divisions: "the Negro leaders themselves have such a hard time arousing the mass of Negro people to put up any kind of fight for themselves." Part of the difficulty in mobilizing the masses rested in local social networks that rarely brought the classes together. While all faced the dehumanizing impact of segregation, their social spheres rarely intersected. Census data indicate that less than 10 percent of the African American population worked in professional fields, while most blacks worked as domestics, common laborers, or service workers. The division between the classes significantly affected one's daily routine. While a professor at Alabama State College would be able to run a hot bath or shower in the morning, more than 82 percent of the black community lacked piped hot water in their homes. Nearly 70 percent of the black community still relied on chamber pots and outhouses, while only 6 percent of the white community lacked flushable toilets.[50]

Neighborhood demographics and social networks among professionals reinforced these divergent living conditions. Although African Americans lived throughout the city, they primarily clustered in three neighborhoods that had distinct socioeconomic features. The largest group lived just west of downtown, in the second ward. This community consisted primarily of poor unskilled service workers and domestics. Just east of downtown sat the second-largest black enclave. Although this section of town included a poor area, it also housed a professional community near the Alabama State College campus and another middle-class cluster and small business district on or near South Jackson Street, which is where the Dexter parsonage was located. The poorest black section of Montgomery was in the northern part of the city, in the shadows of warehouses, manufacturing mills, and other industries. Those who were part of the professional class often filled their lives with memberships in social service organizations and clubs. Although a few churches brought together the working and professional classes on Sunday, this was one of their few connections. Professional blacks might respond to physical needs and hardships that caught their attention, but for the most part they did not know the daily lives of working-class blacks in their own town. While philanthropy, service, lobbying, and court cases may have benefited the entire African American community, such an agenda was unlikely to "arouse the masses." In the political arena, particularly following the *Brown v. Board of Education* decision, most local leaders set their sights on challenging Jim Crow segregation while relegating economic and quality of life issues to a secondary position.[51]

King happened to be the pastor of an African American church with a professional "silk-stocking" reputation. Although he enjoyed preaching to an educated congregation, he was never comfortable with the perceived exclusivity of Dexter. While he appreciated their staid responses to his preaching, he bristled at the undertones of haughtiness that often went hand in hand with a congregation largely comprised of professionals. Convinced that true worship would transcend class distinctions, King challenged Dexter to become more educationally and socioeconomically inclusive: "Worship at its best is a social experience where people of all levels of life come together and communicate with a common father. Here the employer and the employee, the rich and the poor, the white collar worker and the common laborer all come together in a vast unity. Here we come to see that although we have different callings in life we are all the children of a common father, who is the father of both the rich and the poor." King's earliest preaching experiences had been at his father's primarily working-class church in Atlanta. He did not want Dexter to become Ebenezer, but he did want Dexter to become a place where any member of his father's congregation would be welcomed and embraced. King's desire to build ties with the working class played a significant role in uniting the people in the days to come.[52]

King also hoped to build bridges with the white community. Recognizing the presence in Montgomery of men and women like Aubrey Williams, Clifford and Virginia Durr, and Clara Rutledge reaffirmed King's belief that goodwill was possible from the white race. While he did not dismiss the persistence of white racism, King encouraged his congregation to overcome the temptation to paint all whites with the same brush: "The Negro who experiences bitter and agonizing circumstances as a result of some ungodly white person is tempted to look upon all white persons as evil, if he fails to look beyond his circumstances." King offered an extremely positive assessment of the potential of whites who are "some of the most implacable and vehement advocates of racial equality." Highlighting the role of whites in the founding of the NAACP, King noted the organization still "gains a great deal of support from northern and southern white persons." Therefore King could encourage his congregation to "wait on the Lord," confident that "God's goodness will ultimately win out over every state of evil in the universe." King concluded, "We as Negroes may often have our highest dreams blown away by the jostling winds of a white man's prejudice, but wait on the Lord." A tragedy in the neighboring state of Mississippi provided a stark reminder to King and to African Americans throughout the country of the "jostling winds of a white man's prejudice."[53]

Earlier in the summer of 1955, fourteen-year-old Emmett Till had traveled to visit family near Money, Mississippi. After the young African American from Chicago allegedly said "bye, baby" to a white lady working at the general store in town, many blacks in the area were prepared for the worst. Tragedy struck about a week later, when the woman's husband and brother-in-law picked up Till in the middle of the night, shot him in the head, and dumped his body in a river. The arrest and trial of the murderers happened quickly. So did the jury's acquittal of the men, as they deliberated for less than an hour before declaring the defendants "not guilty."

For many African Americans, the murder of young Emmett Till served as a brutal reminder of the depths and horrors of racism. Countless blacks would never forget the picture of Till's battered corpse published in *Jet* magazine. The acquittal of the murderers by an all-white Mississippi jury further demonstrated that justice did not exist for blacks in the South. The verdict amounted to a sanctioning of white supremacy and brutality. The case did not escape King's notice. In a sermon delivered the week following the verdict, King lamented, "That jury in Mississippi, which a few days ago in the Emmett Till case, freed two white men from what might be considered one of the most brutal and inhuman crimes of the twentieth century, worships Christ." In response to those who "worship Christ emotionally and not morally," King paraphrased words from Isaiah 1:13–15: "Get out of my face. Your incense is an abomination unto me, your feast days trouble me. When you spread forth your hands, I will hide my face. When you make your loud prayer, I will not hear. Your hands are full of blood."[54]

In the wake of the Till verdict, King angrily lamented the brutal consequences of systematic injustice. He turned to the parable of the rich man, traditionally known as Dives, and Lazarus, in which an affluent man failed to fully address the needs of a beggar named Lazarus, resulting in eternal punishment for the wealthy man. For King, the man's sin was not that he created the injustice but that "he felt that the gulf which existed between him and Lazarus was a proper condition of life. Dives felt that this was the way things were to be. He took the 'isness' of circumstantial accidents and transformed them into the 'oughtness' of a universal structure." King connected the parable to life in America in 1955: "Dives is the white man who refuses to cross the gulf of segregation and lift his Negro brother to the position of first class citizenship, because he thinks segregation is a part of the fixed structure of the universe." Like the rich man from Jesus' parable, Alabama's white denominations and organizations either failed to directly challenge the injustice of segregation or attempted to maintain the racial status quo.[55]

Some of the white businessmen in Montgomery became increasingly frustrated by the inability of local politicians to move the city forward following World War II. Concerned with the community's economic dependence on the air force bases, they believed Montgomery desperately needed to embrace industrialization. In response, a number of leading businessmen chose to form a new organization: the "Men of Montgomery." The group first met in October 1955 under the slogan "We Mean Business." As this group of influential citizens examined the challenges facing their city, they did not recognize the crippling effects of systemic discrimination and segregation. Rather than lobby for a more inclusive city, this group hung their hopes for a new Montgomery on the construction of a cutting-edge terminal at the city's airport.[56]

Alabama's Southern Baptists also sought to overcome many of the challenges facing Montgomery and their home state. In a report submitted for the denomination's statewide meeting, they addressed the issue of race relations, unable to turn a blind eye to what was an increasingly charged atmosphere following the *Brown* decision and the Till verdict. The denomination's Christian Life Commission rendered the following report:

In the south it is primarily a matter of the black and the white. The recent supreme court decision on desegregation is one of serious moment to the south. Only a dreaming idealist could close his eyes to the stark realities of that problem. On the other hand, the Christian must strive to his utmost to find a proper solution to the circumstances. Feeling runs high in the south as exemplified by the Till case in Mississippi. There is an unfortunate example of parties choosing to fan the emotions rather than seek to make the best usage of an extremely unfortunate situation. Hatemongers on both sides have played upon the emotions of all otherwise reasonable people. It is not good and we earnestly urge thoughtfulness and patience. Without passing judgment on the "White Councils" organized in certain southern states we cannot help but raise the question, "Is it the best?" We look askance at these movements believing that they will divide us further rather than offer an answer.

The Southern Baptists in Alabama were aware of the challenges facing the South but were unwilling to take a clear stand on any of the big issues, including school desegregation, White Citizens Councils, or even the verdict in the Emmett Till trial. Such passivity by Christians in the South must have become more and more obvious to King the longer he lived in Montgomery.[57]

Meanwhile, the White Citizens Council sought to establish itself in the city. Roughly 450 people showed up for an October 3 organizational meeting at city hall. Temporary chairperson Luther Ingalls attempted to rally those gathered by shouting: "The house is on fire. We've got to wake up!" Alabama state senator Sam Englehardt offered an address in which he accused the NAACP of having ties to the Communist Party. In their analysis of the event, the Alabama Council of Human Relations newsletter seized on an editorial printed in the *Montgomery Advertiser* that noted that because they failed to attract any "face cards"—that is, no significant Montgomery leaders "were within a mile of the meeting"—the event was "harmless." While the first meeting was not particularly well attended, the WCC would grow in strength over the next several months.[58]

In the face of the alarming passivity of some and the blatant racism of others, King's concern for radical structural change continued to influence his preaching as 1955 drew to a close. In a very unorthodox interpretation of Jesus' parable of the Good Samaritan, King questioned the long-term effectiveness of the story's protagonist: "He was concerned merely with temporary relief, not with thorough reconstruction. He sought to sooth the effects of evil, without going back to uproot the causes." King had come to realize that many southern whites were in the same boat. They might privately question the Till verdict, keep their distance when the White Citizens Council came to town, and offer assistance to a destitute African American that crossed their paths, but they were unwilling to challenge the dehumanizing system known as their "way of life." King concluded his sermon by calling his congregation to couple the compassion of the Good Samaritan with a willingness "to tear down unjust conditions and build anew instead of just patching things up." Within a few weeks, King would have the opportunity to make a major contribution in collaboration with others seeking significant structural change in Montgomery.[59]

As 1955 drew to a close, King found himself in the midst of the struggle for civil rights in the heart of the South. The doctrine of white supremacy cast a pall over the entire city of Montgomery. Although a handful spoke against the system, the vast majority of whites either wholeheartedly endorsed segregation or tacitly sanctioned its existence. Despite the apparent intransigence of Jim Crow segregation, some African Americans in Montgomery were challenging the status quo. They demanded meetings with city commissioners, held a political forum for local political candidates, attempted to integrate city schools, and rallied around the arrest of teenager Claudette Colvin when she refused to give up her seat on a city bus. Still, Montgomery's black community was divided. Although conflicts among some leaders explained part of the problem, the day-to-day gulf between professionals and the working class proved more debilitating.

A resident of Alabama for fewer than eighteen months, King was not yet at the forefront of community activists. He did provide a new type of leader on the local scene, however. He combined the education and pedigree of the most accomplished black professionals in the city with a heart for connecting with working-class people. He also articulated a powerful message of hope that inspired people to radical love and bold labor with the confidence that segregation would soon pass away. King's sermons during 1954–1955 reveal that challenging racism's various manifestations became a regular feature of his preaching and psyche. As he encountered Robert Hughes, Juliette Morgan, Aubrey Williams, and Virginia Durr, he was encouraged by the willingness of some whites to join the struggle for justice. Through the courageous and tireless efforts of Jo Ann Robinson, E. D. Nixon, Mary Fair Burks, Rufus Lewis, and Rosa Parks, he saw examples of people making contributions toward the effort to end discrimination and segregation. Inspired by their lives, King was ready to join the front lines of the battle himself.[60]

4 "They Are Willing to Walk"

> We shouldn't give people the illusion that there are no sacrifices involved, that it can be ended soon. My intimidations are a small price to pay if victory can be won. We shouldn't make the illusion that they won't have to walk. I believe to the bottom of my heart that the majority of Negroes would ostracize us. They are willing to walk.
> —Martin Luther King Jr., January 30, 1956

Rosa Parks would not be moved. It was Thursday afternoon, and she had just completed a long day's work as a seamstress in a downtown department store. When she boarded the bus, Parks located a seat in the first row of the African American section, only to be ordered to move a few minutes later to accommodate a boarding white passenger. As Parks continued to sit, the bus driver got the police involved, who placed her under arrest. Word soon spread around town, and a few were ready to act. They had waited for the day when the city's bus laws could finally be challenged in court. E. D. Nixon later remembered: "I have told the press time after time that we were doing these things for years before December 1955, but all they want to do is start at December 1 and forget about what happened. They say that Mrs. Parks is the lady that sat down on the bus and then they want to start talking about what happened December 5. But that leaves a whole lot of folks out and ignores a lot of what was done over a long period of time to set the stage." Those who had "set the stage" in Montgomery did not waste any time seizing the moment. Clifford and Virginia Durr joined Nixon in bailing Parks out of jail. They then went to her apartment, where they talked with Parks and her husband at length about the possibility of making her arrest a constitutional test case of bus segregation. She agreed to move forward legally should she be found guilty in court the following Monday.[1]

After a little more than a year in Montgomery, Parks's arrest thrust

King into the front lines of a local movement for civil rights. His theological discussions of evil would become much more than rhetoric bolstered by occasional reminders of the ugliness of racism in the segregated South. He would experience a daily battle, facing weapons as varied as the spoken word, letters, phone calls, and even bombs. Pushed into the role of spokesperson for the newly formed Montgomery Improvement Association (MIA), King flourished, galvanizing the African American community with his inspired Holt Street address. Behind the scenes, King continued to lean upon and learn from the people of Montgomery, who were the backbone of the movement. Without the organizational efforts, commitment, and examples of Nixon, Jo Ann Robinson, and Mary Fair Burks, coupled with the daily sacrifices of the people, the bus boycott would have never happened and King might well have settled into a reflective and secure career, never personally engaging the battle himself. Because the people of Montgomery were willing to walk, King had the opportunity to lead.

Jo Ann Robinson was better prepared for this moment than King. When she heard of Parks's arrest, she went right to work, laboring through the night mimeographing thousands of fliers describing a one-day bus boycott on Monday, December 5. Her statement explained that another African American had been arrested for not yielding her seat to a white person. Noting that it was the second such arrest since the Claudette Colvin case that spring, Robinson charged: "Negroes have rights, too, for if Negroes did not ride the buses, they could not operate. Three-fourth of riders are Negroes, yet we are arrested, or have to stand over empty seats." In an attempt to personalize the situation, she continued, "The next time it may be you, or your daughter, or mother." The note encouraged "every Negro to stay off the buses Monday in protest of the arrest and trial. Don't ride buses to work, to town, to school, or anywhere on Monday." Her task was urgent if she was to circumvent any conservative impulses on the part of Montgomery's African American ministers, many of whom tended to be reticent to take such bold steps.[2]

Attorney Fred Gray remembered the cautious attitude embodied by many of the local clergy: "Initially, the Women's Political Council (led by Mary Fair Burks and Jo Ann Robinson), E. D. Nixon, and Rufus Lewis were more interested in the Protest than were the ministers." According

to Robinson, the town's clergy supported the proposed boycott only after realizing that many of their parishioners were already backing the protest: "One minister read the circular, inquired about the announcements,
and found that all the city's black congregations were quite intelligent
on the matter and were planning to support the one-day boycott with or
without their ministers' leadership. It was then that the ministers decided
that it was time for them, the leaders, to catch up with the masses." To
ensure the masses were aware of the planned protest as soon as possible,
Robinson mobilized the WPC on Friday morning to spread the word.
Some, like fellow Dexter Avenue member and Alabama State professor
J. E. Pierce, were not initially supportive. He did not believe the people
would actually support even a one-day boycott. Others were more recep-
tive, however, including Nixon.[3]

At first, King was reluctant to join the proposed bus protest. When
Nixon called early Friday morning asking for his involvement and support, King was hesitant. Nixon later recalled: "The third person I called
was Martin Luther King. He said, 'Brother Nixon, let me think about it
awhile and call me back,' and I called him back. He said, 'Yeah, Brother
Nixon, I decided, I'm going to go along with you.' And I said, 'That's
fine, because I called 18 other people and I told them they're going to
meet at your church this evening.'" Meanwhile Robinson and a few of her
students had left the anonymous boycott notices at a local church where
a clergy meeting was scheduled for that morning. Soon nearly every pastor in Montgomery knew of the proposed boycott, and they joined other
community leaders at Dexter that evening.[4]

When she returned to the Alabama State College campus, Robinson
discovered that the college president, H. Councill Trenholm, wanted to
see her immediately. Trenholm confronted Robinson regarding her role
in making the 52,500 leaflets that were distributed. Fearing she might
be fired, Robinson explained the conditions that had led to the proposed
boycott and the significant role of the WPC in bringing these injustices
to light. Trenholm's response was more positive than she expected: "Your
group must continue to press on for civil rights." The president did require her to reimburse the school for the mimeographed copies she had
made and let her know that her role in the protests must be behind the
scenes, not involving the school directly. Assured that her job was safe at

least for the time being, Robinson headed to Dexter that evening for the proposed organizational meeting.[5]

The gathering at Dexter proved contentious. Since Nixon had left town early Friday to fulfill work commitments, Reverend L. Roy Bennett, the president of the Interdenominational Ministerial Alliance, presided at the meeting. According to King, Bennett attempted to stymie debate by eliminating any group participation or discussion and instead charged ahead with concrete plans for the upcoming boycott. After nearly an hour of filibustering, Bennett agreed to open up the floor for questions and discussion. The majority voted to proceed with the one-day boycott and began working on an ad hoc transportation system to be put in place on Monday to help African Americans get around town without using the buses. They also revised Robinson's original statement, removing a reference to Claudette Colvin and adding information about a mass meeting to be held on Monday evening at Holt Street Baptist Church. King and Abernathy used Dexter's mimeograph machine to again produce thousands of leaflets for distribution throughout the city. While working, they discussed the leadership needs the hour demanded. According to Abernathy, King was wary of Bennett, believing he would elevate the clergy into strategic positions at the expense of the people whom they were asking to make the real sacrifice by not riding city buses.[6]

On Saturday, ministers and other community leaders worked to distribute the leaflets. Mary Fair Burks and Jo Ann Robinson ran into their share of challenges: "Despite our early start, progress was slow. Often we not only had to take time to explain the leaflet, but also first to read it to those unable to do so." This experience interacting with the city's poorer citizens proved an eye-opening experience for Burks, who taught at Alabama State College, as boycott communication efforts forced her out of her middle-class world: "It was my first encounter with masses of the truly poor and disenfranchised. I remember thinking that not even a successful boycott would solve the problems of poverty and illiteracy which I saw that day." Burks was not alone in her observations. Many pastors also encountered the challenging living conditions faced by many of Montgomery's African American residents for the very first time. Edgar French, the pastor of Hillard Chapel AME Zion, noted: "Although there was not time for pastoral visits, ministers had been closer to the realities of living in slum areas than ever before. They had really been among poorly-clad and undernourished children, alcoholics, and many other forms of human deprivation they hardly realized existed. The stark evils of social and economic injustices experienced in those few hours made it easy for many of the ministers to discard their well-prepared manuscripts at the Sunday worship hour, and to speak concerning the evils of their day." The task of communicating about the planned boycott proved to be as galvanizing for Montgomery's African American community as Parks's arrest had been.[7]

That evening, Mary Fair Burks also experienced the aloofness of some of Montgomery's black professionals. Due to delays in explaining the handbills that announced the proposed one-day boycott to the masses in Montgomery, Robinson and Burks were an hour late to a scheduled bridge party. Burks remembered: "Our partners were irate, despite our explanations. . . . And so about one hundred black women played bridge a scant thirty-six hours before the boycott began, much like Nero had played his fiddle while Rome burned. That was the black middle class before the boycott." Although not every African American understood or embraced the proposed protest, Burks and Robinson worked tirelessly to make sure everybody, regardless of economic class, would know about the boycott by Monday morning.[8]

In addition to the leaflets, nearly all the African American congregations heard about the boycott from their pastors that Sunday. Stories in both the *Alabama Tribune* and the *Montgomery Advertiser* bolstered efforts to inform the entire black community about the one-day protest. Local television news stations also highlighted the effort in their broadcasts. While some wanted the plot to remain a secret to surprise the city, the media coverage served to inform those who had not yet heard of the plan and to legitimize the effort in the minds of others. Many united around the proposed boycott, arousing interest that circumvented the typically rigid class distinctions. Rosa Parks's standing in the community contributed to this widespread support. As Mary Fair Burks put it: "Mrs. Parks's arrest penetrated the indifference of the middle class and shook the passivity of the masses. The educated class realized that what had happened to her could happen to any one of them. Most of the passive masses did not know Rosa, but when the boycott was called, they identified with her situation. They had experienced it all too often." Though most black residents did not know Parks, the majority of black leaders and professionals did not know the so-called "passive masses." Before the arrest of Parks and the subsequent planned protest, they had crossed paths primarily in the public sphere. Most black civil rights leaders in Montgomery did not have enough evidence to determine how passive the working class was until this moment, when the masses proved more than ready to get involved.[9]

The boycott of city buses allowed a disparate African American community to unite to unleash a perfect storm upon white leaders in Montgomery. Black professionals saw Rosa Parks as a respectable citizen who was mistreated and abused for conducting herself with silent dignity. No matter how much African Americans in the Jim Crow South had accomplished, they remained vulnerable second-class citizens subject to the whims of white authority figures. They also saw the opportunity to challenge the dehumanizing system of segregation that affected every black regardless of class or degree of respectability. Meanwhile, the working class bore the brunt of the specific dehumanizing experience of riding buses in Montgomery. They endured the racist abuses of some of the drivers. They identified with how tired and weary Parks was on the night of her arrest. The situation on the city buses was a quality-of-life issue for the working class of Montgomery, and they proved ready to sacrifice to change the situation.

On the Sunday morning following Parks's arrest, King chose to address the "awful silence of God" with his Dexter congregation. King suggested that although throughout history people had "appealed to God in desperate tones" to bring justice, "evil continued to rise to astronomical proportions." King admitted that, in a world filled with evil and injustice, maintaining the necessary faith to fight for change would not be easy. Despite the enormity of the challenge, King called on his congregation to join a citywide, one-day boycott of city buses. While not brushing aside experiences to the contrary, King called for action to overcome "the iron feet of oppression." King's text for the sermon, found in Isaiah 45:15, asserts, "Verily thou art a God that hidest thyself, O God of Israel, the Saviour." The context of the verse, however, proclaims the creative and redeeming power of God leading to the salvation of Israel and the downfall of their oppressors. Over the next two months, thousands in Montgomery proved willing to walk so God's justice would no longer be hidden by the wickedness of white supremacy. Inspired by God and the people, King would learn to lead as they courageously encountered the depths of evil together.[10]

As Monday morning dawned, many watched city buses go by their homes and places of business, wondering how successful the boycott would be. To their great surprise and satisfaction, the boycott was nearly 100 percent effective. Ralph Abernathy credited another element of good fortune that helped make the effort so successful. The previous day, the city's police commissioner had appeared on local television and radio assuring police protection for blacks who chose to ride despite "goon squads" that would threaten them. "The Commissioner also said that there would be two squad cars—one in front and one behind every bus that rolled on Monday morning." According to Abernathy, "Negroes who had not really been swept into the spirit of the movement, upon seeing policemen riding behind the buses, felt they were there to force them to ride, and rebelled against it by joining with those who were walking." During a testimony time at a mass meeting held during the boycott, a participant recounted how she had joined the boycott upon seeing police at her bus stop that morning. Given the reputation of white police officers for violence against African Americans, she decided to avoid the bus stop and walked to work instead. In the end, only a handful of Montgomery's African American citizens rode the bus that Monday, December 5, 1955. It proved to be an extremely successful beginning of what would become a yearlong protest.[11]

Early that morning, Fred Gray left a meeting with King and Robinson and headed to the courthouse as the defense attorney for Rosa Parks's trial, which was scheduled to begin at 9 a.m. Gray had to weave through hundreds of people to make it into the packed courtroom. After originally intending to charge Parks under a city code demanding segregation, the state instead convicted her in violation of chapter 1, section 8, of an obscure 1945 Alabama law requiring segregation on buses. The court sentenced Parks to either pay a ten-dollar fine or face fourteen days in jail. Fred Gray immediately appealed the ruling on Parks's behalf. Nixon later remembered the community's response: "On December 5, 1955, the black man was born again in Montgomery. On that morning when they tried Mrs. Rosa Parks, the whole courtroom and all out in the street was crowded with black men. They was saying, 'Brother Nick, Brother Nick, what's happening?' I tells them she's found guilty. They was mad then. They said, 'Brother Nick, if you don't come out, you know what we gonna do? We gonna come in there and get you.' There must've been over five hundred men there." Parks's guilty verdict, coupled with the early success of the boycott, further galvanized the city's African American community as they prepared to meet at Holt Street Baptist Church that evening.[12]

In the afternoon, community leaders gathered in an attempt to organize in the wake of the success of the one-day boycott. They met at Reverend Bennett's Mt. Zion African Methodist Episcopal Church, with Reverend Bennett again presiding. The decision to have the meeting at Mt. Zion reflected both the low level of trust between many of the city's pastors and an attempt to remain united as the protest developed. Many believed the non-Baptist ministers would not have attended had the meeting been held at the Baptist Center under the direction of Reverend Hubbard, who served as president of the Baptist Ministers Conference. Therefore they chose to meet at a Methodist church in order to bolster whatever frail unity existed in the moment. As had been the case a few days earlier, the meeting began with attempts to wrest control away from Reverend Bennett, who again held onto the floor. At this point, Robert Matthews of the NAACP suggested that some in the meeting were trying to spy on the proceedings in order to report back to white leaders. In the midst of the chaos, those gathered finally decided to form an executive committee that would meet behind closed doors to determine the shape of the organization and make plans for the mass meeting that evening. According to Abernathy, eighteen people were chosen to serve on the committee.[13]

When the executive meeting began, Abernathy suggested they call their new organization the "Montgomery Improvement Association (MIA)," a proposal that was quickly accepted. The meeting's momentum soon slowed as several leaders wanted to be able to keep their affiliation with the MIA secret. Most local clergy had learned to be cautious in challenging racial mores, as they balanced advocating for their race while not unduly offending white officials. Nixon was incensed: "We are acting like little boys. Somebody's name will have to be known, and if we are afraid we might just as well fold up right now. . . . We'd better decide now if we are going to be fearless men or scared boys." Chastised by Nixon, those present agreed to publicly endorse an indefinite continuation of the one-day boycott until certain conditions were met.[14]

As one of their first orders of business, the MIA selected officers. Many of those gathered had served in various leadership capacities over the years. Few of them would have ridden buses that day even if a boycott had not been in effect. While the new organization needed a leader who would command the respect of the people in the room, they also needed someone who would be able to connect with those who were making the real sacrifice by giving up the use of public transportation. Although Nixon had the strongest connection with the black working class, his unlearned use of the English language and lack of education prevented many professionals from uniting behind him. Rufus Lewis and NAACP chair Robert Matthews did not have the support of the working class. The more established clergy, such as Baptist Ministers Conference president and Bethel Baptist Church pastor Hillman H. Hubbard, or Interdenominational Ministerial Alliance president Reverend L. Roy Bennett, had a history of compromise with city fathers that disqualified them, while younger pastors, like Uriah J. Fields of Bell Street Baptist Church, had not yet earned the respect of the more established leaders.

Those gathered had to navigate the distrust, rivalries, and jealousies while also finding a spokesperson who could connect with African Americans across class lines. Independently, Nixon and Lewis believed King was the person who could become a unifying figure for the trying days ahead. When the nominations for president opened, Lewis hastily submitted King's name, and he was unanimously elected to the position. When he later reflected on this turn of events, King claimed that if he had taken time to consider the position, "I would have declined the nomination." When some friends had encouraged him to pursue the presidency of the local NAACP chapter a few weeks earlier, he and Coretta had decided he "should not then take on any heavy community responsibilities, since I had so recently finished my thesis, and needed to give more attention to my church work." Without the time to contemplate the possible implications of his new role, King became president of the newly formed MIA.[15]

Not everyone was enthusiastic about the decision to place King in charge of the new organization. Uriah Fields coveted the job as well. Years later, Fields claimed: "It was given to King because some of the older ministers didn't want it. I feel that there was a strong feeling as to whether King or I should've had that position. Because of what I had been involved in. But it went to King. And notice that immediately after they selected King president, they elected me secretary." Despite the undercurrents of jealousy that were bound to emerge among the town's leaders, all united behind King. Before adjourning, they organized a subcommittee to continue meeting in order to draw up a list of demands they would bring to the city and the bus company.[16]

Nixon, Abernathy, and Reverend Edgar French had the responsibility of drawing up a list of demands as conditions for ending the boycott. The first was a plan that the WPC had been pushing for several years: Seating on the buses would be first-come, first-served, with blacks filling the bus from the back to the front, and whites from the front to the back. Once patrons had filled all the seats, no one would be expected to yield their seat to an oncoming passenger. Second, they called for more courteous treatment of customers by the bus drivers. The third demand concerned hiring black bus drivers for predominantly African American routes. This idea, which Uriah Fields had included in a letter to the editor of the *Montgomery Advertiser* over a year and a half earlier, reflected Nixon's desire for black economic development to be one of the significant desired objectives of the protest. French typed up these three demands later in the day so they could be presented at that evening's mass meeting.[17]

The demands did not include an end to segregation on the city's buses. In an interview conducted during the boycott, Jo Ann Robinson attempted to explain why: "There is a state law requiring segregation, and all we do must come under that law. We cannot change the law by protesting. It must be declared unconstitutional through the courts. We can get our demands under the present law, however, this protest is more far reaching than that. It is making the white man more respective of the Negro, and it shows him that the Negro can be a threat to his economic security which has kept him in his position of superiority to some extent." *Alabama Tribune* editor Emory O. Jackson basically agreed with Robinson's assessment, noting that the boycott was only "incidentally a protest against segregation. That is the first observation, it seems to me, which should be emphasized and kept in mind. What has happened is the release of pent up resentment over the recurring, unceasing and unrelenting abuse, humiliation and disrespect accorded Negro passengers, especially the lady folk." Jackson applauded the efforts of Montgomery's black citizens: "For placid, conservative yielding Montgomery leadership to get worked up into what has been described as a 'boycott' had to be something that touched more sharply than racial segregation, must have been a reaction from segregation more painful than the mere shameful practice of an annoying discrimination." The African American people of Montgomery were ready to act.[18]

King made his way to Holt Street Baptist Church aware that he had been thrust into a position that he had neither expected nor sought. King later admitted: "When I went to Montgomery as a pastor, I had not the slightest idea that I would later become involved in a crisis in which non-violent resistance would be applicable. I neither started the protest nor suggested it. I simply responded to the call of the people for a spokesman." He had little time to prepare for what would be the most significant address of his young life. He felt the burden of the task as he attempted to construct "a speech that was expected to give a sense of direction to a people imbued with a new and still unplumbed passion for justice." With only enough time to prepare a brief outline, King set out for Holt Street. Traffic was so thick around the church that he had to park several blocks away. The service began with two hymns, prayer, and Scripture, followed by what would be the first of many memorable addresses delivered by King.[19]

In his Holt Street address, King reminded the large audience of the long history of intimidation on the city's buses and discussed the specific circumstances surrounding Parks's arrest. Employing a phrase he had used the day before in his sermon at Dexter, King charged, "And you know, my friends, there comes a time when people get tired of being trampled over by the iron feet of oppression." Aware of the history of divisions among the city's black community, King called for unity as they worked together for justice. In his stirring conclusion, King proclaimed: "Right here in Montgomery, when the history books are written in the future, somebody will have to say, 'There lived a race of people, a black people, "fleecy locks and black complexion," a people who had the moral courage to stand up for their rights. And thereby they injected a new meaning into the veins of history and civilization.'" King later remembered the enthusiastic response to his speech: "As I sat listening to the continued applause I realized that this speech had evoked more response than any speech or sermon I had ever delivered, and yet it was virtually unprepared." Few who were there would ever forget the impact that King's speech had on them that early December evening.[20]

Thousands heard the speech, either from seats in the auditorium, through a public address system in the church basement, or on make-shift speakers placed outside of the building. Many saw in the people's response the dawning of a new day for Montgomery's African American citizens. Rufus Lewis claimed the speech "stimulated the people more than anything has ever stimulated them as long as I've been here."[21] The Montgomery resident Idessa Williams Redden was so moved by King's speech that she shouted, "Lord, you have sent us a leader." Not surprisingly, Nixon's perspective on the evening was different; he described the mass meeting as "the most amazing and the most heartening thing I have seen in my life. The leaders were led. It was a vertical thing." While the speech did inspire the people and elevated King's stature in the minds of the community, the converse is true as well. The response of the crowd stimulated something in King. He had risen to the occasion, and the people's response emboldened him. King was not a regular patron of the city's buses. He was not boycotting anything. The African American people of Montgomery allowed him to participate in the boycott in the role of the president and spokesperson of the MIA. As Nixon aptly stated, King was led, and his life and ministry would never be the same.[22]

No longer a one-day event, the bus boycott galvanized Montgomery's African American community. Organizers of the protest launched creative solutions to accommodate those whose jobs necessitated significant daily travel. Their first transportation alternative was to enlist African American–owned taxis to offer service at a reduced rate equivalent to local bus fares. In response, the city enacted a law that set a minimum rate for taxis and threatened full prosecution for any who dared to break this mandate. Again ingenuity prevailed, as boycott leaders set up an intricate carpooling system that allowed residents to get the transportation they needed. The car pools served to further unify the community as strangers and casual acquaintances began to spend significant time together each day. Those wealthy enough to own vehicles volunteered to drive working-class citizens, further breaking down barriers between the classes. As they rode, they shared the joys and trials of the boycott with one another. Alabama State College history professor Norman Walton emphasized the significance of the car pool in solidifying the cohesion of the participants: "It has closed the gap between the Negro groups based on education, income and position. In Montgomery, there is unity, the lowest person doing her humble task, rides to work in a Cadillac, a jalopy or a truck. The college professor talks with the maid and the drunkard to the minister, but with a common interest that brings them together." These unplanned conversations and burgeoning relationships did as much to solidify the boycott as any speech or mass meeting.[23]

Meanwhile King continued to shepherd Dexter Avenue Baptist Church. After a guest speaker filled the Dexter pulpit on December 12, King preached the following three Sundays to his home congregation, including a Christmas sermon entitled "The Light That Shineth amid Darkness." In the midst of the darkness of white stubbornness, hatred, and exclusion, King emphasized the necessity of love to his congregation that Christmas morning. His words had more force now, however, as his descriptions of darkness were not theological abstractions but morally tangible and politically all too real. Over the coming months, King's sermons would continue to grow in depth, urgency, and power. A technically accomplished preacher before the boycott, King's speaking was now imbued with a passion that stirred his congregation, his community, and eventually the nation.[24]

Although he was pastor of a silk-stocking church in Montgomery, King's time at Ebenezer had prepared him for dealing with both the professional and working-class citizens of Montgomery. His decisions to take on summer jobs as a teen doing manual labor helped him more effectively communicate with those who had depended on the buses for daily transportation. Since his arrival at Dexter, he had hoped to attract more working-class and poor blacks to his church. Even if changing the makeup of his congregation proved difficult, King enjoyed the opportunity to address the working class regularly at mass meetings. He also attempted to listen to and learn from those who were sacrificing most so the boycott could continue. King's ability to effectively interact with even the boycott's most vulnerable participants impressed Jo Ann Robinson: "There was no other leader there with the humility, with the education, with the know-how of dealing with people who were angry and poor and hungry. . . . If King had not been prepared to talk with all of them, make all of them feel that they were making a contribution—and they were. Even that man who couldn't give a straight sentence was letting you know how he felt, and maybe representing the people from his area."

Not only did King encourage and inspire the poor and working-class participants; he was encouraged and transformed by their commitment as well. One of his favorite anecdotes from the boycott was about an elderly woman known to the black community as Mother Pollard, who dismissed suggestions by concerned friends and pastors that she go ahead and ride the bus due to her age. In response, she simply replied, "My feets is tired, but my soul is rested." As he witnessed the resilience of people like Mother Pollard, King was more prepared to make personal sacrifices.[25]

Aware that the boycott represented a radical challenge to the status quo in Montgomery, leaders of the Alabama Council on Human Relations (ACHR) got involved, hoping to serve as an intermediary body between the protesters, the city leaders, and the bus company. Local leaders of the ACHR included the council president, Thomas Thrasher, who was pastor of the Church of the Ascension, Montgomery's largest Episcopalian congregation, and Robert E. Hughes, a Methodist minister who served as the organization's executive director. An interracial organization, the ACHR had the advantage of relationships with all the local parties involved. They moved to set up a meeting in the hope that a settlement could be reached. There was reason to be pessimistic about the ability of the ACHR to broker an agreement. Following the *Brown v. Board of Education* decision, they had tried and failed to bring white and black ministers together to merely discuss the implications of the ruling. While Hughes did not shy away from speaking about racial justice, he was more interested in developing relationships than engaging in debates with staunch segregationists. Together Hughes and Thrasher parlayed their unique positions in the community to arrange a December 8 meeting between the MIA and the city commissioners.[26]

The meeting was held at city hall as a dozen MIA leaders met with the city commissioners as well as the local bus manager, J. H. Bagley, and the attorney for Montgomery City Lines, Jack Crenshaw. Crenshaw would not yield, claiming the bus company could not violate a city ordinance to accommodate the protesters' request. According to King, "the more Crenshaw talked, the more he won the city fathers to his position. Mayor Gayle and Commissioner Sellers became more and more intransigent." With the meeting going nowhere, the mayor asked a smaller contingent to meet behind closed doors. Again Crenshaw quelled any hope for an agreement, claiming, "If we grant the Negroes these demands they will go about boasting of a victory that they had won over the white people; and this we will not stand for." As a next step, the MIA sent a letter to the bus company headquarters in Chicago, apprising them of the bus conditions that had led to the boycott. After delineating the three proposals that bus company officials and the city commissioners had denied, they pleaded, "Since 44 % of the city's population is Negro, and since 75 % of the bus riders are Negro, we urge you to send a representative to Montgomery to arbitrate." A few days later, MIA leaders issued a press release regarding the rationale for the protest in which they argued that a settlement was possible: "We feel that there is no issue between the Negro citizens and the Montgomery City Lines that cannot be solved by negotiations between people of good will and we submit that there is no legal barrier to such negotiations." Despite good-faith efforts to further negotiations, both bus and city officials refused to yield to the MIA's seating proposal.[27]

A few of Montgomery's white citizens supported the boycott, including Hughes, Virginia Durr, and the Trinity Lutheran pastor, Robert Graetz, each of whom assisted with the car pool by driving protesters around the town. Graetz, who served as pastor of a predominantly African American congregation, attended the Holt Street meeting. Impressed by the reasonableness of the MIA demands, he pushed fellow clergy in the white ministerial association to support the boycott's objectives, but they refused. Inspired by his congregation's resolve and the just cause of the protest, Graetz decided to join the MIA himself, proving to be the lone white pastor to participate in the organization during the boycott.[28]

A week after the boycott began, librarian Juliette Morgan penned a letter to the editor of the *Montgomery Advertiser*. She compared the goals and methods of the protestors to the effective efforts of Gandhi in India a few decades earlier. Impressed by the significance of the event, Morgan wrote: "One feels that history is being made in Montgomery these days, the most important in her career. It is hard to imagine a soul so dead, a heart so hard, a vision so blinded and provincial as not to be moved with admiration at the quiet dignity, discipline, and dedication with which the Negroes have conducted their boycott." Morgan's letter affirmed the ill-treatment of African American passengers by some of the bus drivers. Morgan and a few other white citizens in Montgomery were willing to stand up and be counted by supporting the efforts of the protestors.[29]

Reverend Graetz attempted to draw greater national publicity to the boycott. In late December, he typed a letter to the news editor of *Time* magazine in which he called the nascent protest a story "that may be just as explosive as the Till case." Frustrated with what he deemed to be slanted local coverage by Montgomery's white media, he urged the magazine to send a reporter to the city so they could "get a good look at the way a one-race press and a one-race police force band together to discredit fifty thousand people who are tired of being treated like animals on the city buses, and who are registering their feelings by refraining from riding those buses."[30]

In the early days of the boycott, Nixon was an essential contributor both in his role as MIA treasurer and as a strategist. While many black professionals did not believe Nixon could effectively serve as leader of the protest, they recognized the critical role he played in making the boycott a reality. Dexter deacon Robert D. Nesbitt Sr. noted, "Mr. Nixon had already been laboring in the community to secure rights for black people and his commitment to the advancement of his race was well known." After claiming that Nixon could not have effectively led the effort, he quickly added: "He was a dynamic community man. Securing the release of Mrs. Parks and calling the meeting, seizing the moment to initiate a protest, and helping engineer the election of Martin are evidence of his insight." Rufus Lewis saw things differently, believing Nixon had wanted the prestige of leadership for the movement he had helped engineer: "Mr.

Nixon did not initially want Reverend King. The former wanted to be the leader. Nixon was ambitious, but he did not have the force or background necessary to command a large following." Dexter member Mrs. Thelma Austin Rice stressed Nixon's significant contributions, however: "The bus boycott was basically Mr. E. D. Nixon's idea. He made such a claim on several occasions and I believe it. Mr. Nixon had the wherewithal, the tenacity, and commitment needed to make things happen, but lacked the ability to communicate with all people and groups. He had the necessary raw skills. Reverend King brought the refined dimension required." As Rice suggested, Nixon's perspective was vital in developing the grassroots nature of the boycott, having earned the trust of working people over the previous two decades. Nixon also brought his union experiences to the table as his organization skills proved invaluable to the MIA. As part of A. Philip Randolph's Brotherhood of Sleeping Car Porters, Nixon understood the opportunities that can materialize when people are organized and united. He also knew how much work would be needed for the effort to last beyond the first few weeks.[31]

Soon after the boycott began, the NAACP held a special meeting. King had been on the local board since August and attended the December 13 gathering called by Mr. W. C. Patton, who served as a NAACP field secretary. In notes recorded by Rosa Parks, the local branch commended the MIA for their efforts in the bus protest. The organization sought to work in tandem with the MIA, whose focus would be the local boycott, while the NAACP would press forward with Parks's legal case. For her part, Parks was willing for the "NAACP to take case to fullest extent of the law." The organization gave attorney Fred Gray a $100 retainer and named Ralph Abernathy as the chair of the fund-raising efforts to cover anticipated legal expenses.[32]

While some were amazed at the cohesiveness and sacrificial efforts of the people of Montgomery, J. E. Pierce believed the leadership in Montgomery had "finally caught up with the masses," who had "been ready for a long time, but until now they have been without leadership." For Pierce, the leaders who were finally stepping up were the town's clergy, for he was well aware of the long-standing efforts of fellow Dexter Social and Political Action Committee members Jo Ann Robinson and Mary Fair Burks to bring substantive change to the city. The leaders who were most ready for this day were Nixon and the women of the WPC. Based on their sacrificial response, the people were also ready. They simply needed local black leaders to move beyond paternalism, recognizing that they could be equal participants in a movement to bring substantive change to their lives. The bus boycott tapped into their willingness to take action.[33]

By the dawn of 1956, any hope of a quick end of the boycott had faded. Four weeks into the protest, and with no end in sight, King delivered a sermon at Dexter titled "Our God Is Able." As would be true numerous times over the coming year, King emphasized God's power and ability in the face of difficulties. He boldly told his congregation: "The God we worship is not a weak God, He is not an incompetent God and consequently he is able to beat back gigantic mountains of opposition and to bring low prodigious hilltops of evil." Despite this theological truth, King admitted that sometimes circumstances lead to "times when each of us is forced to question the ableness of God." He next turned to evidence of God's power, noting the intricacies of creation and the ultimate triumph of good over evil: "This is ultimately the hope that keeps us going. Much of my ministry has been given to fighting against social evil. There are times that I get despondent, and wonder if it is worth it. But then something says to me deep down within God is able, you need not worry. So this morning I say to you we must continue to struggle against evil, but don't worry, God is able." Thematically similar to "Death of Evil upon the Seashore," which King had preached the previous summer, on this occasion his words seem stronger, filled with passion. The theological assertion that God is able took on deeper meaning now that King was personally active in the struggle.[34]

As King stepped into the pulpit throughout 1956, he was preaching to his congregation while also "ministering to his own spirit." Throughout the year, as King's personal involvement in the struggle continued to deepen and intensify, he forged a resilient and hope-filled faith in God in the face of the brutal realities of racism. As James Cone has argued, by participating in the struggle on a daily basis, "King was reintroduced, in a practical manner, to the God of the black experience." King's decision to heed Benjamin Mays's challenge to return to the South had given rise to a spiritual awakening within the young pastor. Through the crucible of the struggle, King remembered and experienced the power and hope Daddy King had been preaching for decades: that "God is able."[35]

The people of Montgomery also sharpened King's faith and understanding. Early in the boycott, King had a conversation with Myles Horton, who ran the Highlander Folk School. King asked him for any advice he might lend, to which Horton replied: "draw your strength from the people. You are not going to get it from any kind of ideology. That is fine to have. We all need it and I am all for it, but practically speaking you've got to listen to the people and learn to respond to their feelings and needs and be intuitive." Horton believed King followed his advice and indeed drew "his strength from the people."[36]

Among the people King leaned on most were Robinson and Burks, who wielded great influence during the early months of the protest. According to Erna Dungee Allen, who served as the secretary of the WPC, the women "were kind of like the power behind the throne. We really were the ones who carried out the actions." Allen also asserted: "When all the dust settled the women were there when it cleared. They were there in positions to hold the thing [MIA] together. We took the position that if anything comes up, all you have to do is whistle and the men will be there. They'd come. But the little day-to-day things, taking care of the finances, things like that, the women still take care of that." In Allen's view, King benefited from the committed people around him, men and women alike: "He listened a lot and he thought a lot. He got by himself a lot. But he had a lot of help from the other men. And they exchanged ideas and he accepted ideas. And they usually came up with a good decision out of all of the exchanging of ideas." While King may have had the responsibility of making final decisions and communicating those to the people, in the early days of the boycott King benefited from the collective wisdom, passion, and ideas of the gifted people around him.[37]

No one played a greater role than Robinson. Less than two months into the boycott, the Fisk researcher Donald Ferron wrote: "I sense that in addition to Reverend King, there is another leader, though unknown to the public, of perhaps equal significance. The public recognized King as the leader, but I wonder if Mrs. Robinson may be of equal importance." King later described Robinson as "indefatigable" and as a person who "was active on every level of the protest. She took part in both the executive board and the strategy committee meetings. When the MIA newsletter was inaugurated a few months after the protest began, she became its editor. She was sure to be present whenever negotiations were in progress. And although she carried a full teaching load at Alabama State, she still found time to drive both morning and afternoon."[38]

Not all was harmonious inside the leadership of the MIA, however. In an early January edition of the *Montgomery Advertiser*, an editorial appeared by MIA secretary Uriah Fields. He used strong language throughout, arguing: "On our side there can be no compromise with this principle involved. In the first place this is a compromise to begin with. We should have demanded complete integration which does away with Jim Crow, and what our constitutional rights guarantee to all American citizens." Raising the stakes even higher, Fields concluded: "We shall never cease our struggle for equality until we gain first-class citizenship, and take it from me this is from a reliable source of Negro citizens of Montgomery. We have no intention of compromising. Such unwarranted delay in granting our request may very well result in a demand for the annihilation of segregation which will result in complete integration." While Fields's words may have represented the true sentiments of the majority of Montgomery's African American citizenry and the leaders of the MIA, the leadership did not want their views broadcast in the local media. Fields had sent in the editorial without informing the rest of the MIA leadership. King and other leaders were angry with Fields, whose words served to heighten the vitriolic rhetoric between the parties and blunted the claim of the protesters that they were not seeking an end to segregation. A few weeks later, at an executive board meeting, the decision was made to curtail any such letters in the future: "The President at his discretion may make releases to the press. All other releases must be approved by the exec. comm., and such releases must be in writing with the newspaper having a copy and copy (duplicate) kept by the committee as a protective measure." This would not be the last time Fields's comments caused a crisis for the MIA and headaches for King.[39]

In an effort to clarify their position, the MIA and a group of African American pastors wrote a letter to Montgomery officials. They reiterated that their boycott was in part a response to "the present seating arrangement," though they added that it was "not a request for the abolition of segregation on buses but for a fair and reasonable seating of passengers so as to assure all passengers equal treatment." The mayor and city commissioners refused to budge, citing their commitment to uphold city and state law.[40]

Despite the internal controversy, the *Alabama Tribune* editorial director, Emory Jackson, remained impressed by the boycott as it entered its sixth week. He stressed not only the unity of the people and the quality of leadership, but also the economic benefit the protest yielded for the community's African American citizens, noting Montgomery "has demonstrated the power of mobilized purchasing power" and that "the dollar can be made to perform a double duty in a democracy." Instead of patronizing city buses, blacks hired carpool drivers and purchased gas from black-owned service stations. The boycott of buses also meant most African Americans had less time, opportunity, and inclination to patronize downtown Montgomery's predominantly white-owned businesses.[41]

The bus boycott galvanized the African American community around a common protest, but that was not all that bound the people together. As Jackson's editorial suggests, one consequence of the boycott was the establishing of a parallel black economy in the city. Instead of spending their dollars in white-owned businesses downtown, African Americans increasingly depended upon one another, creating new business and job opportunities. While the working class bore the brunt of the protest by not riding city buses, some did benefit from the broader galvanizing of the black community surrounding the boycott. Not only were some new jobs created, such as driving vehicles for the car pools, but numerous relationships were forged across class lines. The economic dimensions of the boycott must have particularly pleased Nixon, who not only longed for symbolic victories to challenge segregation, but who also desired substantive changes in the daily lives for all of Montgomery's black citizens.

As he tried to respond to the controversy caused by the Fields editorial, King delivered a sermon titled "How to Believe in a Good God in the Midst of Glaring Evil." Among King's responses to the problem of evil was his assertion that "disbelief in a good God presents more problems than it solves. It is difficult to explain the presence of evil in the world of a good God, but it is more difficult to explain the presence of good in a world of no God." The sermon contained no easy answers. His philo-sophical responses seem hollow given the challenges facing both he and his congregation. Perhaps they knew no high-minded theological treatise could substitute for the daily experience of God's presence, even in the midst of glaring evil. King and his congregation would lean on their faith often over the coming weeks.[42]

As January dragged on, the ACHR director, Robert Hughes, still hoped some type of settlement could be brokered. Though Hughes pri-vately believed the demands of the protest were legitimate, his role with the ACHR limited how much he could say publicly. He did not believe a boycott was the most constructive approach to solving the problem, noting it "is too much like the way the citizens' council work." Hughes clarified his distaste for the protest: "I think it is wrong to take measures that deprive people of their livelihood, that you should work things out in some way that will not cut off a man's income because he feels differently than you do." Hughes hinted at an underground effort of those who want to try to solve the boycott that was scheduled for January 20, but when pressed on the details, he was sketchy and evasive. Like many other liberal whites in Montgomery, Hughes affirmed the injustice of the cur-rent conditions but did not endorse the means by which the MIA chose to challenge the injustice. In the guise of being part of a bridge organiza-tion between whites and blacks, he evaded taking a clear public stand on any of the principles involved.[43]

On January 20, the ACHR held their monthly meeting at Dexter Av-enue Baptist Church. Around forty people attended to hear a discussion of the pastor's role in race relations. Panel members included Reverend E. Tipton Carroll of Cloverdale Christian Church, Dr. Crockett of Ala-bama State College, and Reverend Thomas R. Thrasher of the Church of the Ascension. King was originally scheduled to be on the panel but was out of town. In notes taken at the meeting, the Fisk University re-searcher Anna Holden commented that each of the respondents believed there were times when one should risk one's position to take a stand, and they all admitted a reluctance to do so. In the question-and-answer period, Clara Rutledge recommended a recent *Reader's Digest* article to the group titled "The Churches Repent," which examined the outcome for some churches that chose to integrate. At the close of the meeting,

Hughes asked for prayer for Reverend Robert Graetz, who had received many threats. Among those present at the meeting were Fred Gray and Coretta King.[44]

In a surprising development, the *Montgomery Advertiser* announced on January 22 that city officials had reached a settlement of the bus boycott with some prominent African American leaders. There had been a meeting with three relatively obscure black pastors who were not a part of the MIA in which they agreed to what King called "conditions that had existed prior to the boycott." The MIA moved quickly to refute the story, calling local clergy late at night to ensure they would let their congregants know during their worship services the following morning that the boycott was still on. Recognizing that many would not be in church the next day, King joined a group who visited African American nightclubs and pool halls until one o'clock in the morning to let them know that any rumors of a settlement were false. Reflecting on his long night, King noted, "For the first time I had a chance to see the inside of most of Montgomery's night spots." The fraudulent settlement ended up backfiring on city leaders as King and others reinforced ties with the broader black community through their late-night crusade through taverns and bars. The boycotters responded angrily to the purported agreement, serving notice to all that they were not interested in any outcome based on promises of possible future changes. MIA leaders also issued a press release in which they argued that any ministers who did meet with city officials "do not represent even a modicum of the Negro bus riders." Claiming that more than 99 percent of the city's black community supported the boycott, they emphasized that "the bus protest is still on and it will last until our proposals are given sympathetic consideration through our appointed leaders."[45]

The day after responding to the supposed settlement of the boycott, King told his congregation that "Christianity has never been content to wrap itself up in the garments of any particular society." He urged his audience to take seriously Jesus' call to go "into all the world and preach the gospel," arguing that the one who most needed to hear about universal dimensions of the Gospel was "the white man," noting "he is pagan in his conceptions." As an example, King referred to those who murdered Emmett Till. He also sharply criticized white concern for foreign missions while they continued to trample "over the Negro" in the United States. King's proposed method for reaching out to southern whites included exploring "the root of the problem," loving them, and sitting down and preaching to them. He concluded the sermon by calling his congregation to "be maladjusted." In the wake of a manipulative attempt to end the boycott, King called for a vigilant movement to redeem the souls of southern whites. Less than two months into the boycott, King's dream for the South was bigger than the end of segregation; he envisioned the creation of what he often called the beloved community.[46]

Even after the MIA vehemently debunked the spurious settlement announced by city officials, the rector of the Episcopal Church of the Ascension, Thomas Thrasher, hoped a compromise could still be reached. A board member of the ACHR who had served nine years in the city, Thrasher believed black leaders had not sought full integration because "Nigras here are used to operating within the framework of the state laws and that they feel more comfortable when they stay within the bounds of the law." The real roadblock to a settlement was Crenshaw, the lawyer for the bus company, whom Thrasher called "rabidly anti-Nigra and a disturbed person." While Thrasher hoped to find some middle ground, he also faced pressure from some in his congregation to remain silent on racial matters. Among those urging the rector to keep his moderate views quiet was Luther Ingalls, a parishioner in Thrasher's church and the primary organizer of the White Citizens Council (WCC) in Montgomery.[47]

Boycott participant and WPC member Irene West was not interested in any brokered settlement dreamed up by Thrasher. Although she was a wealthy widow of dentist A. W. West Sr., she recognized the critical role played by the working people in the struggle. She had been involved in attempts to advance the quality of life for African Americans in Montgomery for decades, even hosting Ella Baker at her home during a trip by the NAACP branch director in the early 1940s. The bus company was financially dependent on laborers who rode the buses to work each day. These were "the ones who keep this movement going. The leaders could do nothing by themselves. They are only the voice of thousands of colored workers." West believed a significant change had occurred in white-black relations since the *Brown* decision, as white clerks in the town's stores began interacting with African American patrons with "a steely glare in their eyes." Emphasizing the economic power wielded by the black community, West claimed no compromise would happen and that the demands were only a first step. Next would be an all-out assault on "the unconstitutionality of the state statute. From this point we can wipe out state wide segregation on city bus lines." Six weeks into the boycott, she believed the protest might "last another month or a year, but so long as it does, I'll get up at 4:00 a.m. and help people get to work and everything else I can to make it a success. We have reached the point of no return." King later applauded West's exemplary commitment to the cause: "Every morning she drove her large green Cadillac to her assigned dispatch station, and for several hours in the morning and again in the afternoon one could see this distinguished and handsome gray-haired chauffeur driving people to work and home again."[48]

In an MIA board meeting a few days later, King speculated the settlement announcement betrayed an attempt by the mayor to portray the African American community as divided. Debate in the meeting revealed there were very real differences within the MIA leadership. The majority argued that they should give up on their demand for black bus drivers, while a few felt that having bus drivers was the most important of the boycott objectives. Early on, several MIA leaders began to waiver on the demand for black bus drivers. While the executive board vowed to stand firm on their three conditions, King later admitted: "considering the possibility that there were no imminent vacancies and taking into account the existence of certain priorities due to union regulations, it was agreed that we would not demand the immediate hiring of Negro bus drivers, but would settle for the willingness of the bus company to take applications from Negroes and hire some as soon as vacancies occurred." Their willingness to be flexible on this point reflects the presence of varying priorities on the part of the leaders of the MIA. This wavering also led many in the area to view this last demand as little more than a bargaining chip when negotiations began, as the ACHR director, Robert Hughes, believed: "I can't say this publicly and this is of course confidential, but it seems to me that the demands for Negro drivers was tacked on for purposes of compromise—I think it was something the leaders added to use as a bargaining point and I think it will be dropped when they are ready to end the thing, whenever that is."[49]

While MIA leaders tried to stay unified, the city commissioners announced a "get-tough policy" after their bogus settlement fell apart. A few weeks earlier, Commissioner Clyde Sellers had joined the Montgomery White Citizens Council, claiming "I'll stand up and say I'm a white man." The crowd roared as Sellers joined an organization that now numbered as many as twelve thousand people from the Montgomery area. Following the ill-fated compromise attempt, all three commissioners claimed they "felt betrayed," and at a rally on January 24, Mayor Gayle and City Commissioner Parks joined Sellers as members of the White Citizens Council.[50]

Responding to the news that all the city commissioners were now members of the WCC, the ACHR chair, Reverend Raymond Whatley, declared that "the Mayor has declared war on the Nigras of Montgomery." In an attempt to explain this overreaction by white authorities, Whatley added that "they see this as an opening wedge leading to mixing in the schools and in people's homes." In the wake of Sellers joining the WCC, Whatley had preached a sermon on Herod, noting the Roman leader ordered the deaths of innocent infants out of fear that this newborn King of the Jews would threaten his rule. Whatley claimed that some modern-day public officials were like Herods who were willing to join the WCC to preserve their reign of leadership. Soon after, Whatley got a note from the vestry board asking him to not mention blacks and segregation from the pulpit. He was later forced by his church board to resign from the ACHR, as both chair and member. Over the coming months Whatley decided to leave the firestorm at St. Marks to become the pastor at a small country church.[51]

Following this new "get-tough" policy by Mayor Gayle, the number of threats made against boycott participants grew significantly. King continued to be one of the primary recipients of hate-filled letters and phone calls. One night late in January, the phone rang just as King was heading to bed. A threatening voice told King that by "next week, you'll be sorry you ever came to Montgomery." At that moment, the torrent of threats and the stresses of leadership overwhelmed King. Unable to sleep, he made some coffee and deliberated how to gracefully remove himself from the leadership of the MIA. Exhausted and overwhelmed, King decided to practice what he preached by bringing his situation to God. He later remembered the tenor of his prayer: "I am here taking a stand for what I believe is right. But now I am afraid. The people are looking to me for leadership, and if I stand before them without strength and courage, they too will falter. I am at the end of my powers. I have nothing left. I've come to the point where I can't face it alone." In a later recounting, King remembered: "At that moment I experienced the presence of the Divine as I never had experienced Him before. It seemed as though I could hear the quiet assurance of an inner voice saying: 'Stand up for righteousness, stand up for truth; and God will be at your side forever.' Almost at once my fears began to go. My uncertainty disappeared. I was ready to face anything." This prayer would serve as a defining moment of his personal faith and his leadership of the Montgomery movement.[52]

King emphasized this kitchen table experience in later stories about the boycott and recounted it in sermons around the country for years. Many King scholars have followed King's lead, emphasizing this prayer as a critical turning point. Keith Miller emphasizes the "social gospel twist" of the story: "Unlike the narrators of traditional conversions, he faltered not from personal weakness or temptation, but from the strain of leading a social crusade. His description testifies to a social gospel, for God offered him strength—not to resist personal temptation—but to continue leading the bus boycott. By translating the social gospel into a conversion narrative, he expertly blends this-worldly and otherworldly redemption." James Cone claims this was the moment when King first made the God of the African American experience his own. Mervyn Warren asserts that the vision at the kitchen table transformed King from "a mere pastor to a minister with innumerable inner resources." Lewis Baldwin also credits what he calls King's "vision in the kitchen" with solidifying a spiritual conception of his social leadership. Baldwin goes on to qualify his perspective, however, suggesting this was not a unique experience, but rather was one reflective of many such encounters King had over the course of his civil rights leadership.[53]

King did not mention this epiphany publicly for nearly a year, when he was quoted as telling his church that he had a vision in which God told him to "stand up and die for the truth, stand up and die for the righteousness." Given the distance between the incident and any public account, it is quite possible King used this event as a rhetorical device to capsulate a yearlong journey marked by a consistent struggle with fear and doubt. Throughout the year, and for the remainder of his life, King fought to retain his faith in God's ultimate power and presence. King's sermons suggest a need by both King and the community to be reminded again and again that "our God is able" and that one can indeed "believe in a good God in the midst of glaring evil." While his vision at the kitchen table was significant, it was but one in a series of crises that King faced during the year of the boycott. King's faith in God and in his own ability to lead developed in the midst of many moments of truth throughout the year.[54]

A few days later, King called a special executive board meeting of the MIA to deal with some urgent issues. The minutes reflect that the first item they addressed was whether to accept a new settlement proposal made by "white friends" to Reverend Binion, who was on the MIA finance committee and served on the executive board. After explaining that this proposal had been floated before the so-called compromise, Binion suggested that a vastly reduced number of seats reserved for whites on predominantly black bus routes might be amenable to the city commissioners and provide some grounds for an agreement. Nixon dismissed the suggestion immediately, noting the board was "going to run into trouble" with the foot soldiers of the movement should they make such a compromise. Nixon wanted no part of such a compromise: "If that's what you're going to do, I don't want to be here when you tell the people." King quickly sided with Nixon: "From my limited contact, if we went tonight and asked the people to get back on the bus, we would be ostracized. They wouldn't get back. We shouldn't give people the illusion that there are no sacrifices involved, that it could be ended soon. My intimidations are a small price to pay if victory can be won. We shouldn't make the illusion that they won't have to walk. I believe to the bottom of my heart that the majority of Negroes would ostracize us. They are willing to walk." King knew this was no time to grow timid or turn back. If the people were willing to walk, the leaders of the MIA needed to demonstrate their commitment through bold leadership. They took a courageous step when they concluded their meeting with a commitment to file suit in federal court to seek a ruling that would ensure full integration on city buses.[55]

That evening, a mass meeting was held at Ralph Abernathy's First

Baptist Church. In King's keynote address, he told the people: "If M. L. King had never been born this movement would have taken place. I just happened to be here. You know there comes a time when time itself is ready for change. That time has come in Montgomery, and I had nothing to do with it." Referring to his recent arrest and fine for speeding at the hands of Montgomery police, King continued, "If all I have to pay is going to jail a few times and getting about 20 threatening calls a day, I think it is a very small price to pay for what we are fighting for." As the meeting was winding down, King received word that a bomb had exploded at his home where his wife, Coretta, and their new baby were resting.[56]

King rushed home, making his way through a gathering crowd to discover a hole in the front porch and several shattered windows. He quickly located his wife, Coretta, and was relieved to discover that she and their young baby had not been harmed. King next turned his attention to the angry crowd, which was primarily comprised of a number of Alabama State students and some working-class blacks who had sacrificed significantly over the previous few months. From his badly damaged front porch, King urged them not to resort to violence but to continue to love their enemies. He then reiterated a theme he had sounded at the mass meeting earlier in the evening, reminding them that "if I am stopped this movement will not stop. If I am stopped our work will not stop. For what we are doing is right. What we are doing is just. And God is with us." After encouraging the crowd to return to their homes, King added, "We are not hurt and remember that if anything happens to me, there will be others to take my place."[57]

Many scholars have reflected on the significance of this front porch speech. Keith Miller characterizes it as "the most important address this man ever made. If he failed to control his emotions, if he failed to talk nonviolence, if he failed to preach love, and—most importantly—if he failed to disarm the mob, nonviolence would fail, the boycott would fail, love would fail, and he would fail." King's comments suggest the moment was about much more than King, however. This was a moment for the people of Montgomery. How they responded to this blatant act of violence against their leader and his family said much more about the character of the movement than King's speech did. As the boycott entered its third month, the protest belonged to the people. It was not his to bargain away. It was not dependent on his rhetoric in a time of crisis. Rather, the movement's future rested with the African American citizens of Montgomery, and with God, who walked with them.[58]

Several months later, the MIA's effort to get bus segregation declared unconstitutional went to trial. In the courtroom, the defense lawyer Walter Knabe interrogated Claudette Colvin, who had been arrested for violating the city's bus segregation laws a year earlier. He charged that the MIA had changed their goals since December 5, to which Colvin responded: "No, sir. We haven't changed our ideas. It has been in me ever since I was born." Later Colvin responded to a question about leadership of the boycott: "Did we have a leader? Our leaders is just we ourself." When Knabe pressed another witness to affirm that King had originally made three demands at the beginning of the boycott, none of which were for desegregation, another witness noted, "The Reverend King did not ask that, the Negroes asked that." She later added, "We employed him to be our mouth piece." The women who signed on to the lawsuit that would change the segregation laws in Montgomery rejected the notion that King or anybody else was the leader of the movement. Rather, they credited the people with being their own leaders. By the end of January 1956, the most significant change for King was that he was now fully a part of the people. As one movement participant commented in a mass meeting, if anybody in the city wanted to kill King, they were too late "because Martin Luther King is in all of us now, and in order to kill Martin Luther King, you'll have to kill every black in the city of Montgomery." Thanks to the crucible of the past few months, the people were in King as well. Their courage and commitment had inspired King, motivating him as a leader and inspiring him as a speaker. They proved willing to walk together.[59]

5 "Living under the Tension"

They begin to wonder all over the nation, how is it we can keep walking in Montgomery? How is it we can keep burning out our rubber?
How is it we can keep living under the tension? And we can cry out
to the nation, "We can do it because we know that as we walk, God
walks with us."
                                    —Martin Luther King Jr., September 1956

Just a few short days after the bombing of his home, King delivered a
sermon at Dexter with a title he could easily embrace: "It's Hard to Be
a Christian." The past two months of King's life had been extremely
challenging. As the most visible face of the bus boycott, he had become
a lightning rod for criticism, threats, and even violence. Despite his suf-
ferings, King reminded the people of Dexter that the Christian faith is by
definition costly. This was not time to substitute "a cushion for a cross"
or to have "a high blood pressure of creeds and an anemia of deeds." He
called for a more authentic Christianity that is by definition "hard because
it demands a dangerous and costly altruism. It demands that the 'I' be
immersed in the deep waters of 'thou.'" The people of Dexter knew they
were not the only Christians in Montgomery. That same morning, hymns
were emanating from the all-white Dexter Avenue Methodist Church just
a block away. The hypocrisy of many of Montgomery's white Christians
was fair game this Sunday, as King blasted "white people who are for
justice" but who are "afraid to speak." King concluded by reminding his
congregation that Christianity demands "putting our whole being in the
struggle against evil, whatever the cost."[1]

The coming eleven months would prove to be costly for many involved in the local struggle. In addition to facing varied and perpetual
manifestations of white racism, King and other boycott leaders tried to
keep the community united in purpose. Accusations that the MIA had

115

mismanaged funds would add to the pressures facing King and other leaders. In response, they sought to maintain unity by closing ranks. Vigorous debate over the direction of the local movement became less regular as clergy gained greater power within the MIA. Meanwhile, E. D. Nixon's role diminished over the course of the year. Living under the tension of segregation, white attacks, and internal conflict, leaders fixed all their energies on a skirmish over bus policies while economic initiatives were relegated to the back burner. Much of the early promise for a local sustained assault on white supremacy never materialized. They failed to develop concrete plans for African American economic development after the boycott. The MIA would win the battle over buses, but the tension they lived under each day would leave the larger war for equality and justice unresolved.

The January 30, 1956, bombing of King's home was but the most sensational result of the "get-tough" policy toward boycott participants of Montgomery mayor William "Tacky" Gayle. Despite the onslaught, King and the people did not back down. Instead they went on the offensive, going ahead with plans to file suit in federal courts claiming bus segregation was a violation of the Fourteenth Amendment. Filing the lawsuit ran contrary to the original demands of the MIA, but as early as the evening of Parks's arrest, Nixon and others had in mind the notion of a test case to strike down segregation on the city's buses. The intransigence of the city commissioners coupled with the use of violence convinced the leadership of the MIA that only the courts would settle this issue, and that meant challenging segregation.[2]

The MIA leadership could not ignore the violence. An attempted bombing of Nixon's home on February 1 reinforced the sober reality that any of them might be next. At an executive board meeting just a few days later, King addressed a recent "increase in the amount of violence" and innumerable threats since the city's commissioners "joined the white Citizens Council." In response, the MIA beefed up security measures for mass meetings, but King insisted: "We're not going to give up; they can drop bombs in my house every day. I'm firmer now than ever."[3]

The first task for attorney Fred Gray in developing the case that would become *Browder v. Gayle* was finding a group of people willing to serve as plaintiffs. He elected not to make Rosa Parks part of the case so as not to complicate her criminal proceedings. Aurelia Browder, a Montgomery housewife, became the named plaintiff for the case, which was filed the morning of February 2. She was joined by seventy-seven-year-old Susie McDonald, two teenagers named Claudette Colvin and Mary Louise Smith, and Mrs. Jeanetta Reese. Once the suit was filed, the city moved to try to discredit both the legal maneuver and Fred Gray, the attorney representing the MIA. After Gray launched a legal attack on segregated buses, Jeanetta Reese pulled out under pressure from white authorities. As a result, some white leaders engaged in a concerted effort to have Gray disbarred in the state. A similar strategy had proven effective a decade earlier, when Montgomery officials convinced a court to disbar African American attorney Arthur A. Madison, who had led a large group of blacks to register to vote at the county courthouse in the fall of 1943. When they were all summarily rejected, Madison filed suit on behalf of sixteen of the applicants. In February 1944, six of the plaintiffs claimed they had not authorized Madison to file the lawsuit. Most of these were public school teachers and were thus vulnerable to white backlash expressed through the termination of their jobs. Authorities arrested Madison for filing false court documents, fined him $2,500, and disbarred him in the State of Alabama.[4]

On the day Gray filed the lawsuit, the board of the MIA already had heard rumors that Reese had withdrawn her name from the case. Although she had retained Gray as her attorney, she later claimed that he acted without her consent. Segregationists moved swiftly, as reports had Reese going to the mayor's office the very day the lawsuit was filed. Once word spread about Reese's involvement in the case, threatening phone calls to her followed. Reese worked for a high-ranking police official who brought a lot of pressure on her to drop her role in the case, which she did. MIA leaders responded with resolve, reassuring the rest of the plaintiffs that they had the full support of the organization. The intimidation efforts were directed at Rosa Parks as well. She reported to the MIA executive board that "some strange men have been coming in my neighborhood inquiring about the woman who caused all of this trouble." In response, the MIA decided to ensure that Parks had protection at night.[5]

In addition to intimidation, violence, and legal maneuvers, some local white Baptists sought to strip the MIA of their office space. Early on the MIA had set up offices at the Baptist Center, a facility donated by the Southern Baptists to assist with ministry among the city's African American population. During the early 1950s, the center was a source of pride in the Southern Baptist's annual reports. The Baptist Center director, Reverend Glasco, an African American member of the MIA board, reported that the superintendent of missions had decided the MIA would have to move their offices "due to the lengthy run of the movement and since it has taken on a political angle." Glasco added that prior to this, every decision regarding the center's operation had been made by African Americans, but this was imposed by whites. King responded to this news decisively, noting: "I think the position of the white Baptists is that they're just against it. I don't want to accept anything from them." After exploring various alternatives, the board elected to move the offices to Ralph Abernathy's First Baptist Church.[6]

King's response to the barrage of white reprisals did not end with his leadership of the MIA. He also took personal steps in an attempt to provide a greater degree of protection for his family. Less than a week after the bombing of his home, King agreed to an interview with Fisk University researcher Donald Ferron. While King's public announcements that week were bold, notes from the interview reveal he was definitely on edge. At one point, King stood up, looked out the front window, and said, "I thought somebody was putting something on the porch." This nervousness and fear led him to have a meeting with Governor Jim Folsom, who had a reputation as being supportive of greater rights for blacks. According to King, following the bombing of his parsonage Folsom had "promised us protection and said he would talk to the mayor."[7]

At the MIA board meeting on February 2, King noted that he had gone to the sheriff's office in an attempt to get a gun permit for the men who were guarding his house but he "couldn't get one." King argued the sheriff's denial of a gun permit was tantamount to saying, "you are at the disposal of the hoodlums." In the interview, Ferron asked King about effective strategies for racial change, to which King replied: "Somebody told me a whale puts up its biggest fight after it has been harpooned. It's the same thing with the Southern white man. Maybe its [sic] good to shed a little blood. What needs to be done is for a couple of those white men to lose some blood; then the Federal Government will step in." While it would be a stretch to say that King embraced violence as a strategy, he had not yet adopted nonviolence as a life commitment. King's response to the bombing demonstrates that his overall commitment to nonviolence had not fully formed.[8]

Over the next few weeks, however, King had the opportunity to spend time with Bayard Rustin and Glenn Smiley, two avowed pacifists who helped King infuse his love ethic with the ideology of nonviolence. Rustin, a civil rights veteran, arrived in Montgomery at the behest of novelist Lillian Smith, who believed King and the MIA would benefit from greater instruction in nonviolence. Rustin had spent time working with the Congress on Racial Equality (CORE) and the Fellowship of Reconciliation (FOR), and in 1956 was serving as the executive secretary of the War Resisters League. Rustin was a close associate of the president of the Brotherhood of Sleeping Car Porters, A. Philip Randolph, and a student of Gandhian nonviolence. He also had a past that, if discovered, could embarrass the Montgomery movement. In addition to a brief period when he was a part of the Young Communist League, Rustin had served a prison sentence for resisting the draft and had been convicted for sodomy just three years earlier. Because of these concerns, some of Rustin's associates encouraged him not to go to Montgomery at all, but in the end Randolph and pacifist A. J. Muste deemed his value to King and the nascent Montgomery movement significant enough to justify his visit. Upon his arrival in the city, Rustin was struck by the tension he witnessed. He noted that both King and Abernathy had shifts of men watching their homes every night. MIA leaders warned Rustin that he would be under white surveillance and therefore ought to take necessary precautions.[9]

As an outsider, Rustin spent his first few days attempting to better understand the climate in the city. One evening he went to visit Jeanetta Reese, who had withdrawn her name as a plaintiff from the lawsuit filed by Fred Gray. He was shocked by what he found at Reese's home: "Although the police had provided no protection for King and Nixon after their houses had been bombed, I found two squad cards parked before Mrs. Reese's home." After negotiating with police to be allowed to approach Reese's home, all he could get her to say was, "I had to do what I did or I wouldn't be alive today."[10]

King invited Rustin to participate in nearly all MIA events during his visit. The two men also had several extensive discussions regarding the principle of nonviolence. A few days after Rustin's arrival, Glenn Smiley, a white FOR official, joined Rustin in Montgomery. Like Rustin, Smiley had the opportunity to spend significant time with King discussing the principles of the movement, including the relevance of Gandhi's leadership and ideas to what was happening in Montgomery. According to Smiley's reflections on the conversations, King admitted regarding Gandhi, "I will have to say that I know very little about the man." King had heard of Gandhi many times at Morehouse, but he had never studied his thought in depth.[11]

Soon after Smiley's arrival, a letter came to him from New York informing him that Randolph and others had decided Rustin needed to leave Montgomery, in part due to a lukewarm response to his presence by many in leadership with the MIA. Several local leaders feared Rustin wanted to influence the direction of the movement and receive credit for some of its successes: "There is some danger that Bayard is indicating that he has had more to do with what is happening, than he actually has." Although Smiley proved less forceful and abrasive to the MIA leadership, he shared a paternalistic attitude toward those in Montgomery: "we can learn from their courage and plain earthly devices for building morale, etc., but they can learn more from us, for being so new at this, King runs out of ideas quickly and does the old things again and again. He wants help, and we can give it to him without attempting to run the movement." Rustin and Smiley would both be significant figures in continuing to shape and develop King's thoughts and philosophy regarding nonviolence by providing a philosophical framework for what was happening in Montgomery. Their impact on the boycott itself was minimal, however. Although King was not a complete advocate of nonviolence prior to the boycott, he passionately expressed a commitment to an ethic of love and nonviolence in both the December 1955 Holt Street address and in his unprepared remarks following the bombing of his home in January 1956. Rustin and Smiley helped sand and polish King's philosophy of nonviolence, yet it was the people's willingness to boycott Montgomery's buses that brought King's nonviolent leanings to the surface in the first place.[12]

The MIA struggled to find appropriate responses in part because white attacks came from so many different directions. Many working-class whites expressed their solidarity with the city commissioners by joining the local White Citizens Council, which became the community's largest white organization by the end of January. On February 10, more than ten thousand turned out for a WCC gathering to hear Mississippi senator James Eastland. During the rally, the crowd applauded the resolve of city leaders in the face of the bus boycott. Using the methods of intimidation and economic reprisals against those participating in the boycott, the ranks of the WCC were bolstered by union members, who had a history of local resistance to interracial policies advocated by the national AFL-CIO. In the wake of the *Brown v. Board of Education* decisions, many local unions even threatened to break away from their national organizations. Four of the seven members of the Montgomery WCC executive board were union members, leading attorney Clifford Durr to label most of the members of the citizens' council "riff-raff" rather than people of any real prominence. Despite Durr's dismissive appraisal, the numbers of laborers who joined the council made it an organization of significant white resistance during the boycott. Union members continued to bolster the ranks as each round of bus-driver layoffs sparked greater anger and bitterness. During the boycott, Montgomery's Carpenters Hall, where many unions met for their meetings, even became a locus of Ku Klux Klan activity.[13]

White resistance to racial equality included the clergy. During the week after the bombing of King's home, a Fisk university researcher interviewed G. Stanley Frazier, who served as the pastor of St. James Methodist Church in Montgomery. A member of the WCC, Frazier attacked the MIA for attempting to use "the church as an instrument to destroy segregation." Frazier claimed that "both races prefer segregation" and that the boycott was ultimately an attempt to force integration on the people of Montgomery.[14]

Political leaders also dug in their heels as the boycott wore on. Montgomery mayor, William "Tacky" Gayle, when asked what was the root cause of the bus boycott, responded: "Segregation. They want to destroy our whole social fabric. We have laws that they want to ignore." Gayle complained that white women who were driving their maids to work and back were partly responsible for the success of the boycott. Virginia Durr recalled the response of many of Montgomery's white women: "If the mayor wants to do my washing and ironing and cooking and cleaning and raise my children, let him come out here and do it." Durr was quick to point out that most white women did not overtly support the boycott. Still, their self-interest prevailed over the social and legal issues that were in play.[15]

Former city commissioner Dave Birmingham, a year after his electoral defeat, weighed in on the boycott as well. He cited four primary causes for the protest, including "the tendency of mulattoes to want to bring about integration," the end of segregation in the armed forces (particularly significant with the proximity of Maxwell Air Force Base), the *Brown v. Board of Education* rulings, and the Claudette Colvin and Rosa Parks cases. Although Birmingham had received significant African American support during his candidacy, he was not a supporter of the boycott. MIA attorney Fred Gray believed that had Birmingham been in office, the boycott may not have happened.[16] Certainly his relationship with Nixon could have served as a conduit for negotiations during the early weeks of the protest. His opportunity for real influence would have been very early in December, however. If an early settlement had not been brokered, it is very doubtful that Birmingham would have greatly influenced the course of the boycott in any substantive way.[17]

Joe Azbell, an editor with the *Montgomery Advertiser*, was one of many whites who believed blacks simply lacked gratitude for all the whites had done for them over the years. Claiming African Americans benefited from "85 % of every tax dollar" while paying only 15 percent of local taxes, he questioned their wisdom in upsetting the paternalistic relationship that had served the city so well for decades. In Azbell's opinion, the boycott was "a slap in the face after all [whites] have done for them and all that good feeling that was there has been destroyed." He believed whites were not concerned about the boycott and "are glad the 'Nigra' are off the buses. They don't want them back on, they don't care if they never ride the buses again. I have had lots of calls from white people since my column asking me why I wanted to settle it—they said they were glad the black bastards were off the buses and to let them stay off. That is how the white people feel." He then attacked the morality of blacks, claiming they purchased 80 percent of the whiskey sold in the city. Azbell's reckless reliance on spurious racialized statistics demonstrates how little empathy he had for the MIA or its cause.[18]

Other whites took bold countercultural stands in support of the boycott, often at great personal cost. Librarian Juliette Morgan, who had written an editorial to the *Montgomery Advertiser* in December praising the boycott, faced significant backlash. Some patrons claimed they would no longer take advantage of library services as long as Morgan remained on the payroll. Although Morgan's mother, Lili Bess Olin Morgan, did not support her daughter's views, she did allow Juliette to stay with her during the first few months of the boycott. Some of the feedback to Morgan's letter was positive, revealing the complexity of the white community's attitude during this season of tension and upheaval. Morgan even claimed that most of the responders to her editorial "agreed with me, and said they would have liked to say the same thing themselves, but they couldn't for various reasons. Most of them are afraid—the kind of fear that is silly in the long run, but I guess in the short run, maybe there is something in it." Morgan also reflected on her controversial standing in the community: "I feel like we don't have much to gain, or to lose, in this life and none of it is worth much if we feel like we can't stand up for the things we believe in. Maybe I'm an exception and I'm more secure than most people, but I feel like what I have to lose isn't worth being silent. I pay for it in my stomach, but I would pay for it more if I didn't say the things I think I should. I think that the real basis for silence in situations like this is greed. Not greed in the ordinary sense, but greed in the sense that people are fearful of losing what they have." While Morgan continued to support the boycott throughout, she remained frustrated by the silence of prominent whites "who want to say something, but are afraid to speak out."[19]

Like Morgan, the women of the Fellowship of the Concerned were not afraid to challenge white supremacy. The local organization conducted a workshop in March at Trinity Lutheran Church titled "The Supreme Court Decision—Building Community Understanding." Olive Andrews attended the workshop and commented on the intentional mispronunciation of "Negro": "We here in Montgomery know how to pronounce Negro, for our Negroes are our heroes." Later Andrews noted that the city ordinance against segregated meetings did not apply to churches.

Clifford and Virginia Durr also worked behind the scenes to assist the protestors. The Durrs had joined E. D. Nixon in bailing Rosa Parks out of jail and were present as Nixon attempted to convince Parks and her family to allow her arrest to be a test case to challenge the city's segregation laws. As the boycott continued, Clifford Durr immersed himself in the legal challenges facing the MIA. Although he was never the attorney of record, he provided extensive legal assistance to Fred Gray.[20]

They were joined in their efforts by Robert Graetz, the only white clergy member to join the MIA. Graetz believed that there were a number of whites in the city who were in favor of change, citing the presence of the Alabama Council on Human Relations. In his view, the largest segment of white support for the boycott came from the wives of businessmen in the city. Graetz also believed that about half the white ministers in the city were on the side of the boycotters, and hoped many of these would stand up and be counted in the near future.[21]

Some white business leaders tried to play a mediating role as the conflict continued. The previous year they had developed a group known as the Men of Montgomery in an attempt to help the city advance economically. Although many segregationists belonged to the organization, King felt "they were open-minded enough to listen to another point of view and discuss the problem of race intelligently." They were particularly concerned about the negative national press directed toward Montgomery thanks to the boycott. In February, the group set up meetings with both the city and some MIA leaders in an attempt to broker a settlement. G. T. Fitzpatrick, who ran Empire-Rouse Laundry, described their talks in extremely patronizing terms: "we had several long sessions with them and while we were dealing with what you might call the upper crust—the ministers and teachers—we had to treat them pretty much like children— lead them along by the hand, so to speak. All of us businessmen agreed we could have done the same thing in two or three hours, but had to sit with it through two or three sessions lasting that long." Despite this paternalism, the conversations between the MIA and the Men of Montgomery held some promise for a solution.[22]

Representatives of the Men of Montgomery met with some MIA leaders on a few occasions during mid-February. Many of the business leaders believed they had reached an agreement to settle the boycott at their final meeting, having secured the endorsement of their plan by both the bus company and the city commissioners. When the proposal was taken to a mass meeting on February 20, it was voted down by a reported margin of 3,998 to 2. Business leader G. T. Matthews noted that the MIA leaders had claimed that they were simply representatives of the organization, and any decisions would be subject to the approval of the people. Matthews did not fully believe this claim, noting "if the leaders wanted to settle it, they could have. The ministers are running the thing and their congregations will follow them. You know how they are. Most of them are ignorant and they will do whatever their preachers tell them." Fitzgerald did concede that the roughly two hundred black workers at his plant had been extremely disciplined throughout the boycott and had continued to be very productive workers, noting "from a purely selfish standpoint, the boycott has been a good thing for my plant." While the business leaders were undoubtedly prejudiced, King later reflected that, had it not been for the "recalcitrance of the city commission," the MIA and Men of Montgomery may have worked out a deal.[23]

Some boycott leaders and participants were surprised more people did not endorse the settlement. The agreement included reserving ten seats at the front of the buses for white patrons and ten at the back for African American riders, as well as a guarantee for greater courtesy on the buses. According to Alabama State College professor Lawrence Reddick, after nearly three months of the boycott many carpool drivers were growing weary. Some were driving four or five hours a day on top of their jobs, family responsibilities, and other obligations. In light of the federal suit filed to attempt to end bus segregation, the outcome of the bus situation in Montgomery no longer seemed to rise or fall based on the continuance of the boycott. In the end, the courts would decide the most pressing questions. Based on these concerns, the leaders elected to submit the Men of Montgomery proposal to the people. According to Reddick, the nearly unanimous rejection of the proposed settlement "revived the morale of the leaders." The MIA did offer their appreciation for the Men of Montgomery's "very fine exemplification of good will and its willingness to see justice prevail in the city for all citizens."[24]

Few white leaders embodied a passion for justice, however. In the wake of the MIA's decision to launch a court case seeking an end to segregated buses in Montgomery, the city decided to take legal action against the boycott itself. While King was delivering a series of lectures at Fisk University in Nashville, the grand jury indicted 115 boycott participants, charging they were in violation of an obscure 1921 law in Alabama prohibiting conspiracies that sought to undermine legal business and commerce. The February 21 indictment charged that King and others "did, without just cause or legal excuse for so doing, enter into a combination, conspiracy, agreement, arrangement, or understanding for the purpose of hindering, delaying, or preventing Montgomery City Lines, Inc., a corporation, from carrying on lawful business." The list of those charged was riddled with errors and inaccuracies that resulted in lowering the total number indicted to eighty-nine. The morning after the grand jury's decision, many boycott participants set out for the police station. Nixon was first to enter, saying: "You are looking for me? Here I am." While white officials were surprised to see such a willingness to submit to arrest, the boldness of the leaders excited and encouraged participants who gathered to watch the proceedings. Meanwhile, King left Nashville early and flew to Atlanta, where Coretta and their daughter, Yolanda, were staying with his parents.[25]

Daddy King was ready for his son's arrival. Concerned that the Montgomery authorities were out to get his son, Daddy King assembled a number of family friends in an attempt to convince King Jr. to remain in Atlanta for the time being. Among those present was King Jr.'s mentor and Morehouse College president Benjamin Mays. Despite the pleadings of his father and many respected elders gathered at his parents' home, King never wavered from his resolve to return to Montgomery. Reflecting on the meeting, King remembered saying: "I must go back to Montgomery. My friends and associates are being arrested. It would be the height of cowardice for me to stay away. I would rather be in jail ten years than desert my people now. I have begun the struggle, and I can't turn back." Hearing King's words, Dr. Mays began to defend the decision to return to Montgomery, and others soon relented as well. Early on February 23, Daddy King joined his son's family as they drove to Montgomery. In what he later described as a "holiday atmosphere," King went to the courthouse, where he was arrested, fingerprinted, photographed, and then released on bail. That evening at a prayer meeting held at Abernathy's First Baptist Church, King addressed a crowd of several thousand. He reminded his audience that their goal was not racial conflict but to bring improvement to "the whole of Montgomery." Should they continue to be "arrested," "exploited," and "trampled over" daily, King called them to not "let anyone pull you so low as to hate them. We must use the weapon of love." King concluded with a word of hope, for although "we stand in life at midnight, we are always on the threshold of a new dawn."[26]

King continued to mix realism and optimism with his congregation the following Sunday. He admitted that recent historic events, both globally and in the South, might justify some in having a negative assessment of human nature: "Within a generation we have fought two world wars. We have seen man's tragic inhumanity to man. We have looked to Mississippi and seen supposedly Christian and civilized men brutally murdering the precious life of a little child. We have looked to Alabama and seen a ruthless mob take the precious law of the land and crush it below their tragic whims and caprices." These realities ought not lead to despair, however, for Jesus' ministry "revealed a deep faith in the possibilities of human nature." Based on faith in the human capacity to change, King predicted the boycott would end as "a victory for justice, a victory for fair play and a victory for democracy."[27]

The month of February had proven a critical one for King. He faced threats and experienced violence, yet his resolve had not faltered. One of King's greatest sources of encouragement was the people themselves. February had proven pivotal for them as well. Those who sacrificed most by not riding city buses had overwhelmingly defeated a proposed settlement brought by the Men of Montgomery. The grand jury had indicted a group of eighty-eight people in addition to King, demonstrating that the boycott was about the people of the city and not the leaders alone. At the last mass meeting of the month, held at Holt Street Baptist Church, King began his remarks by describing the mood of the people: "We have new zeal, new stamina to carry on." While reports at the meeting suggest the arrest did have a negative impact on the car pool, Ralph Abernathy offered some brief remarks: "Thanks must go to 50,000 Montgomery Negroes. This is your movement; we don't have any leaders in the movement; you are the leaders." The African American people of Montgomery had displayed their commitment to the movement that month. They had withstood an onslaught of tactics from those intent on defeating the boycott without cowering in fear or reacting with violence.[28]

With his trial set to begin the next morning, King elected to title his March 18 sermon "When Peace Becomes Obnoxious." He began the sermon with a description of the recent riots in Tuscaloosa that led University of Alabama officials to force Autherine Lucy, the school's first African American student, to leave the university. King cited a local newspaper editorial that claimed, "There is a peace on the campus of the University of Alabama." King blasted the university officials, noting any calm they were experiencing was built on "peace that had been purchased at the price of capitulating to the forces of darkness. This is the type of peace that all men of goodwill hate. This is the type of peace that stinks in the nostrils of the almighty God." King urged his congregation not to accept peace at any price, as "every true Christian is a fighting pacifist." Citing Jesus' words that he did not come to bring peace but a sword, King defined true peace as "not merely the absence of some negative force" but rather as "the presence of some positive force—justice, goodwill, the power of the kingdom of God."[29]

King acknowledged the presence of forces pursuing "obnoxious peace" in Montgomery: "I had a long talk the other day with a man about this bus situation. He discussed the peace being destroyed in the community, the destroying of good race relations." While admitting "if the Negro accepts his place, accepts exploitation, and injustice, there will be peace," King had no interest in this type of "obnoxious peace." He passionately proclaimed: "If peace means accepting second class citizenship, I don't want it. If peace means keeping my mouth shut in the midst of injustice and evil, I don't want it. If peace means being complacently adjusted to a deadening status quo, I don't want peace. If peace means a willingness to be exploited economically, dominated politically, humiliated and segregated, I don't want peace." For the many professionals sitting in the pews of Dexter that morning, King's words defied their most tested strategy of survival in the segregated South: keeping the peace at any cost. As King prepared to enter court the next morning, he was unwilling to seek an easy out. He proclaimed his willingness to "revolt against this peace" so the true peace of God's Kingdom might be established on the earth.[30]

The eyes of the world focused on Montgomery when King's trial began. Reporters from Europe and Asia joined many American journalists to witness the proceedings. The prosecution sought to prove the significant role that King and other leaders had in both the commencement and the continuation of the bus boycott, thus demonstrating a pattern that would violate the state law. The defense argued there had been a long-standing pattern of discrimination and mistreatment on city buses that finally boiled over into a spontaneous protest, providing a "just cause" for the boycott. The truth rested somewhere in between. While leaders had played a critical role in the early days of the boycott, the people passionately supported the idea. Were it not for the overwhelming support of the people for a one-day boycott on December 5, the leaders would not have proposed continuing the protest, nor would they have formed the MIA. Making such a movement successful did require leadership, however, as transportation systems, negotiating teams, and planned mass meetings helped provide a sense of unity and shared purpose.

King was the final defense witness in the trial. He testified that he had not urged members of the MIA to stay off the buses but had advocated that people "let your conscience be your guide, if you want to ride that is all right." Under cross-examination, the prosecution used minutes from the first few MIA meetings in an attempt to show King's definitive direction of the boycott from its inception. Particularly damaging to King's position was the resolution presented by the MIA that Abernathy read at Holt Street on December 5: "That the citizens of Montgomery are requesting that every citizen in Montgomery, regardless of race, color or creed, to refrain from riding busses owned and operated in the city of Montgomery by the Montgomery City Lines, Incorporated until some arrangement has been worked out between said citizens and the Montgomery City Lines, Incorporated." While King did not draft the statement, it did represent the official position of the MIA, and thus accurately reflected his sentiment. The case then depended on whether the judge would find that the MIA had just cause for boycotting the buses. After the four-day trial, Judge Eugene W. Carter found King guilty, sentencing him to either a $500 fine or 386 days of hard labor in Montgomery County. King's attorneys appealed the ruling, leading Judge Carter to suspend King's sentence and postpone the remaining eighty-eight boycott cases until the appeal had been heard. Over a year later, the court of appeals denied King's appeal, as his attorneys had waited too long to officially file the complaint.[31]

Immediately after the verdict, Coretta King joined her husband in a press conference outside the courthouse. Coretta affirmed that she had not wavered from her commitment to her husband and the protest: "All along I have supported my husband in this cause, and whatever happens to him, happens to me." Again King took the opportunity to advocate nonviolence: "there is no bitterness on my part as a result of the decision and I'm sure that I voice the sentiment of the more than forty thousand Negro citizens of Montgomery. We still have the attitude of love, we still have the method of passive resistance and we are still insisting, emphatically, that violence is self-defeating." That evening the community gathered for a mass meeting during which King further reflected on his trial. He began his remarks by confessing to committing three sins: "being born a Negro," "being subjected to the battering rams of segregation and oppression," and "having the moral courage to stand up and express our weariness of this oppression." Remarking on the decision of Judge Carter, King noted that perhaps "he did the best he could under the expedient method. As you know, men in political positions allow themselves to succumb to the expedient rather than reaching out for the moral that might be eternally corrective and true." He also sounded a message of hope in America, which has the capacity "to transform democracy from thin paper to thick action." King applied biblical imagery to the suffering of the people of Montgomery: "You don't get to the promised land without going through the wilderness. Though we may not get to see the promised land, we know it's coming because God is for it. So don't worry about some of the things we have to go through. They are just a necessary part of the great movement that we are making toward freedom."[32]

The following day, *Montgomery Advertiser* editor Joe Azbell interviewed King. Azbell asked him if he was afraid, to which King replied: "No I'm not. My attitude is that this is a great cause, it is a great issue that we are confronted with and that the consequences for my personal life are not particularly important." Convinced that this was his hour to "stand up and be counted," he reflected on the perils of fear: "My great prayer is always for God to save me from the paralysis of crippling fear, because I think when a person lives with the fears of the consequences for his personal life he can never do anything in terms of lifting the whole of humanity and solving many of the social problems which we confront in every age and every generation."[33]

Reverend Thomas Thrasher of the ACHR penned an article in early 1956 describing the feeling on the ground in Montgomery. Thrasher, one of the few white pastors willing to acknowledge the legitimacy of many of the MIA's complaints, highlighted the communication gap between the races: "the patterns of our past communication are breaking, and new patterns are not yet formed. We know them, and yet in our knowing we are aware that we know them not. The nightmare persists even when we hear words and see gestures. They speak. We do not understand." In assessing the prospects for the future, Thrasher bemoaned many of the unintended outcomes of the boycott: "Our experience in Montgomery, a city known in the past for its good race relations, shows us that change, any change, will be painful for some of us, and that sudden change may operate in reverse and bring about what is not wanted. The Negro is surely regretful to see his bus boycott contribute to the growth of the White Citizens' Council." Following King's trial and conviction, the communication gap continued to widen in Montgomery. The city had elected to get tough with the protesters, and the MIA was not about to back down.[34]

On April 23, the U.S. Supreme Court ruled in *Fleming v. South Carolina Electric and Gas Company* that segregation on any public transportation was illegal. In response, National City Lines, the parent company of Montgomery City Lines, ordered its drivers to not enforce local segregation laws on their buses any longer. The following day, Police Commissioner Sellers announced his intention to arrest any bus drivers who permitted integrated seating on their buses. When the bus company vowed to stand behind any arrested bus drivers, Montgomery commissioners threatened to revoke National City Lines' franchise in the city. With the two parties deadlocked in the dispute, King addressed the MIA at a mass meeting, urging the passage of a resolution that would continue the bus boycott until the city chose to abide by the ruling of the Supreme Court. Those present supported the resolution unanimously. At the end of his remarks, King offered a word of encouragement: "Eventually, segregation in public transportation will pass away, eventually. And I think we should start preparing now for the inevitable. And let us, when that moment comes, go into the situations that we confront with a great deal of dignity, sanity, and reasonableness." King continued to pray that Montgomery's leaders would have "the wisdom to see the vision of goodness in the Cradle of the Confederacy." For the time being, his prayers remained unanswered. After over two weeks of haggling between the City of Montgomery and National City Lines, on May 9 Judge Walter B. Jones found that local and state segregation laws were constitutional, and therefore directed bus drivers to once again enforce segregation on Montgomery city buses. The bus company chose to abide by the ruling.[35]

Through his preaching, King attempted to buttress his message of hope with a call to responsible preparation for the challenges and opportunities of the freedom struggle. In a sermon delivered to his Dexter congregation on Mother's Day, King encouraged mothers to take seriously their "responsibility to prepare for this great moment of history." He called for mothers to instill within their children "a sense of dignity and self-respect. Start teaching your child early that he is somebody." Recognizing that a legal victory tearing down segregation would not result in a level playing field, he called for parents to model and expect excellence from their children, conceding that "the Negro must work a little harder than the white man, for he who gets behind must run a little harder or forever remain behind." King also honored mothers of the past "who didn't know the difference between 'you does' and 'you don't,' but who wanted their offspring to 'get it all.'" He added that "mothers not only ought to be praised for their greatness, but for keeping on." The message of simply "keeping on" was apt for the protest movement, as the hot summer months approached with no settlement in sight.[36]

As the boycott entered its sixth month, King and other MIA officials recognized that the battle in Montgomery was more of a distance race than a sprint. King offered suggestions to the MIA board regarding how to better pace themselves for the long haul. Among his recommendations was a reduction of mass meetings down to one each week and limiting this Monday evening gathering to ninety minutes. He also stressed the need to increase the political voice of African Americans in Montgomery through voting and voter registration. He announced that Jo Ann Robinson would edit a bimonthly newsletter to keep people better informed of MIA developments. Additionally, King advocated a plan to increase their "economic power through the establishment of a bank," appointing a committee to apply for a charter in the near future.[37]

The concern for greater economic power had been a part of the agenda of the boycott since its inception. One of the original demands of the boycotters was that Montgomery City Lines hire black drivers to drive on largely African American routes. This condition set by the MIA reflected a felt need among the community for greater economic opportunities. All indications are that the boycott provided a boon to the black economy in Montgomery. Rufus Lewis, who led the transportation efforts for a period, claimed that black businesses were aided: "We buy all our gas from eight Negro filling stations. There is an appeal in mass meetings to trade with Negroes. This whole thing has brought about closer cooperation between Negroes." In an article, King sounded a similar note: "We have observed that small Negro shops are thriving as Negroes find it inconvenient to walk downtown to the white stores," concluding, "we have a new respect for the proper use of our dollar." As summer approached, an end to the bus boycott was nowhere in sight, but the protest had brought an unexpected economic boost to Montgomery's black citizens.[38]

Although the economic effects warrant attention, many argued the greatest significance of the boycott was how it united the African American community in Montgomery. Later accounts typically describe this as a time when a previously divided people came together for a common cause. While the car pools provided a degree of independence from the white economy, the car rides also served as a powerful time for boycott participants to share stories and build community. Many drivers saw their task as far more than transporting people from one place to another. They attempted to lighten the mood, some with jokes and stories about whites that gave some respite from the daily grind. Drivers frequently reminded passengers of the power of God, turning their seat into a pulpit for the duration of the trip. They saw their time in the car pool as crucial to keeping the people united, encouraged, and confident. Jo Ann Robinson noted that by the time folks reached their destination, "they were laughing as if that mood of faith had been with them all day." As many of the drivers represented Montgomery's professionals, and many of the riders were from the working class, the car pools served to provide greater unity among the classes. Robinson even believed "the line between the higher class and the proletariat has broken down—'We are in this thing together' is the spirit on both levels."[39]

The regular mass meetings also provided an opportunity for the community to come together, leading many to view these gatherings as the heartbeat of the movement. The services also allowed boycott leaders, including many of the city's preachers, to play a more public role in the movement. They became a place where the professional classes could join maids and day laborers in a common cause. One veteran pastor who had already earned the respect of many in the city prior to the boycott was Reverend Solomon Seay. King later called him "one of the few clerical voices that, in the years preceding the protest, had lashed out against the injustices heaped on the Negro, and urged his people to a greater appreciation of their own worth." King noted his speeches "raised the spirits of all who heard him." Seay himself viewed the movement as primarily spiritual, with Christianity providing "a common ground upon which everyone could stand." In Seay's mind, the unifying effect of the boycott was best understood "as the work and purpose of God being fulfilled at the historical moment in American history."[40]

Mass meetings would become one of the defining forms of the civil rights movement. Boycott participant Alfreida Dean Thomas credited the gatherings for helping her feel "for the first time that here were people who had been separated just on really fictitious reasons but were now together in oneness of purpose. This alone was enough to make a good feeling." King claimed the attendance at mass meetings included both professionals and the working class: "The vast majority present were working people; yet there was always an appreciable number of professionals in the audience." He went on to claim that "the so-called 'big Negroes' who owned cars and had never ridden the buses came to know the maids and laborers who rode the buses every day. Men and women who had been separated from each other by false standards of class were now singing and praying together in a common struggle for freedom and human dignity."[41]

For many observers of the Montgomery movement, one of the most significant developments among the city's African American community was their willingness to take action. While hosting a workshop at Highlander Folk School in Tennessee with Rosa Parks, Robert Graetz, and Alabama State College professor J. E. Pierce, school director Myles Horton noted that during 1955 he had received letters from Nixon and Aubrey Williams saying "that the Negroes in Montgomery didn't do anything."[42] The belief that the people of Montgomery were not capable of participating in such a movement was shared by many in the city, particularly whites. Pierce affirmed the analysis that Montgomery's African Americans were complacent prior to the protest. These assessments, while perhaps empirically descriptive in the minds of both local activists and onlookers, are overly simplistic. For many, simply surviving another day in the racially repressive South was anything but complacent. Assigning complacency to those whose life situations were barely known speaks to the paternalism of many who longed for social change. Some leaders also distrusted the people's ability to rise together to demand that transformation take place. The boycott helped them overcome any misgivings about the capacity of the masses for constructive action.[43]

The mass meetings provided some window into who was fully supporting the effort, although who actually attended these gatherings is disputed. *Montgomery Advertiser* editor Joe Azbell, noting the quality of clothing worn to mass meetings, claimed they provided a gathering space for car owners and the wealthy rather than "the maids and the janitors and the cooks and the people that are dependent on the bus service." Based on his superficial appraisal, Azbell concluded that "the preachers and the business men and the doctors and the lawyers" were providing leadership and "are the ones who are pushing this thing." He believed the people wanted to return to the buses, "but their leaders won't let them." Azbell's assessments demonstrate the significant cultural gap between blacks and whites in segregated Montgomery. Azbell did not know many of the people who gathered at mass meetings, and was unaware of the importance for many African Americans of wearing nice and respectable clothing when one entered a church sanctuary. The fact that those who attended mass meetings wore nice clothing did not indicate their social standing or how much money they had. He also underestimated the agency and self-determination of the working people who provided the backbone of this movement.[44]

One wonders if the majority of the professional class was ever fully on board with the movement. These more well-to-do citizens did not rely on city buses, so if they stayed out of the limelight they would be able to avoid any negative repercussions from whites in the city. Evidence suggests a lack of concern by some in the professional class that continued throughout the boycott. Mrs. O. B. Underwood, who was a family friend of the Kings, believed laborers were much more supportive of the boycott than many black professionals in the city: "I doubt that many of the middle class blacks felt that Rev. King was doing anything for them because, as you well learned by the time, the middle class blacks didn't help the Montgomery boycotting situation; they did nothing. I don't know any middle class blacks who were involved. There were maybe a handful of people in different situations, but they all had their cars." Reflecting on the boycott years later, Underwood noted that many teachers who were trying to hang onto their jobs were frightened during the boycott. Most professionals who went to mass meetings "were hiding or standing behind bushes or something, wanting to hear, but afraid to be seen." She claims some whites began photographing people coming and going from the meetings in order to exact some type of revenge on those supporting the protest. The result, according to Underwood, was that the visible support of the movement came from the working classes, who had less economic vulnerability to white reprisals.[45]

Mrs. Althea Thompson Thomas, who served as an organist at Dexter, was not supportive of the boycott. She believed churches had become too involved: "The ministers have no business in this and turning the church into a political organization." Believing that "some of these ministers don't know what they are doing," she suggested having the city's black and white "intelligentsia" get together at Alabama State College to settle on some sort of agreement. Thomas did not hide her antagonistic spirit: "I think for myself, and if I want to ride a bus, I ride. That's why I don't go to any of the meetings, because I'll speak my mind." She even suggested that the MIA offered no room for contrary opinions or dissent: "One of my friends told me that if I went to a meeting and told them how I felt, that they would throw me out. So I take no part in it." Clearly not every African American in Montgomery rallied behind the MIA. The city was not as unified as many participants projected or leaders later remembered.[46]

Although Montgomery's African American community was not of one mind regarding the boycott, they could all celebrate the ruling of the federal courts in *Browder v. Gayle*. In a 2–1 ruling, the federal district court found that "the statutes and ordinances requiring segregation of the white and colored races on the motor buses of a common carrier of passengers in the City of Montgomery and its police jurisdiction violate the due process and equal protection of the law clauses of the Fourteenth Amendment to the Constitution of the United States." Buoyed by the victory, the Kings and Abernathys headed to California for some vacation and to raise funds for the MIA. Ruptures within the MIA would force them to return early from their trip.[47]

Meanwhile, Nixon continued to lobby for greater economic independence and development for African Americans in order to make lasting changes. His plans for the future included greater unionization and a higher degree of economic sophistication. He tried to keep the pressure on King to use some of the funds pouring in from around the nation to further develop the community. He looked at the history of the Montgomery bricklayers' local union as an example of black economic initiative, as African Americans got the local charter for the city and hence whites had to apply to blacks for membership into an integrated union.[48]

Nixon had a very significant impact within the MIA and on its leaders. Although his job as a Pullman porter took him away from Montgomery regularly, he consulted with King when he was home: "I never came to town a single trip that the Reverend King and I didn't spend some time together. Strategy meetings and so forth, and then some nights at twelve o'clock at night he was either at my house or I was at his." Nixon had an even greater influence on the tactics and convictions of Pastor Uriah J. Fields. The original recording secretary of the MIA, Fields had written a controversial letter to the editor of the *Montgomery Advertiser* in January, suggesting the true goal of the boycott was an end to segregation on city buses, an objective Nixon had sought from the beginning. Reverend H. J. Palmer, an MIA leader who would later serve as the organization's secretary, claimed Fields's letter had served as a turning point in the city, leading several whites who had been making significant contributions to the effort to withdraw their support. Many whites had been trying to address the stated goals of the MIA, only to discover that part of the leadership really wanted to end bus segregation in Montgomery.[49]

After being reprimanded by the executive committee, Fields had not been faithful in attending MIA meetings, leading a nominating committee to replace him as the organization's recording secretary. At the next mass meeting, Fields angrily denounced his demotion from his leadership position. He then went to the media, claiming the MIA had mismanaged the considerable donations they had received from well-wishers and supporters throughout the country. The local media seized on Fields's charges, while opponents capitalized on the allegations as a way to discredit the boycott. King and Abernathy, who were vacationing and raising funds in California when the story broke, rushed back to Montgomery to respond to the crisis.[50]

At the next scheduled MIA meeting, King introduced Fields, who issued a retraction and an apology to those gathered. Fully engaged in damage control, the next MIA newsletter attempted to marginalize the validity of Fields's allegation while highlighting his retraction. Titled "A Regrettable Incident," the story emphasized that the change in the recording secretary position coincided with the incorporation of the organization and that all previous positions on the executive board had been temporary. The article noted how busy Fields had been, which led to frequent absences from MIA board meetings, resulting in his inability "to render the type of service that the organization needed. He had not been present several weeks before his replacement." The article called Fields's charges of financial mismanagement "preposterous" and thus "unworthy of refutation." In conclusion, the writer claimed: "In a state of human passion and human frailty, he spoke falsely against an organization which he loves. The wrong has been righted, but the blur remains. The minister's mistake has been costly to himself and to the good name of the MIA, but 50,000 of his fellow comrades will neither desert nor forsake him."[51]

Other evidence suggests the matter was far more complicated. Robert Graetz later claimed that Fields's charges of financial mismanagement "reignited my own concerns about the way money was handled." As the movement grew in prominence, leaders had opportunities to participate in MIA fund-raisers around the country. Graetz helped raise thousands of dollars on such events, and had always given all the proceeds, minus travel expenses, to the MIA. He later remembered a conversation with someone from the MIA office after one such trip in which he was asked "Did you keep enough out for yourself?" When Graetz responded that he had raised all the money for the organization, he was told, "I know, but the other speakers normally keep an honorarium for themselves out of the money they raised." Although he was initially shocked, he later felt those keeping part of the money for themselves may have needed it, as some were not well compensated by their congregations. Graetz's recollections reveal a lack of clear economic policy guiding the MIA's fund-raising activities. Nixon also gave some credence to Fields's charge:

> A lot of times a minister would go and make a speech and he'd think that he's entitled to some of it. Everybody didn't do like I done. Why I've known Reverend King to, you know? Reverend King, he spoke up in Canada and he told me, "Brother Nick, when the check come from Canada, that's my personal check." Sure 'nough, when it came I gave it to 'im. No weren't no question about it. A lot of that happened. But Mrs. Parks never accepted anything. Whatever she collected she turned right in. She'd come in three or four o'clock in the evening and turn in anything she'd collected and I'd give her a receipt for it. Everybody didn't do that.

With any growing organization emerging quickly in response to a specific challenge, infrastructure often lags. A lack of clear organization policies and guidelines did allow for MIA monies to be claimed by individuals within the movement, including King. Without clear guidelines or accounting, it is also possible that greed prevailed on more than one occasion, as leaders helped themselves to more of the funds than was warranted. Fields's allegations of financial mismanagement were thus not without merit.[52]

Fields experienced significant backlash for going to the white press with his claims. Johnnie Carr, who attended Hall Street Baptist Church, where Fields had served prior to Bell Street, later remembered the young minister's greed as one of the things that led him to be dismissed from the church. According to Carr, Fields publicly denigrated Hall Street Baptist's treatment of him. Far more egregious in Carr's eyes was Fields's betrayal of the organization in response to a personal offense: "I think very little of anybody who was part of the inside who would go out and try and destroy." B. J. Simms, who headed the transportation committee for the MIA, believed Fields wanted to lead the boycott, and when that did not happen he allowed jealousy to cloud his judgment. Simms asserted, "Fields decided if he couldn't run it, he'd ruin it." This torrent of criticism led Fields to later claim that he "found there's no pressure like pressure from the inside group." Nixon wondered if some of the trouble was not attributable to Fields's willingness to challenge some of King's decisions. In the end, this perceived insubordination led to his dismissal from the executive board, and after his public allegations, "some of King's supporters run that man off."[53]

The MIA used the funds that came into their coffers to keep the car pools going, to pay for legal expenses, and to maintain communication through efforts like the MIA newsletter. According to Erna Dungee Allen, some of the organization's finances also went toward helping people with financial needs in the community. The organization assisted residents with rent, paid energy bills, provided food for those who needed it, and even purchased a few washing machines for families. She believed the MIA engaged in these types of assistance to try "to get along with the people. And usually the folks who weren't participating, who didn't belong to a church or anything, were the ones who came for help. They were usually the poorest ones." Allen remembered King as particularly concerned with the plight of Montgomery's poorest. While he didn't support all the charitable assistance, "he felt like he had to go along with most of it."[54]

Throughout the summer, some whites continued to resort to desperate strategies in an attempt to discourage, intimidate, and hamper those participating in the boycott. As ripples of civil rights struggles spread from Tuscaloosa to Birmingham to Montgomery, it was easier for whites in the state to blame outsiders for the challenges rather than attribute the protest to indigenous dissatisfaction with the racial status quo. As a result, the state outlawed the NAACP in Alabama, citing the organization's refusal to turn over their membership list to the government. In late August, the home of Lutheran pastor Robert Graetz was bombed and nearly destroyed. Soon after word came that insurance providers were unwilling to cover seventeen church-owned station wagons that provided the backbone of the MIA's citywide car pool system. After a brief period of concern, Lloyds of London agreed to pick up coverage on the vehicles.[55]

Despite the white backlash, one of the overriding concerns of the MIA was how to win whites to the cause of justice rather than merely defeat them. At an executive board meeting in September, King urged those present to reach out across racial lines by making "our motives clearly understood by whites of our community" and beginning to "move from protest to reconciliation." The board adopted several strategies to assist in building more bridges with the white community. They elected to get some people associated with the MIA to write essays on the true spirit of the movement that could be carried by local newspapers. Additionally, they hoped to mail these articles to "influential and representative whites in this city, both those favorably disposed to our movement and those who oppose it" including white clergy, the Men of Montgomery, and women's organizations. Finally, they sought to work with radio and television stations to try to get the local media to cover both sides of the boycott story. If local approaches failed, King was to seek an appearance on *Meet the Press*. The primary strategy adopted by the MIA for addressing whites in the community was to use the media. While they had little success in Montgomery, this meeting was a harbinger of a strategy that proved pivotal as the civil rights movement expanded, with national media bringing the story of the movement to whites throughout the nation.[56]

As weariness set in among the protesters, King once again attempted to provide words of encouragement, inspiration, and hope to his Dexter congregation. He reminded them of Jesus' invitation from Matthew 18:21–22: "Come unto me, all ye that labor and are heavy laden, and I will give you rest." God's rest was available to them, for "although we live amid the tensions of life, although we live amid injustice" these conditions will not last forever: "I'm glad the slaves were the greatest psychologists that America's ever known, for they learned something that we must always learn. And they said it in their broken language, 'I'm so glad trouble don't last always.'" King bemoaned the current conditions in the Southland, where white supremacy dominated state and local decision making as men in power dedicated themselves "to keep the Negro segregated and exploited and keep him down under the iron yoke of oppression." King held on to hope, however, as he cried out to his congregation:

> And there is something that cries to us and says that Kasper and Englehardt and all the other men that we hear talking, grim men that represent the death groans of a dying system. And all that they are saying are merely the last-minute breathing spots of a system that will inevitably die. For justice rules this world, love and goodwill, and it will triumph. They begin to wonder all over the nation, how is it we can keep walking in Montgomery. How is it that we can keep burning out our rubber? How is it we can keep living under the tension? And we can cry out to the nation, "We can do it because we know that as we walk, God walks with us."

After months of protest and struggle, King had learned that God's presence with the people represented the only foundation for their efforts to hold on and continue their fight.[57]

King also continued to preach about the importance of love for those committed to the struggle. Warning against the self-righteousness embodied by the older brother in Jesus' parable of the Prodigal Son, King observed that "the tragedy of the elder brother was that he was contaminated with the sin of pride and egotism," noting "his spiritual pride had drained from him the capacity to love. He could not call his brother brother." King encouraged his Dexter congregation to not only strive for personal piety, but to also embody genuine love for others. Bemoaning the fact that the church and culture have tended to elevate some sins while ignoring others, he charged: "The Church has been harder on profanity than on prejudice. It has denounced drunkenness more than stinginess. It was unchristian to gamble, but not to own slaves."[58] Meanwhile a few white Christians in Montgomery continued to display an unwillingness to love, as the MIA car pool once again came under attack.[59]

At the suggestion of Jack D. Brock, the president of Montgomery's printers' union, the city elected to take legal action against the car pool by claiming it was an unauthorized business. Mayor Gayle instructed Montgomery's city attorneys "to file such proceedings as it may deem proper to stop the operation of car pool or transportation systems growing out of the bus boycott." The case went to trial on November 13, with the city not only seeking to end the car pool, but also to gain the lost tax revenues Montgomery would have garnered through bus travel. The MIA faced the possibility of the car pool ending with no alternate plan under development. As King sat at the defendant's table during a brief midday recess, he noticed activity at the back of the courtroom. Word soon came to him that the U.S. Supreme Court had sided with the U.S. District Court, finding segregation on Montgomery's buses unconstitutional. In what proved to be an anticlimactic ruling, Judge Carter supported the city's claim in their lawsuit, effectively ending the car pool. The Supreme Court's ruling did not take effect immediately. Over the following six weeks, as the city exhausted every delay tactic they could find, the boycott continued. MIA leaders scrambled to develop share-a-ride programs in local neighborhoods, although without a centralized transportation system, many elected to walk rather than return to segregated buses.[60]

On the day the Supreme Court ruling reached Montgomery, the 134th Alabama Baptist State Convention was in session in the city. The proceedings included a report from the Christian Life Commission titled *The Race Situation in Alabama*. The Southern Baptists dismissed the legitimacy of Autherine Lucy's protest at the University of Alabama, calling her a puppet of the NAACP. They proceeded to address the boycott in Montgomery, surmising that "emotionalism has affected, we feel, some decisions of the legislators and certain magistrates." They also defended those who had elected to join the White Citizens Council: "Because of a lack of alternate course many white Christians, normally moderate, are finding themselves more closely linked with the stands not of their own persuasion." As a way to proceed, the report recommended meetings between "more independent Negro ministers" and nearby white ministers with the goal of lessening the tension of the situation, noting those involved should be members of neither the NAACP nor the White Citizens Council. While the Southern Baptists continued to identify the problem as tension between the races, King and the MIA described how to live faithfully with the inevitable tensions emerging from a struggle for justice.[61]

On December 20, the Supreme Court's ruling reached Montgomery, instructing the city to operate integrated buses the following morning. At a mass meeting that evening, King concluded with words of faith and expectation: "It is my firm conviction that God is working in Montgomery. Let all men of goodwill, both Negro and white, continue to work with Him. With this dedication we will be able to emerge from the bleak and desolate midnight of man's inhumanity to man to the bright and glittering daybreak of freedom and justice." King woke early to board one of the first fully integrated buses. He did so as a changed man. Over the course of the previous twelve months, the trajectory of King's life and ministry was radically reshaped. Within the crucible of a community in struggle, King found his voice. No longer was King primarily a theoretical advocate of the social gospel. Now King was in the heart of the battle to make social justice a reality. Before coming to Montgomery, King had immersed himself in a life of social gospel oratory, rooted in the power of love. He had had ideas about God's character and about social change, but he had never fully experienced the shared and prolonged struggles that transform theories into convictions and forge authentic, unwavering faith. But by the end of 1956, King was no stranger to living under the tensions of modern life, and as he stared evil in the face daily, he became a preacher of passionate conviction that could stir not only a congregation or even a community, but a nation.[62]

In his memoir of the boycott, King claimed that "The Montgomery story would have taken place if the leaders of the protest had never been born." In many respects, this is true. The boycott idea preceded King's arrival in the city, and the first few days of the protest would have occurred had King not been on the scene at all. The stalemate with the city would likely have happened as well, for Montgomery city officials proved determined to maintain white supremacy in the city by defending segregated buses, and were unwilling to compromise. The MIA had many resolute leaders who were committed to staying the course. Even the emphasis on love and nonviolence would have emerged as a dominant theme without King's presence. The commitments to loving your neighbor and turning the other cheek were deeply rooted in the African American Christian tradition. The fact that the people embodied the nonviolence King articulated demonstrates their predisposition to view nonviolence as a viable strategy.[63]

What then did King contribute to the Montgomery bus boycott? Perhaps most importantly, as he would say the following year, he became a symbol for the movement. He was better educated and more articulate than any of the other black pastors in the city. His winsome personality allowed him to remain above the fray. When conflicts emerged within the movement, King played the role of arbitrator and peace maker, as he did when he met with Uriah Fields following allegations of MIA financial mismanagement. He also had the capacity to connect with professionals and the poor, the highly educated and the illiterate. King became a unifying figure whose capacity for personal growth coupled with his significant social skills made him an ideal person to serve as the face of the local movement. His sense of the moment and calm demeanor under pressure as demonstrated in his Holt Street address and through his reassuring words following the bombing of his home solidified his unique role. J. Pius Barbour, King's friend and mentor from Crozer, wrote during the boycott: "Every now and then God takes a human personality and makes that personality the Symbol of some great social movement. King has become the Symbol of the New Negro in the Negroes struggle. He is the first voice of the new negro. The new negro has had no spokesman. King is the first." While the protest would have begun without King, and the Supreme Court would have found in their favor regardless, the local people may well have fractured without his presence. More conservative leadership might have prevailed at critical moments, leading to compromise and an end to the boycott. King's decision not to compromise coupled with his hope-filled rhetoric held the people of Montgomery together for nearly thirteen months.[64]

There can be no doubt regarding the deep impact the boycott had on King. Jo Ann Robinson and E. D. Nixon had mobilized the community with the idea of a boycott and had invited King to play a critical role. Seizing upon the arrest of Parks, they created a context within which King could blossom. King gleaned from the sacrifices of maids and laborers who bore the brunt of the hardship by giving up buses for over a year. He also gained valuable experience as the president of the MIA, where he had to marshal resources, navigate through controversies and rivalries, and respond to crises with strategic thinking and skillful decision making. In addition, he learned the potentially pivotal role the media could play in swaying the opinions of the nation, as numerous media sources covered his trial and the eventual integration of the city's buses. King experienced the goodwill and assistance of some local whites, providing him evidence that change, redemption, and transformation of hearts was possible. He was emboldened by the intransigence of the city commissioners and their varied attempts to intimidate and dissuade both him and the MIA. Montgomery provided a unique challenge that he would have had a hard time finding elsewhere. No other local movement developed with the longevity and significance of Montgomery until the next decade. It also took a unique situation for a relative newcomer to the city to have the opportunity to be the leader of any organization, let alone a major civil rights protest. From the long view, King may have gained even more from the boycott than the community did.[65]

As the year came to an end, King began planning for the future of the MIA. In December 1956, *Liberation* magazine dedicated its issue to the boycott. In an article titled "We Are Still Walking," King noted future plans for the organization following the November 13 Supreme Court ruling. He also reflected on the past thirteen months of his life in a conversation with New York attorney Stanley Levison: "if anybody had asked me a year ago to head this movement, I tell you very honestly, that I would have run a mile to get away from it. I had no intention of being involved in this way." Once the movement began and King realized the inspiration he provided for those sacrificing for the cause, he "realized that the choice leaves your own hands. The people expect you to give them leadership. You see them growing as they move into action, and then you know you no longer have a choice, you can't decide whether to stay in it or get out of it, you must stay in it." For the remaining days of his life, King stayed in the fight for civil rights, but the setting was rarely Montgomery.[66]

6 "Bigger Than Montgomery"

They had the vision to see this struggle is bigger than Montgomery. And they have been willing to share me with this nation and with the world.
　　　　　　　　　　　　—Martin Luther King Jr., December 5, 1957

In February 1957, King appeared on the cover of *Time* magazine in a story chronicling the successful conclusion of the Montgomery bus boycott. This honor reflected an unintended outcome of the local protest: King became the face for the national struggle for civil rights. He was now one of the most sought-after African American preachers in the nation, having delivered keynote addresses at the annual gatherings of both the NAACP and the National Baptist Convention the previous summer. Speaking opportunities flooded his desk. He accepted an invitation from Kwame Nkrumah to attend Ghana's independence celebration and was in serious discussions to write his memoirs of the boycott. Although his civil rights leadership was born in Montgomery, by early 1957 King had already become bigger than Montgomery.

As King's prominence grew, the local struggle intensified. Once the buses were integrated, a wave of violence swept Montgomery, offering a foretaste of the depths to which some would sink to preserve white supremacy and segregation. By the time the boycott ended, the African American people of Montgomery had secured a major local and national victory. They had stood together to strike a blow against Jim Crow and segregation in their city. In response, a small number of reactionaries unleashed a wave of violence. During the first ten days of bus integration, five white men assaulted a black woman at a bus stop while snipers fired shots at King's parsonage and several city buses. Within a week, the city suspended evening bus service in an attempt to curtail the violence. A few weeks later, bombs struck two homes and four churches, demonstrating that integrated buses did not ensure safety and justice for all Montgomery's citizens.

King's notoriety and leadership grew immeasurably during the boycott. The benefits of the protest did not extend to the daily lives of most of Montgomery's African Americans, however. Many boycott leaders would face difficult and challenging days. The fragile unity that had held during the boycott soon crumbled. By the end of the decade, several of those who had been part of the vanguard of black leadership in Montgomery prior to King's arrival had either left the city or seen their influence stifled by the clergy-directed MIA. Working-class blacks faced significant backlash as well. Many faced increased verbal abuse and frightening threats. Some lost their jobs when whites exacted an economic price on African Americans who had supported the movement. A few became victims of violent acts resulting in the destruction and loss of property, personal injury, and even the loss of life. The boycott had provided an economic boost to the local African American economy, but leaders failed to foster any sustained economic development effort. King shifted his attention to a struggle bigger than Montgomery as the local community labored to sustain the momentum generated by the boycott. The U.S. Supreme Court decision supporting integrated buses in the city proved more of a victory for King and the burgeoning national civil rights movement than it was for Montgomery's African American community.

King's attention turned to broader regional challenges during the first week of January 1957. Sensing an opportunity to capitalize on the momentum of Montgomery, King heeded the advice of Bayard Rustin by calling together several southern black pastors. They agreed to meet at Atlanta's Ebenezer Baptist Church to contemplate a collaborative effort to bring racial change and integration throughout the South. The night before the meeting, a series of bombings rocked Montgomery, reminding King and all who gathered that some would stop at nothing to preserve segregation. King and Abernathy rushed back to Montgomery to inspect the damaged buildings and to reassure the people. Bombs struck several homes, including the parsonages of both Abernathy and Robert Graetz. Among the four church buildings that absorbed significant damage was Abernathy's First Baptist Church. Two of the other church buildings had to be completely rebuilt.[1]

After inspecting the damage, King and Abernathy returned to Atlanta to resume discussions with a group of southern pastors who would form the core of what would later be called the Southern Christian Leadership Conference (SCLC). Like any new organization, the SCLC needed money to launch its ambitious program. As the newest face of the civil rights struggle, King became their most effective fund-raiser, as he traveled around the nation sharing the Montgomery story. In spite of these responsibilities, King intended to more fully engage his pastorate at Dexter once the boycott ended. He also remained president of the Montgomery Improvement Association (MIA), which sought to develop a road map that would lead to additional gains in their city. The bombings reminded King that the local struggle he had been fighting for the last thirteen months was far from over. Given the intransigence of white supremacy, moving forward in Montgomery would prove a difficult challenge.

The wave of violence alarmed Montgomery's white citizens. A group that included *Montgomery Advertiser* editor Grover Hall, several white pastors, and the Men of Montgomery issued a statement condemning the bombings. City police responded to the outcry by arresting seven Ku Klux Klan members, several of whom later confessed to the crimes. One of the men even showed police the stock of explosives they had used, but an all-white jury later acquitted them of all charges. Despite indignant rhetoric in the wake of the violence, white Montgomery lacked the collective will to bring the perpetrators to justice.[2]

Once the bus boycott became a national story, Montgomery became a flashpoint for white backlash. The White Citizens Council grew exponentially, bombings of churches and parsonages became far too common, and economic reprisals were the order of the day. Following the Supreme Court ruling and the official integration of city buses in Montgomery, the backlash only intensified. Many local whites were determined that the victory garnered through the bus boycott would not be replicated. Developing a sustained local movement following the boycott would be that much more difficult because the white community would not again be guilty of underestimating the capacity of Montgomery's African American citizens to galvanize for a cause. Their primary weapon was to terrorize blacks through consistent acts of violence.

In his Sunday sermon following the bombings, King struggled to make sense of the violence: "Where is God while hundreds and thousands of his children suffer merely because they are desirous of having freedom and human dignity? Where is God while churches and homes of ministers are being plunged across the abyss of torturous barbarity?" The following evening at a MIA mass meeting, King further chronicled the tragic details of their shared struggle: "Several of our people have been needlessly beaten, one of our humble ladies—an expectant mother, has been viciously shot, and to climax it all two of our homes and four of our churches have been bombed." While admitting ignorance regarding God's ultimate purpose, he suggested that "it may be we are called upon to be God's suffering servants through whom he is working his redemptive plan." He encouraged those gathered to not become bitter nor turn to violence but to "continue to love" and to "keep standing up." As King was delivering the closing prayer at the gathering, he recalled being "gripped by an emotion I could not control." Despite being overcome, he prayed: "Lord, I hope no one will have to die as a result of our struggle for freedom here in Montgomery. Certainly I don't want to die. But if anyone has to die, let it be me." This open display of emotion brought King some cathartic relief while also prompting many to reach out and reassure him of their support for his leadership even as the community faced uncertain days. Many had hoped the tension would ease once integration orders came from the U.S. Supreme Court. Instead, King and the community struggled to come to terms with the intransigent nature of racism.[3]

Following the bombings, the city briefly suspended bus service. When officials reinstated public transportation, a wave of violence once again fell upon Montgomery. Bombs struck a service station, a cab stand, and the home of an African American hospital worker. Someone also placed twelve sticks of dynamite under King's front porch, although the makeshift bomb was discovered before it exploded. The day this new round of bombings hit, King admitted before his congregation that "I went to bed many nights scared to death" over the previous year, but he had been sustained by a vision in which God told him to "Preach the Gospel, stand up for truth, stand up for righteousness." With divinely inspired boldness, King proclaimed: "So I'm not afraid of anybody this morning. Tell Montgomery they can keep shooting and I'm going to stand up to them; tell Montgomery they can keep bombing and I'm going to stand up to them. If I had to die tomorrow morning I would die happy, because I've been to the mountain top and I've seen the promised land and it's going to be here in Montgomery." Days after being overwhelmed by emotion, King emerged with his usual message of hope and faith. He optimistically spoke of a day when his city would experience a Promised Land, but many of Montgomery's black citizens were destined to wander in the wilderness for many more years.[4]

Clear direction for the Montgomery movement proved elusive. In early February, King appeared as a guest on a national NBC Sunday news program called *The Open Mind*. When asked by the moderator about future plans for the MIA, King admitted: "In Montgomery we have not worked out any next steps, that is, in any chronological order. We are certainly committed to work and press on until segregation is nonexistent in Montgomery and all over the South." While plans were hazy on the local scene, King continued to take full advantage of opportunities to travel, speak, and promote the cause of justice both domestically and abroad. An appearance on the cover of *Time* magazine cemented King's role as the face of not only the MIA, but also the broader civil rights struggle. Among King's many opportunities was a request from Gold Coast prime minister Kwame Nkrumah to attend Ghana's independence celebration. Seeking to solidify his understanding of the relationship between national and international freedom movements, King accepted the invitation. Only twenty-eight years old, King had already earned the status of foreign dignitary. A few days before departing, King preached "It's a Great Day to Be Alive" at Dexter. King told his congregation that the groundswell of freedom movements around the globe demonstrated God's power at work, leading him to be optimistic that the local struggle for social change would prove successful.[5]

Before leaving, King hoped to set in motion a process that would provide the MIA with a blueprint for how they would take full advantage of what King called "a great time to be alive." In a memo to Ralph Abernathy, King urged his deputy to call together a "Future Planning Committee" to chart a course for the future of the MIA. The committee included Abernathy as chair, Jo Ann Robinson and Dr. Moses W. Jones as co-chairs, as well as J. E. Pierce, Solomon Seay, H. H. Hubbard, R. J. Glasco, Rufus Lewis, E. D. Nixon, Mrs. A. W. West, and Robert

Graetz. At the first meeting, the committee discussed implementing an eight-point program for the organization. Proposed initiatives included nonpartisan political education and involvement, an emphasis on interracial communication, providing means for adult education, and improving recreation opportunities for African Americans in the city. They also sought to improve the economic status of Montgomery's black citizens through securing more good jobs, providing better housing, promoting neighborhood businesses, establishing credit unions and perhaps a Savings and Loan, and continuing financial relief efforts. Finally, the committee hoped to pursue better cooperation with the police while recognizing the need for an "impartial investigation of alleged intimidations and discriminations" by law enforcement.[6]

Soon after King's return from Ghana, the committee settled on a plan for the future of the MIA. They began their written blueprint for the organization with an idealistic preamble:

> Recognizing that every community has the basic potential for the solution of social problems and the implementation of legal decisions which redefine the ideals set forth by the founders of this nation, and that ultimately the local community is the proving ground for the social progress of the nation; and recognizing that the only feasible solution to the problems of group relations and race relations is through the Christian and non-violent approach; and recognizing that enforced segregation is a social evil which must be eradicated before any group or people can reach their full social, political, economic, and moral maturity; and desiring to provide a far-reaching MIA program that would embrace both the immediate and the remote problems, and at the same time center its aims upon the building of a bigger, a better, and a more beautiful community, wherein good group relations and good race relations exist; we therefore set forth the following ten-point program.

Despite consistent backlash from segregationists, the MIA dared to dream big as they prepared for the future. They believed Montgomery would continue to be a primary proving ground for the burgeoning civil rights movement. Over the coming years, all Montgomery would prove was that the nation had a long way to go.[7]

King used his first sermon at Dexter following his return from Ghana to reflect on his trip, emphasizing the tragic stories of colonialism and slavery that deeply affected the continent of Africa and her people. Citing the groundswell of independence movements throughout the world, he asserted that "there is something in the soul that cries out for freedom." When King heard the chants of freedom emanating from the people at the hour of Ghana's independence, he remembered "that old Negro spiritual once more crying out: 'Free at last, free at last, Great God Almighty, I am free at last.'" Although Ghana had experienced their liberation, the local struggle continued for Dexter's parishioners: "Don't go back to your homes and around Montgomery thinking that the Montgomery City Commission and that all the forces in the South will eventually work out this thing for the Negroes." The lesson of Ghana was that "freedom only comes through persistent revolt, through persistent agitation, through persistently rising up against the system of evil. The bus boycott is just the beginning. Buses are integrated in Montgomery, but that is just the beginning." Emphasizing the theme of nonviolence, he instructed his congregation to "fight with love, so that when the day comes that the walls of segregation have completely crumbled in Montgomery, that we will be able to live with people as their brothers and sisters. Oh, my friends, our aim must be not to defeat Mr. Engelhardt, not to defeat Mr. Sellers and Mr. Gayle and Mr. Parks. Our aim must be to defeat the evil that's in them. But our aim must be to win the friendship of Mr. Gayle and Mr. Sellers and Mr. Engelhardt." King embraced the MIA's belief that Montgomery could become a proving ground for the development of genuine cross-racial relationships.[8]

On Easter Sunday, King shared some of his heartfelt questions regarding the persistence and power of evil in the world. As he contemplated the implications of Christ's resurrection, he confessed his doubts: "Every now and then I become bewildered about this thing. I begin to despair every now and then. And wonder why it is that the forces of evil seem to reign supreme and the forces of goodness seem to be trampled over." He admitted struggling to understand why "the forces of injustice have triumphed over the Negro, and he has been forced to live under oppression and slavery and exploitation? Why is it, God? Why is it simply because some of your children ask to be treated as first-class human beings they are trampled over, have their homes bombed, their children are pushed from their classrooms and sometimes little children are thrown into the deep waters of Mississippi?" King's specific questions for God reveal his commitment to wrestle along with the people through the most perplexing challenges of life in the segregated South. While happy the boycott was successful, they experienced in its wake the full onslaught of racist resistance to social change. In the face of such hatred, King's faith remained steadfast as Easter "answers the profound question that we confront in Montgomery. And if we can just stand with it, if we can just live with Good Friday, things will be all right. For I know that Easter is coming and I can see it coming now. As I look over the world, as I look at America. I can see Easter coming, in race relations. I can see it coming on every hand. I see it coming in Montgomery."[9]

King's frequent travels meant he had fewer opportunities to see Easter coming in Montgomery. When *Pulpit Digest* requested that King provide a sermon on race relations for publication, King declined, citing "an extremely crowded and strenuous schedule for the last two or three years, I have not had the opportunity to write most of the sermons that I preach. In most cases I have had to content myself with a rather detailed outline." His energies were increasingly directed toward achieving national objectives. In May, King joined A. Philip Randolph of the Brotherhood of Sleeping Car Porters and Roy Wilkins of the NAACP in calling for a march on Washington, D.C., dubbed the "Prayer Pilgrimage for Freedom." Set for the third anniversary of the *Brown* decision, the organizers stressed that "eight states have defied the nation's highest court and have refused to begin in good will, with all deliberate speed, to comply with its ruling." In their attempt to garner participants for the march, the sponsors noted the passivity of law enforcement while "ministers have been arrested, threatened and shot," "churches and homes have been bombed," and "school children have been threatened with mobs." William Holmes Borders, the pastor of Atlanta's Wheat Street Baptist Church, attended the organizational meeting for the march and responded with a brief note to King. Concerned that there was no concrete plan for action beyond the event, Borders suggested an agenda that included integrating buses in several southern cities, registering more voters, testing integration at southern restaurants, and "continuous intelligent agitation for implementation of the Supreme Court Decision." While Borders lobbied for a more clearly defined agenda for the Washington, D.C., event, his civil rights agenda reflected the typical concerns of activist professionals who were only marginally concerned with economic issues, but instead focused on integration and the right to vote.[10]

Bayard Rustin did encourage King to adopt a more aggressive economic agenda by emphasizing connections between the objectives of civil rights leaders and the national labor movement. Given the critical role that labor leader A. Philip Randolph played in bringing the march together, Rustin saw this event as a great opportunity to elevate the potential partnership between labor and civil rights. He argued that "equality for Negroes is related to the greater problem of economic uplift for Negroes and poor white men. They share a common problem and have a common interest in working together for economic and social uplift. They can and must work together." When King took the podium in front of the Lincoln Memorial for his address before a crowd of roughly twenty thousand participants, he eschewed any emphasis on furthering a relationship between the civil rights agenda and labor or broader economic concerns. Instead he focused squarely on the desperate need for African Americans to have full voting rights, demanding again and again, "Give us the ballot."[11]

While King's star continued to rise nationally, trouble brewed in Montgomery. Six months after the end of the boycott, Nixon sent King a letter of resignation from his post as treasurer of the MIA. In the caustic correspondence, Nixon expressed anger that local leaders continued to minimize his contributions while treating him "as a newcomer to the MIA." Noting he had been a treasurer only "in name and not in reality," he reminded King and the MIA board that it had been his "dream, hope and hard work since 1932" that had tilled the soil for change in the community. A few weeks later, King and Abernathy met with Nixon in an attempt to pacify the fiery Pullman porter. They managed to convince Nixon to remain with the organization as treasurer, suggesting they would change some of the organization's financial practices that had caused him concern for some time. Despite the truce, distrust between the parties continued unabated. Even as King gained an audience with Vice President Richard Nixon and was awarded the NAACP's Spingarn Medal "for the highest and noblest achievement" by an African American over the previous year, he was losing his grip on the local scene.[12]

The summer of 1957 proved tragic for one of Montgomery's most outspoken white advocates for justice and civil rights. In January, librarian Juliette Morgan had written an editorial to a paper in Tuscaloosa in which she attributed the crisis in the South to the cowardice of white males who were afraid to stand up for justice and equality. Following the article, pressures on Morgan escalated, leading her into a deep depression. Morgan's mother, while not supportive of her daughter's stand for civil rights, did all she could to help in this time of need. Morgan began seeing a psychiatrist in Birmingham from whom she received shock treatments. Although she briefly rallied, in early July she overdosed on pills, leading to her death.

Many of Montgomery's African American women wanted to honor Morgan by attending her funeral. Virginia Durr called the church rector to receive permission for the women to attend, but was told that approval for an interracial gathering would take too long. Although she had put her reputation at risk to argue for an end to segregation in her hometown, Morgan's funeral was a fully segregated, white-only affair.[13]

Morgan's willingness to courageously challenge white supremacy had an impact on King. He mentioned her in his memoir of the boycott, recognizing she was the first to connect the boycott to Gandhi's nonviolent struggle for Indian independence. King also observed the onslaught of abuse she faced in the wake of her fearless public attacks on the racial mores of Montgomery. Morgan's life and tragic death impressed upon King the high cost to southern whites who openly supported the fight against segregation.[14]

If whites could expect to encounter significant backlash if they were too closely tied with the struggle for justice, King began to embrace his symbolic association with the growing civil rights struggle. In an August 1957 sermon, King admitted his growing notoriety often tempted him to believe that he was special: "I can hardly walk the street in any city of this nation where I'm not confronted with people running up the street, 'Isn't this Reverend King of Alabama?' Living under this isn't easy, it's a dangerous tendency that I will come to feel that I'm something special, that I stand somewhere in this universe because of ingenuity and that I'm important." King claimed he prayed to God daily to "help me to see myself in my true perspective. Help me, O God, to see that I'm just a symbol of a movement." Noting "a boycott would have taken place in Montgomery, Alabama, if I had never come to Alabama," King admitted that "this moment would have come in history even if M. L. King had never been born." But King had been in Montgomery, and his leadership of the movement had opened many doors for him even as they slammed shut on many African Americans in the city. Unfortunately, King's potent oratory was not accompanied by concrete local action.[15]

Despite lofty goals from the MIA, the lives of boycott participants continued to be plagued with difficulty. Rosa Parks's financial situation was particularly dire. While her arrest and personality had served the movement well, she was unable to find regular employment both during and after the boycott. As early as February 1956, Virginia Durr wrote Highlander Folk School director Myles Horton regarding Parks's tenuous financial situation: "She has lost her job and had her rent raised and I am at the moment trying to raise some money for her to live on. It is fine to be a heroine but the price is high." By November 1956, Durr had raised around $600 to assist Parks's family. In a letter to Horton, Durr lamented that the funds raised to that point were "hardly enough to live on and she has had a hard time. As you know she has a terrible problem with her husband [alcohol abuse] and her mother is sick a lot and she has real troubles and cannot leave them." As the boycott neared its conclusion, Durr was concerned about how the MIA seemed to be treating both Nixon and Parks: "the time has now gone by I am afraid for Mr. Nixon to start the voting office. I think the MIA will do it on a big scale and it should be a great success but Mrs. Parks won't have a job there (the jobs will all go to the college people) and Mr. Nixon won't be in charge. Perhaps he can start the Progressive Democrats again. In the meantime Rosa is still in need."[16]

The MIA attempted to assist Parks during the first few months of 1957. In a memo written prior to his departure for the Gold Coast, King had directed the MIA vice president, Ralph Abernathy, to take action regarding Rosa Parks's financial struggle. He told Abernathy that "she is in real need, and because of her tremendous self respect she has not already revealed this to the organization. After studying her situation and realizing that the whole protest revolves around her name, I am recommending that $250.00 be given to her from the Relief Fund." He later added, "You may make it three hundred dollars ($300.00) if you feel so disposed." Minutes from an early March relief committee meeting indicate Parks received $300 from the MIA. While Nixon and Virginia Durr remained frustrated by what they deemed to be insufficient local support for Parks, the action by the MIA indicates that King was trying to do something on her behalf.[17]

By midsummer, after enduring over eighteen months of harassment and threats while struggling to find consistent employment, Parks elected to leave Montgomery. In response, the MIA declared August 5 "Rosa Parks Day" and held a program on her behalf that evening. They provided her a gift of around $800 collected from area churches. A few weeks later, Parks penned a letter to King thanking him and the MIA board for their generosity. She was sad that she had to leave Montgomery but believed living near her brother in Detroit would be better for her mother and husband. While Parks left gracefully, some believed movement leaders had neglected to provide her with enough support and adequate opportunities. Nixon claimed that on the evening of the program held in her honor, he "almost cussed at Mt. Zion," the church that hosted the event. He later added:

> It's a shame before God, here is the women responsible for this thing and got to leave home for bread. Raising a little pitiful seven or eight hundred dollars and give her then stick your chest out and think you've done something. But the people got carried away with Reverend King and forgot about everyone else. And like a woman told me coming down on the airplane one day, "Mr. Nixon, I don't know what those black folks would have done in Montgomery if Reverend King had not come to town." I said, "If Mrs. Parks had gotten up and given that cracker her seat you'd never heard of Reverend King," which is true.

King did not disagree with Nixon's assessment of Parks's role in the boycott. In early September, King and Parks saw one another at Highlander

Folk School in Tennessee, where King delivered a keynote address to commemorate the institution's twenty-fifth anniversary. He acknowledged that Parks was in the audience, claiming "you would not have had a Montgomery story without Rosa Parks." Parks herself had delivered a report for the anniversary meeting in which she described Montgomery as an "integration beachhead." Parks would no longer be a part of this beachhead, however. As the summer of 1957 drew to a close, Nixon was estranged from King and the pastoral leadership of the MIA while Parks had left the city altogether. Parks and Nixon, who for years had toiled for the NAACP on both the local and statewide levels, became outsiders. As others attempted to further their labors and dreams, they found themselves on the outside looking in.[18]

In October, King offered his annual report to his Dexter congregation. He thanked the church for its "willingness to share me with the nation. Through the force of circumstance, I was catapulted into the leadership of a movement that has succeeded in capturing the imagination of people all over this nation and the world." The ramifications of King's frequent absences from the city led him to confess that "almost every week—having to make so many speeches, attend so many meetings, meet so many people, write so many articles, council with so many groups—I face the frustration of feeling that in the midst of so many things to do I am not doing anything well." King expressed his appreciation for the ongoing support of Dexter as evidenced in not complaining when some tasks were left undone, providing support when he and his family faced physical danger, and encouraging him when opponents sought to tear him down.[19]

King also continued to challenge his congregation to live out Jesus' command to love one's enemies. Because the practice of genuine concern for the well-being of one's opponents seemed so alien to human nature, he told the people of Dexter they could expect to hear about this topic at least once a year. Although a year later King would publish an essay titled "My Pilgrimage to Nonviolence," in this sermon he referred to love for enemies rather than nonviolence as his "basic philosophical and theological orientation." He encouraged his audience to remember "that love has within it a redemptive power" and advocated looking into the eyes of every person in Alabama and around the nation and saying, "I love you. I would rather die than hate you." He maintained the belief that "through the power of this love somewhere men of the most recalcitrant bent will be transformed. And then we will be in God's kingdom." For King, the language and tactics of nonviolence became a vehicle to express a more consistent and enduring commitment to the radical love ethic found in the teachings of Jesus.[20]

An MIA newsletter penned by Jo Ann Robinson demonstrated the difficulty of embodying genuine love for one's enemies in Montgomery. Although she recognized that both races seemed to have accepted integrated buses in Montgomery, Robinson also acknowledged that the MIA faced "a dark future just now, with some conditions getting worse, with no obvious efforts on the part of proper authorities to inaugurate 'the equalization plan' in their so-called separate-but-equal doctrine." Several events led to Robinson's negative assessment, including a gerrymandering of nearby Tuskegee that had resulted in nearly twenty-seven thousand blacks being zoned out of the city limits, preventing them from voting in local elections. In Montgomery, city architects had recently designed a $900,000 library for whites while only allotting $100,000 for a branch library for blacks. The city failed to provide adequate park and recreation facilities for Montgomery's African American community. Robinson also noted the recent arrest of Fred Gray for sitting in the white section of the Montgomery Airport, the recent firings of African American employees from grocery stores and as truck drivers, and the stiff resistance by election officials when blacks attempted to register to vote.[21]

Although the MIA failed to gain any real traction in 1957, they went ahead with their "Institute on Nonviolence and Social Change" on the second anniversary of the boycott's commencement. King offered a keynote address titled "Some Things We Must Do." In his opening comments, King applauded the corporate commitment of Montgomery's African American community, noting over the past year he had received more than sixty awards, but "the award really should be duplicated in about fifty thousand awards. Montgomery is not a drama with one actor, but it is a drama with fifty thousand actors, each playing their parts amazingly well." After offering appreciation to fellow clergy and his wife, Coretta, King took a moment to thank the members of Dexter who "haven't had much of a pastor the last two years" but did not complain as "they had the vision to see that this struggle is bigger than Montgomery. And they have been willing to share me with this nation and with the world." King had dedicated more and more time beyond the local community, traveling nearly every week. While the local struggle frayed at the edges, he found appreciative national audiences eager to hear his speeches and contribute to the cause of civil rights. King had found that sometimes the bigger, broader, more idealistic struggles were easier to fight than the tedious, slow, grassroots struggles of the local community. Significantly, in a speech on how the community should proceed, he avoided identifying specific local initiatives. King naturally gravitated to issues and battles that were "bigger than Montgomery."[22]

Reporter Trezzvant W. Anderson of the prominent black newspaper the *Pittsburgh Courier* wrote a series of articles on the situation in Montgomery a year after the boycott's completion. His first article argued that press coverage of the boycott had "projected into a position of world eminence . . . a young Georgia-born Negro minister, the Rev. Martin Luther King, Jr., who was named to head the movement strictly by force of circumstances and not by any planned action." Anderson claimed the "real dynamo" that launched the protest was Nixon, who had been "the true leader of Montgomery's Negroes over a span of a quarter century." According to Anderson, King's international prominence had resulted in "some deep scars on Montgomery Negroes. There are scars which will never be healed in our lifetime, all growing out of that unfortunate imbalance which disregards the sacrifices and toils of all and focuses on one individual while others work hard, if not harder."[23]

Anderson also questioned the true objectives of the protest. In an interview, King told Anderson that the boycott "cannot be said to have had a purpose in the sense that it was planned from the beginning to achieve a certain end. It is easy to see and understand this when one remembers that the MIA is a 'spontaneous outgrowth' from a precipitant incident— the arrest of Mrs. Rosa Parks. The protest continued as an expression of the dissatisfaction among Negroes for the discourteous treatment which they received in a system which allowed them to be segregated against." King also reflected that "the movement took on a characteristic of love for one's enemies and non-violent resistance which captured the imagination of men throughout the world. The purpose from this moment on was to stand firm before the world and before God with a calm and dignity of person that is unquestionably Christian." Anderson compared King's vague objectives with the three demands the MIA made at the beginning of the boycott: seating on a first-come, first-served basis, with blacks beginning at the back and whites at the front of the bus; drivers treating all passengers with courtesy; and the hiring of black bus drivers for primarily African American bus routes. The city still did not have black bus drivers a full year after the end of the boycott. On the positive side, Anderson emphasized the MIA's successful carpool program "which cost the MIA approximately $1,000 a day to operate. It was effective as an economic weapon in that it caused the bus company to lose $2,000 a day for over a year."[24]

In his next article, Anderson discussed the circumstances surrounding Rosa Parks's decision to leave Montgomery. He charged that the MIA, which received thousands of dollars from around the nation and the world, "failed to sustain and nourish the woman who had caused it all!" While the MIA hired a personal secretary for King at $62.50 a week and paid $5,000 annually to Mose Pleasure to serve as the executive secretary of the organization, they failed to offer office work to Parks, who had extensive experience as a secretary with the NAACP. He also insinuated that the MIA had focused almost exclusively on King's plight while ignoring the trials of other local leaders including Nixon, who told Anderson that "they bombed my house too, but you never heard anything about it. . . . They didn't put any lights around my house" as they did King's after his home was bombed. Anderson charged that the leaders of the MIA became enamored with publicity: "In Montgomery the theme grew to such a proportion that if one of the MIA leaders went down to the corner he had to do it to the accompaniment of a press conference."[25]

The series unearthed the lack of economic development for many African Americans in the wake of the boycott. Anderson stressed that the MIA had not delivered on a promised credit union to aid the city's African American citizens. He also exposed the difficult financial situation facing many of those who had sacrificed most. Although they could now ride on integrated buses, many could not find employment as a result of white backlash propagated by the White Citizens Council. Many black laborers "were feeling the pinch, and there seemed to be no help for them."[26]

An attempt by the MIA to discredit the series appeared in the December 7 edition of the *Pittsburgh Courier,* when Lawrence Dunbar Reddick claimed the articles were "based upon false assumptions and filled with insinuations and inaccuracies. The main false assumption is that the test of the success of the Montgomery movement is to be found in what it has done for the Negro community of this city." Had those who had both endured the indignity of segregated buses and sacrificed most during the yearlong protest been aware of Reddick's views, they might have been befuddled. While not opposed to being an inspiration to others around the nation, they would have been troubled by the assertion that the true impact and effectiveness of the boycott was demonstrated by its "positive national and international effect, far more significant than any local effects." Although Reddick acknowledged that Montgomery had improved as a result of the boycott, his views must have felt like a slap in the face to the foot soldiers of the movement.[27]

Despite Reddick's public relations on behalf of the MIA's leadership, the series continued with an exploration of the employment challenges facing many working-class people in the city. Anderson cited King's response to suspicions of a job squeeze against local African Americans: "We are helping these people as much as we can and piecing together the information and evidence that we can put our fingers on in the hope that we will find some clear-cut case to handle in this regard. We are certain that some elements in the white community are using punitive economic measures against Negroes, but we can only serve in a relief capacity to these persons until we can establish the economic discrimination as a fact." While King recognized the problem and was attempting to provide assistance to those most affected, there was no real strategy by the MIA to address the economic injustices that continued to affect the daily lives of many African Americans in the city. Although the conclusion to Anderson's series included qualified praise for one day of door to-door registration efforts by MIA leaders, he concluded with a stinging critique: "Frankly, this was the only positive action I observed or learned about at the MIA headquarters, except for the 10-point program outlined for the organization."[28]

King did not exert significant energy in Montgomery to try to silence the critics of the MIA. Instead he devoted the early part of 1958 to the SCLC's Crusade for Citizenship, an effort to urge "every Negro in the South to register to vote." Following an executive meeting of the organization in late January, King offered a list of talking points on the campaign for SCLC speakers and members. The memorandum described the goals of the effort as doubling the number of African American voters in the South while also "liberating all Southerners, Negro and white, to extend democracy in our great nation." On the birthday of Abraham Lincoln, the SCLC launched their voting registration campaign in twenty-one cities throughout the South. In a keynote address for a rally in Miami, King cited the fight for women's suffrage as an example of the kind of struggle and persistence needed to gain the vote. Determined to make their "intentions crystal clear," King announced: "We must and we will be free. We want freedom now. We want the right to vote now. We do not want freedom fed to us in teaspoons over another 150 years. Under God we were born free. Misguided men robbed us of our freedom. We want it back, we would keep it forever."[29]

While King continued to travel on behalf of the SCLC's Crusade for Citizenship, challenges in Montgomery continued. In March 1958, King responded to E. D. Nixon's letter from a few months earlier in which he had officially resigned as treasurer of the MIA. In his November letter, Nixon had charged King and Abernathy with not following through on commitments made the previous summer: "You both agreed on some of the points raised by me, and promised to correct them. To date nothing has been done about it." King's letter acknowledged Nixon's resignation and expressed his thanks "for the very fine service you have rendered to the Association since its inception." King ended the letter acknowledging "the support you have given me all along. Let us continue together in the great struggle ahead." Dexter deacon Robert D. Nesbitt Sr. later surmised that Nixon left the MIA because he felt he was "lost in the turn of events and receiving too little attention." While Nixon's desire for greater publicity played a role in his enmity with King, he was also frustrated with the lack of continuity on the ground in Montgomery. He was concerned that a largely symbolic victory over segregation had overshadowed more significant economic needs in his hometown. Nixon would remain frustrated with the outcomes of the boycott for the rest of his days.[30]

Although his relationship with Nixon remained tense, King learned a great deal from the outspoken Pullman porter. At pivotal moments during the boycott, King listened to Nixon's voice above all others. It was Nixon who challenged all MIA leaders to have the conviction and fortitude to be publicly identified with the new organization when the boycott began. Inspired by Nixon's strong words, King immediately agreed. Less than two months later, as the MIA leaders contemplated settling for a compromise with city leaders, Nixon spoke plainly that he would not agree with any attempt to sell out the people. Again King sided with Nixon, noting that the people are "willing to walk," and any compromise would not reflect the desires of the community. King also learned how to try to work with an internal critic who disagreed with aspects of his leadership. Nixon was not the last outspoken idealist who would both challenge and frustrate King. In future years, Fred Shuttlesworth, Ella Baker, and Stokely Carmichael would offer similar challenges. King's experiences with Nixon helped prepare him for future internal conflicts. Nixon exemplified the type of tireless sacrifice necessary in the struggle for racial justice.

Before the dawn of the boycott, Nixon had devoted countless hours to the NAACP. One of the organization's major concerns had been the conviction and death sentence of Jeremiah Reeves, who in 1952 was indicted and found guilty of raping a white woman. Still in high school at the time of his arrest, Reeves had confessed to the rape under police interrogation, though his defense attorneys later claimed his confession had been unjustly coerced. Many African Americans in Montgomery held that the white housewife and Reeves were having an affair. When discovered, the woman claimed she had been raped. On March 28, 1958, Jeremiah Reeves was executed at Kilby State Prison. Following the execution, King joined around two thousand people in a prayer pilgrimage to the Alabama Capitol to protest the state's action. He addressed the crowd, claiming the gathering was "an act of public repentance for our community for committing a tragic and unsavory injustice." Acknowledging that they did not know definitively whether Reeves was guilty or innocent of the charges, King questioned "the severity and inequality of the penalty" he received, noting "full grown white men committing comparable crimes against Negro girls are rare ever [sic] punished, and are never given the death penalty or even a life sentence." King took the opportunity to challenge the pattern of injustice perpetuated by the court system: "Negroes are robbed openly with little hope of redress. We are fined and jailed often in defiance of law. Right or wrong, a Negro's word has little weight against a white opponent." A few days later, a group of three hundred white clergy and church leaders in the community issued a statement denouncing the Easter demonstration, suggesting that instead local African American leaders should participate in organized dialogue with white leaders. When King and the MIA asked for a meeting to begin such discussions, they received no reply.[31]

King continued to take advantage of opportunities to speak on the national stage. In 1957, he began writing answers to readers' questions in a column titled "Advice for Living" published in *Ebony* magazine. He also participated along with other African American leaders in a meeting with President Eisenhower on June 23, 1958. Following the meeting, King joined A. Philip Randolph of the Brotherhood of Sleeping Car Porters, Lester B. Granger of the Urban League, and Roy Wilkins of the NAACP in crafting a statement to President Eisenhower. They urged the president to ensure national law would be enforced throughout the land, sought a White House conference to deal with the integration rulings of the U.S. Supreme Court, and pleaded for full protection for those seeking to register to vote.[32]

A few months after meeting with President Eisenhower, Montgomery police once again arrested King. He was charged with loitering as police claimed King failed to cooperate with a request to "move on" as he tried to gain entrance to the trial of Edward Davis, a man who had attacked Ralph Abernathy the previous week. King countered by accusing the officers of using unnecessary force including trying to break his arm, choking him, and kicking him once he got to his cell. The court found King guilty of loitering and fined him ten dollars in addition to four dollars for court fees. Following his conviction, King informed the judge that he "could not in all good conscience pay a fine for an act that I did not commit." Instead he agreed to "accept the alternative which you provide, and that I will do without malice." Although King intended to serve time in jail, the Montgomery police commissioner, Clyde Sellers, paid the fine in order to avoid further negative publicity for his city.[33]

A few days after the trial, King received a letter from Nixon. While Nixon thought King had been foolish to take the chance of allowing the police an opportunity to assault him "behind closed doors," he applauded the decision to serve time rather than pay a fine, calling it "the most courageous stand in that direction since Bayard Rustin, serve time [sic] in Carolina. And because of your courage in face of known danger I want to commend you for your stand for the people of color all over the world, and especially the people in Montgomery." King thanked Nixon for his letter a few days later, noting: "I am sorry that I have not seen you in a long, long time. I hope our paths will cross in the not-too-distant future."[34]

Nixon's letter to King demonstrates the competing agendas that added to the difficulties for the Montgomery struggle following the boycott. King had stressed that the struggle was "bigger than Montgomery," and Reddick claimed that the local movement's effectiveness was demonstrated primarily through its "positive national and international effect, far more significant than any local effects." In contrast, while Nixon acknowledged the global dimension of King's willingness to go to jail to confront injustice, he was "especially" pleased that King had stood for "the people in Montgomery." As King, Abernathy, and Reddick concentrated on building a regional civil rights movement, Nixon's heart remained first and foremost with the people of his city. Nixon longed for a return to a civil rights struggle defined by the plight of Montgomery's African American citizens and fortified by the courageous action of local people. King's attention was elsewhere.[35]

In the summer of 1958, the few whites working for racial change in Montgomery continued to experience significant backlash for their support of integration. Some simply decided to leave town. Robert Graetz, the only white clergyman in the MIA, accepted a call to pastor a Lutheran Church in Columbus, Ohio. Soon after, the interracial woman's group called the Fellowship of the Concerned decided to hold a daylong meeting at the Father Purcell Unit of St. Jude's Hospital. Someone got wind of the meeting and proceeded to go through the hospital parking lot writing down the license plate numbers of those in attendance. They used this information to get the phone numbers of those affiliated with the Fellowship of the Concerned. Threatening and harassing phone calls soon followed, and participants' names appeared in a segregationist paper called the *Montgomery Home News*. Olive Andrews recalled:

"They didn't publish names of black women at all but they published names of white women and their addresses and their telephone numbers. They gave the husbands' names and their business addresses and their telephone numbers."[36]

Andrews later reflected that the fallout from the meeting at St. Jude's was the first time she felt serious opposition in Montgomery to her organization. She speculated that the reason for the turmoil was that the group had elected to meet in space provided by a white institution. She had been excited about the event and had mailed out hundreds of invitations throughout the area, inadvertently alerting somebody at the post office that the interracial event was taking place. They violated a sacred southern taboo that day by eating together. They shared carry-out boxed lunches because no restaurant in Montgomery would have served them. Some of those harassing the Fellowship of the Concerned made a flier they put on windshields throughout Montgomery telling about a meeting at St. Jude's where "nigger men and nigger women" ate together with whites.[37]

Despite the repressive atmosphere perpetuated by many white churchgoers in Montgomery, King continued to believe the church had the opportunity to be an incredible beacon for peace and justice. He attributed some of the hypocrisy found in people who attend church while failing to be advocates for justice to the types of sermons preached in many churches. Instead of addressing deep spiritual needs, some clergy offered messages filled with positive thinking and plans for personal achievement. In a sermon titled "A Knock at Midnight" delivered in Chicago, King bemoaned the church's failure: "Hundreds and thousands of men and women in quest for the bread of social justice are going to the church only to be disappointed." King challenged the church to provide the bread of faith, hope, and love to a desperate world.[38]

In the fall of 1958, Harper and Brothers published *Stride toward Freedom,* King's memoir of the Montgomery bus boycott. In conjunction with the release, King embarked on a publicity tour that included several days in New York City. During a book signing appearance at a Harlem bookstore, a mentally unstable woman named Izola Curry stabbed King. While the wound did not prove fatal, he was hospitalized for several days. The stabbing forced King to adopt a slower pace for several weeks while he recovered at the home of pastor and family friend Sandy Ray in Brooklyn. When he finally returned to Montgomery over a month later, he was greeted warmly by a large crowd at the airport. In his remarks to those gathered, King announced: "I have come back, not only because this is my home, not only because my family is here, not only because you are my friends whom I love. I have come back to rejoin the ranks of you who are working ceaselessly for the realization of the ideal of Freedom and Justice for all men." Reflecting on the outpouring of goodwill he had received after the stabbing, King surmised that "this affection was not for me alone. Indeed it was far too much for any one man to deserve. It was really for you. It was an expression of the fact that the Montgomery Story had moved the hearts of men everywhere. Through me, the many thousands of people who wrote of their admiration, were really writing of their love for you."[39]

The stir caused by *Stride toward Freedom* in Montgomery was not all related to King's subsequent stabbing. According to Dexter member Thelma Rice, tempers flew when the book came out: "Some people felt they were left out of the publication and their contributions to the struggle diminished or overlooked." Others believed the book failed to properly credit the labors that took place in Montgomery before King's arrival on the scene. Many of the fractures in the town's African American community that Trezzvant Anderson highlighted in his *Pittsburgh Courier* articles were further exacerbated by the appearance of King's book.[40]

The stabbing forced King to delay his annual report to Dexter by several weeks. When he finally submitted his chronicle of the previous ministry year, he thanked his congregation for their ongoing support and encouragement. Calling the year "rather difficult" personally, he noted that he faced "the brutality of police officers, an unwarranted arrest, and a near fatal stab wound" that had affected him greatly. Dexter remained supportive through "thoughtful, considerate gestures of goodwill" that helped provide King "the courage and strength to face the ordeals of that trying period."[41]

The dawn of 1959 provided King with additional opportunities on both the national and international stage. In late January, a group of seventy-five Alabama African American leaders convened at Abernathy's First Baptist Church to respond to the consistent roadblocks preventing many blacks from voting in the state. At the conclusion of the meeting, they sent a telegram to President Eisenhower seeking "more serious concern for the potentially dangerous state of racism in Alabama and to act with firmness consistent with the noblest democratic traditions of America and make real for Negroes the rights guaranteed by the US Constitution." King also had opportunity to assess the continued contributions of some local whites, describing Alabama Council on Human Relations executive director Robert E. Hughes as "a fine person, a dedicated Christian and a white southerner who is deeply devoted to the principles of freedom and justice for all."[42]

In February, Lawrence Reddick and the Kings departed for India in an effort to better understand the life, teachings, and impact of Gandhi and the Indian independence movement. At a press conference held upon his arrival at his hotel in New Delhi, King was asked by an Indian reporter about the degree of transformation experienced by whites in Montgomery. His response hinted at the continued resistance that had caused the local movement to stagnate: "I wish that I could say that our movement has transformed the hearts of all of Montgomery—some, no doubt; but there is a degree of bitterness and a refusal to accept a new way of human relations." While King's trip provided him the opportunity to interact with many Indian leaders including Prime Minister Nehru, the Quaker guide for the trip was frustrated at what he observed as the priorities of the Kings and Reddick: "All three had almost fanatical interest in snapshots, pictures, and newspaper publicity. Many Indians noticed this and even commented on it. Almost before greeting a person or group they were posing for the camera (they carried three wherever they went)." He later added that "constantly they had their eyes on the USA and the impact the trip would be making there. And so much of their conversation as we were traveling about concerned this same subject." While the guide's letter chronicles miscommunications that are common with international travel, his observations do raise the question of the gap between image and reality. King was certainly sincerely interested in the life and legacy of Gandhi, but the letter suggests King's focus often drifted to how he and the movement could use this trip to further his leadership in and the effectiveness of the fight for justice in the United States.[43]

Following their time in India, the Kings and Reddick visited the Holy

Land, which was the backdrop for King's Easter sermon a few weeks later. He shared his experience as he visited the traditional site of Jesus' crucifixion: "something within began to well up. There was a captivating quality there, there was something that overwhelmed me, and before I knew it I was on my knees praying at that point. And before I knew it I was weeping. This was a great world-shaking, transfiguring experience." King was so moved that he elected to return to his hotel alone "to meditate on the meaning of the cross and the meaning of the experience I just had." In his reflections on Jesus' death, King accented his willingness "to be obedient to unenforceable obligation." He added that "the cross is an eternal expression of the length to which God is willing to go to restore a broken community." In King's mind, human beings had "broken up communities" and "torn up society. Families are divided; homes are divided; cultures are divided; nations are divided; generations are divided; civilizations are divided." King then commented on Jesus' empty tomb: "the important thing is that that Resurrection did occur" and "that grave was empty," meaning "all the nails in the world could never pierce this truth. All of the crosses of the world could never block this love. All of the graves in the world could never bury this goodness."[44]

Montgomery's spring elections provided some hope that goodness could indeed triumph in Montgomery. In the April 1959 MIA newsletter, Jo Ann Robinson celebrated local political changes, noting that "March 16 and March 23, 1959 are memorable days in the political life of Montgomery, Alabama." She emphasized the defeat of both Clyde Sellers and Mayor Gayle, both of whom had been primary adversaries of the MIA during the boycott. Robinson credited successful voting drives for making the difference: "The relentless efforts on the part of Negroes to get qualified as voters bore some fruit in the election. The total number of qualified voters in this group was less than two thousand five hundred (2,500). But leadership on the part of Mr. Rufus A. Lewis and the precinct workers coupled with a spirit of unity and determination paid off." Leaders of the White Citizens Council did not share Robinson's enthusiasm. They stressed the pivotal role African Americans had played in the defeat of Mayor Gayle, arguing most had done so "in obedience to instructions given them by the Negro bosses of the Montgomery Improvement Association acting in the absence of, but, as we believe, with the approval of Martin Luther King. All evidence is absolutely conclusive that in Monday's election the Negro votes will decide who will be mayor of Montgomery unless the white voters wake up, fight Negro bloc voting with white bloc voting, get behind one of the two candidates and thus take the balance of power out of control of race agitators."[45]

Perhaps taking their cue from the WCC, in April the board of Trinity Presbyterian Church sent a letter to Mrs. Arnold Smith, who was serving as president of the congregation's women's ministry. The letter instructed Smith to stop being so outspoken regarding the need for racial justice in Montgomery, noting "We would earnestly recommend to you that in your program of work you avoid these questions and leave them out of your consideration entirely." Some chose to use violence rather than letters to communicate their displeasure with those agitating for racial change. Throughout Alabama, there were "several serious incidents of beatings and kidnappings" of African Americans. Fred Shuttlesworth, the president of Birmingham's Alabama Christian Movement for Human Rights, sent King a letter seeking more direct organization and action throughout the state. Shuttlesworth had grown weary of conferences and summits that failed to produce "positive action." He urged King to recognize the limits of oratory, for "when the flowery speeches have been made, we still have the hard job of getting down and helping people to work to reach the idealistic state of human affairs which we desire." In late May, three Montgomery African Americans were severely beaten and MIA member Horace G. Bell disappeared near a lake in Selma. When Bell's body was recovered a few days later, authorities claimed he had drowned, but local blacks suspected he had been but the latest victim of racial violence. The incidents led King to write to the Alabama governor, John Malcolm Patterson, seeking prompt action as "to allow these incidents to go without public cognizance of them will encourage greater and more frequent acts of violence by these irresponsible persons."[46]

During the summer of 1959, King continued to lobby for structural change while also attacking the illogical nature of common racist arguments. King believed that in order to effectively work for social change in Montgomery, one must realize that biblically based and logically sound arguments would not sway those committed to segregation. In a sermon titled "A Tough Mind and a Tender Heart," King argued: "There are those who are soft minded enough to argue that racial segregation should be maintained because the Negroes lag behind in academic, health, and moral standards. They are not tough minded enough to see that if there are lagging standards in the Negro community they are themselves the result of segregation and discrimination." The real danger is that politicians often prey upon soft-mindedness to preserve power at the expense of justice: "Little Rock Arkansas will always remain a shameful reminder to the American people that this nation can sink to deep dungeons of moral degeneracy when an irresponsible, power-thirsty head of state appeals to a constituency that is not tough minded enough to see through its malevolent designs."[47]

King also challenged the continual temptation to conform and remain silent during threatening times. Five years into his pastorate, he still faced the tepid qualities of many professionals in his congregation. Emboldened for a season during the boycott, many gave into their inclination to not rock the boat after the protest ended. King directly challenged their passivity: "We cannot win the respect of the white people of the South or the peoples of the world if we are willing to sell the future of our children for our personal and immediate safety and comfort. Moreover, we must learn that the passive acceptance of an unjust system is to cooperate with that system, and thereby become a participant in its evil."[48]

King and the Southern Christian Leadership Conference faced growing criticism as the year wore on. When *Jet* magazine published an article questioning the organization, King wrote a letter to the periodical's Washington bureau chief defending the SCLC by claiming "our aim is neither to grab headlines nor have a multiplicity of mass meetings on the question of registration and voting; we are concerned about getting the job done." He emphasized the grassroots efforts of some in the organization, noting "more than fifteen of the leading ministers of Montgomery, Alabama took a day off and went into numerous homes to determine how many people were registered and encourage those who were eligible to do so." This growing national criticism of the SCLC for their lack of tangible accomplishments led a growing number of members to urge King to relocate to Atlanta so he could devote more time to the floundering organization.[49]

Convinced of the pressing need for stronger day-to-day leadership of the SCLC, King decided to accept an offer from Ebenezer Baptist Church in Atlanta to join his father as co-pastor of the church. It was a difficult decision to leave Dexter, but King announced his resignation following Sunday services on November 29, 1959. A draft prepared for the occasion included the following notes: "Little did I know when I came to Dexter that in a few months a movement would commence in Montgomery that would change the course of my life forever. . . . Unknowingly and unexpectedly, I was catapulted into the leadership of the Montgomery movement. At points I was unprepared for the symbolic role that history had thrust upon me. Everything happened so quickly & spontaneously that I had no time to think through the implications of such leadership." Many in the church responded with words of encouragement, including deacon T. H. Randall, who wrote a letter appreciating "the kind of life" King had lived as pastor, noting his "sermons and talks have served as a compelling force in our lives—urging us to live the full life thus broadening the horizons of our responsibilities beyond our own church."[50]

A few short days after his resignation from Dexter, King addressed the MIA at the organization's annual conference on Nonviolence and Social Change. His speech included a detailed update on progress in the local struggle for integration and justice. Noting the MIA "is still attempting to make this community a better place to live" and remained "active and deeply committed to its task," King highlighted its contributions to many community projects, including a $20,000 gift to construct a new YMCA and $11,000 to support Vernon Johns's Farm and City Enterprise, a cooperative grocery store in the area. King hoped Farm and City would "stand as a symbol of what the Negro could do by pooling his economic resources." He also stressed the increased patronage of African American–owned businesses since the boycott, a tactic regularly encouraged at MIA mass meetings. The organization had also contributed money to several legal cases, including the defense of Jeremiah Reeves. Perhaps the biggest contribution of the MIA in King's mind was its role as the first and best place for the community's African American citizens to go when they had some difficulty. The MIA provided "an organization, with its doors opened everyday in the week, that will fight" for justice and help ensure the well-being of Montgomery's most vulnerable citizens. By taking on this role, the MIA was "doing a day to day job that is a persistent threat to the power structure of Montgomery."[51]

King went on to highlight specific issues that faced the community. Regarding the dearth of recreation facilities for African Americans, the MIA had chosen to go to court to seek equity and access to all parks. In response, the City of Montgomery elected to close down all city parks, a policy that remained in effect for several years. He also noted that the county school board had failed to respond to a three-month-old letter asking that a plan for integration be spelled out for the citizens of the county. As the school year began, the MIA executive committee wrote a letter to the Montgomery County Board of Education noting that over five years had "elapsed and no discernable move has been made toward integrating the schools of Montgomery." The letter was not intended as "a threat nor an ultimatum" but as a call for the board "to begin in good faith to study the idea, and then provide a reasonable start." Given that the letter received no response, King announced, "we have no alternative but to carry this issue into the federal courts."[52]

Near the end of his speech, King called those present to remember that "the freedom struggle in Montgomery was not started by one man, and it will not end when one man leaves." He encouraged them to unite behind the new president of the organization as "new divisive forces are at work in our community. In the mad quest to conquer us by dividing us they are working through some Negroes who will sell their race for a few dollars and a few cents." King concluded by noting his own personal faith as they faced the days ahead: "I have no doubt that the midnight of injustice will give way to the daybreak of freedom. My faith in the future does not grow out of a weak and uncertain thought. My faith grows out of a deep and patient trust in God who leaves us not alone in the struggle for righteousness, and whose matchless power is a fit contrast to the sordid weakness of man."[53]

King rightly noted the central role the MIA now played in Montgomery. Before the boycott began, however, both Nixon and the WPC had served as a clearinghouse for many in Montgomery's African American community. The WPC president, Jo Ann Robinson, had enough influence to gain an audience with the mayor and city commissioners. When working people faced legal troubles, they had turned to Nixon.

As people looked to the MIA after the boycott, the roles for both Nixon and the WPC became less clear. Following his resignation from the MIA, Nixon turned his attention back to union work through his membership in the Brotherhood of Sleeping Car Porters. By contrast, the MIA had become Robinson's primary outlet for community engagement. Other WPC members also faced persecution from local authorities. WPC member Thelma Glass remembered the slow demise of her organization after the boycott: "the city began to retaliate. We began to lose members, they got threats—if they stayed in the council, [they'd lose] their teaching jobs—people had children to feed and all that, and you know, about the situation. So gradually, membership just dropped and dropped until on campus I remember there were just four of us left, Jo Ann Robinson, and J. E. Pierce and Mary Frances Burkes and myself." In the years following the boycott, the power of the MIA rendered many other African American community organizations and leaders ineffective and inconsequential.[54]

King's decision to leave Montgomery was not only a response to the needs of the SCLC. According to many who were in the city at the time, some in the congregation were ready for a new pastor who would prove less controversial and would be more available to attend to the day-to-day pastoral responsibilities. King family friend Mrs. O. B. Underwood later remembered "rumors all over Montgomery that Dexter did not want Rev. King, and they wanted to get rid of him." Underwood also reflected on the division between some of the younger members at Dexter and those with longer tenures in the congregation. College students and other young adults felt like they were excluded from "the workings and operations of Dexter." Underwood believed part of the problem was "that many people might have felt threatened by him." Dexter member Warren Brown also credited internal tensions within Dexter as a motivation for King's decision to leave Montgomery. Brown emphasized the pressure applied to many professionals who attended Dexter due to their association with King and thus the local civil rights efforts: "Some of the church members complained that the pastor was hurting their cause. Working persons were being threatened by their employers. The old comfort zones were being disturbed." According to Brown, King challenged those who sought to avoid involvement: "Reverend King stood in the pulpit and said one Sunday: 'Those who are working and have jobs might not lift a finger or say a word in support of or in defense of the movement, but they think no more of you than they do of those who are protesting. In fact, they (meaning the local white establishment) do not think as much of you as they do those who are protesting. When it is over, whatever the outcome, you will benefit just as much as anyone else, even those who will lose their lives.'" Although King could issue such bold challenges, his words to Deacon Robert Nesbitt Sr. when he informed him of the decision support Brown's contention: "The explanation was not long in coming: 'Pressure is being put on the teachers and professional people in the congregation. They are having to take abuses that they could avoid, if I were out of the picture.'"[55]

Local barber and Dexter member Nelson Malden also believed the pressure from many professionals at Dexter was a major influence on King's decision to leave the city: "in carrying out his mission, Reverend King was interfering with the bread and butter of some of the folk in the church. I sensed he wanted to remain in Montgomery." Dexter member Claressa W. Chambliss came to a similar conclusion, noting that she "began to notice a change in my pastor. Many of his followers and supporters were withdrawing. I could tell from his sermons he was a little disgusted and hurt. He was being so brave and his followers were getting weak. People started coming forward as if they wanted to be a leader. There was a definite turn in Reverend King's disposition. One could hear it in his sermons and speeches." Dexter deacon Richard Jordan concurred: "Some of the leaders of the movement and open supporters began to withdraw from Reverend King. His Montgomery power base was beginning to weaken. People were not distancing themselves from him because they really wanted to withdraw. Pressure from certain corners forced them to put some distance between themselves and Reverend King." While in part King was pulled toward Atlanta by a chorus of voices urging him to take a much more active role in guiding the SCLC, the timing of the decision was affected greatly by the push from a portion of his Dexter congregation who longed for a more attentive and less controversial pastor to lead them.[56]

On Sunday January 31, 1960, King preached his last sermon as the pastor of Dexter Avenue Baptist Church. Reflecting on his six years in

Montgomery, King gave a sermon titled "Lessons from History." He emphasized a theme he had first sounded even before the boycott began: that throughout history God has triumphed over evil. King also took the opportunity to critique militarism, calling it "suicidal" and the "twin of imperialism." In a closing charge to his congregation, he reminded them that "a great creative idea cannot be stopped" and that "the quest for human freedom and dignity" was coming to fruition around the globe.[57]

Later that evening, Dexter offered a special program to honor the King family. In his remarks, King affirmed the leadership of Ralph Abernathy, who succeeded him as president: "I believe that under his leadership, Montgomery will grow to higher heights, and new creative things will be done. I hope that you will be able to find a pastor to this church who will join him and the movement in this city and will carry you on to higher heights and do many of the things that I wanted to do and that I couldn't do." He also took a few moments to reflect on how he had grown since arriving in the city nearly six years earlier:

> And I know this God enough to know that He's with us. I've come to believe in prayer stronger, stronger than ever before, since I've been in Montgomery. And I'm convinced that when we engage in prayer, we are not engaging in just the process of autosuggestion, just an endless soliloquy or a monologue, but we are engaged in a dialogue. And we are talking with a father who is concerned about us. And I've come to believe that. Maybe this is rationalization. Maybe I have believed more in a personal God over these last few years because I needed Him. But I have felt His power working in my life in so many instances, and I have felt an inner sense of calmness in dark and difficult situations, an inner strength I never knew I had.

Among the many contributions Montgomery made to the life and ministry of King was as the location where his faith became personal and sustaining.[58]

The following evening, the MIA held a banquet to honor the Kings. In his address to an organization he had led since its inception, he downplayed the role he had played: "although you've been kind enough to say nice things about me, Martin Luther King didn't bring about the hour. Martin Luther King happened to be on the scene when the hour came. And you see my friends, when the hour comes you are just projected into a symbolic structure. And even if Martin Luther King had not come to Montgomery, the hour was here." He added that when the boycott began there was already "a preexisting unity here that caused you to substitute tired feet for tired souls and walk the streets of Montgomery until segregation had to fall before the great and courageous witness of a marvelous people."[59]

When King first announced his plans to relocate to Atlanta to devote more time to the SCLC, the organization issued a press release to communicate the rationale for the decision that included some poignant musings from a Dexter member: "Rev. King will not truly be leaving us because part of him always will remain in Montgomery, and at the same time, part of us will go with him. We'll always be together, everywhere. The history books may write it Rev. King was born in Atlanta, and then came to Montgomery, but we feel that he was born in Montgomery in the struggle here, and now he is moving to Atlanta for bigger responsibilities." It would be hard to find better words to describe the fundamental impact King's six years in Montgomery had upon his life and preaching.[60]

King came to Montgomery well prepared to both pastor an African American Baptist church and to play a supporting role in the growing struggle for civil rights. In many ways, King left Montgomery the same as when he arrived six years earlier. His theology and commitments had changed very little. He continued to be suspicious of the excesses of capitalism, to call for greater international cooperation and an end to colonialism, and to hope for an end to segregation and racism through the establishment of a redeemed and beloved community in America. In other ways, however, King was a transformed person. Evil was no longer a theory, but something he and his fellow activists faced day in and day out. Its passing was not inevitable, but would require tireless struggle and sacrifice. He knew full well the resolve of those in power to maintain the status quo. And King was prepared to suffer and even die to resist this evil. This was possible because his faith had moved from an intellectual theory to a heartfelt belief. No longer was King's call to ministry only understood as a way to contribute to society. Now ministry was about leading a community to trust in the power and justice and righteousness of God even when evil seemed to triumph.

Through the crucible of a local struggle for justice, King's oratorical skills shined brightly. After learning how his words could stir a congregation, he set his sights on stirring a nation to fulfill its promises of justice and equality. King also grew in his capacity for connecting with professionals and the working class, black and white. His sermons and speeches demonstrate his effectiveness in speaking the language of people from all walks of life. As he assumed local leadership, King began to adjust to being the symbol of the movement. He and his family became targets. Exploding dynamite and the steely blade of a knife reminded King that being a symbol had its price. Despite threats and even violence, King maintained hope in the prevailing power of God when it is unleashed through the love-infused strategy of nonviolence.

After the boycott, King found it easier to turn his attention to regional and national struggles, as he pulled away from the local battle. Although he would be involved in many local campaigns over the remaining eight years of his life, never again would he play such a pivotal role from start to finish. King was more than just a symbol in Montgomery; he was a part of the movement and critical to its success. He learned a great deal from the city about God, about leadership, and about sacrifice. During a mass meeting shortly after the bombing of King's home, Dr. Moses Jones told the crowd that the city had waited too long to kill Martin Luther King Jr., claiming that King "is in all of us now." The people of Montgomery were also in King, and he would be a different man the rest of his days. Although King's civil rights leadership may have been conceived in Atlanta, Georgia, in Montgomery he was becoming King.[61]

Epilogue

On February 1, 1960, hours before King delivered his final address as president of the Montgomery Improvement Association, four young African American college students staged a sit-in at a Woolworth's lunch counter in Greensboro, North Carolina. Over the following weeks, hundreds of college students staged similar protests in cities throughout the South, including Montgomery. Alabama State University (ASU) students began their protest on February 25 by requesting service at the cafeteria of the Montgomery County Courthouse. Although no arrests were made, Alabama governor John Patterson demanded that ASU president H. Councill Trenholm expel the students who participated in this direct action or risk losing state funding for his institution. In early March, Trenholm wrote letters to several students informing them that the State Board of Education had directed him to expel them from the school, citing their participation in "conduct prejudicial to the school and for conduct unbecoming a student or future teacher in schools of Alabama, for insubordination and insurrection, or for inciting other pupils to like conduct."[1]

Immediately after the expulsions of their fellow classmates, several Alabama State students gathered to protest the expulsions at Dexter Avenue Baptist Church and then proceeded to march to the nearby Capitol building. In response, the Montgomery police deputized dozens of white citizens in response to the sit-ins, and used many of these new deputies to cordon off the Capitol building and prevent the protestors from reaching their destination. Virginia Durr commented regarding the response to the sit-ins and demonstrations: "You never saw such unanimity in your life as there seems to be in the white community, although privately some dissent, but not many." Meanwhile, the campus of Alabama State was divided over the issue, with some professors supporting the protestors, while others worked to preserve their jobs. Still, for the first time since the end of the bus boycott over three years earlier, students from Alabama State took the lead in a sustained protest that lasted several weeks. The leadership for this new protest came not from the MIA or other established local civil rights organizations, but from young college students, who were part of a much larger movement that would soon organize as the Student Nonviolent Coordinating Committee (SNCC).[2]

Young college students were willing to risk a great deal in an effort to break down segregation in their city. The timing of their sit-ins was undoubtedly influenced by events in Greensboro and Nashville and throughout the South. The fact that these Alabama State students sat down at segregated lunch counters, risking arrest and abuse, was also a part of the legacy of their community. Many of their professors had been at the forefront of the boycott just a few years earlier. Several of these students had been on campus or in the broader community during the epic year of the bus protest. They were ready for this moment, in part because of the brave men and women who had stepped forward four years earlier. Despite white backlash and the floundering of local civil rights organizations over the previous three years, there were still young men and women ready to act in Montgomery to bring about substantive change and greater justice.

The State of Alabama seized on the sit-ins and protests by students to finally go after some of the more active faculty members at Alabama State whom they suspected had been a part of the boycott years earlier. Even before the sit-ins had begun, the state had sent representatives from the state's department of education into the classrooms of Alabama State professors they believed had been involved in the local movement, taking notes throughout class in an attempt to intimidate the instructors. Recognizing her teaching job was in jeopardy, Mary Fair Burks wrote a letter to her former pastor expressing her concerns. Claiming "Jo Ann [Robinson], [Lawrence] Reddick and I expect to be fired," her biggest surprise was that they had not yet lost their jobs. King was disappointed in the ASU president: "I had hoped that Dr. Trenholm would emerge from this total situation as a national hero. If he would only stand up to the Governor and the Board of Education and say that he cannot in all good conscience fire the eleven faculty members who have committed no crime or act of sedition, he would gain support over the nation that he never dreamed of. And indeed jobs would be offered to him overnight if he were fired." King tried to reassure Burks, claiming he would "do all that I possibly can to assist you and your colleagues in getting work for the Fall." After the spring term, Burks, Reddick, and Robinson were among seventeen professors who either resigned under pressure or were dismissed from ASU.[3]

Burks and Robinson, the two women most responsible for the effectiveness of the Women's Political Council and the initial launching of the bus boycott, had to leave the city in search of employment. The same year, Thomas Thrasher, an active participant in the Alabama Conference on Human Welfare and one of the few white pastors to challenge white supremacy, was transferred by the Episcopal Church to the chaplaincy of the University of North Carolina due to his outspokenness on racial issues.[4] Four years after the conclusion of the boycott, supporters continued to experience retribution for their involvement, preventing any reemergence of a sustained local movement for civil rights.

Over the coming years, Montgomery remained a part of the struggle for civil rights, but more as a staging ground for national protests than as a result of local agitation. On May 20, 1961, an angry white mob physically assaulted Freedom Riders as they departed their bus at the Montgomery bus station. The following day, King joined his friend and the MIA president Ralph Abernathy at First Baptist Church for a mass meeting, noting that "over the past few days Alabama has been the scene of a literal reign of terror." As King spoke inside First Baptist Church, a white mob gathered outside, threatening violence and preventing meeting participants from departing. King took the microphone to try to calm the agitated crowd: "Now, we've got an ugly mob outside. They have injured some of the federal marshals. They, they've burned some automobiles, but, we are not, we are not giving in for what we are standing for." King continued a few moments later: "The first thing we must do here tonight is to decide that we aren't going to become panicky, and we're gonna be calm, and that we are going to continue to stand up for what we know is right, and that Alabama will have to face the fact that we are determined to be free. The main thing I want to say to you is, fear not, we've gone too far to turn back, let us be calm, we are together, we are not afraid, and we shall overcome." By dawn the mob had dispersed, allowing officials to restore order. The Freedom Rides did result in an integrated bus terminal in Montgomery, a fact the MIA celebrated in a November 1961 newsletter. Despite this symbolic victory, the City of Montgomery had still not met one of the original demands issued at the commencement of the boycott six years earlier: the hiring of black bus drivers.[5]

On July 6, 1962, Montgomery finally hired their first two black bus drivers.[6] Later that year, the MIA president, Solomon Seay, still found himself lobbying with city commissioners to hire additional black drivers to serve a clientele that remained primarily African American.[7] Less than two months into the bus boycott, the demand for black bus drivers had already proven to be a low priority. When the MIA developed a plan to chart a new direction for the organization in early 1957, they made no concrete mention of their desire to see integrated employment policies in public transportation. The failure to hold out until officials met this demand, or even to continue to vigorously lobby for greater access to working class jobs in Montgomery, demonstrates the absence of a local plan that would affect the daily lives of marginalized blacks in the years after the boycott. As professional leaders sought to integrate public parks, economic goals faltered. No sustained movement emerged to build on the successes of 1956. The Montgomery movement floundered, leaving few tangible benefits for those who had sacrificed most during the boycott.

The national civil rights spotlight returned to Montgomery one last time on March 25, 1965. A few weeks earlier, police officers had bludgeoned marchers in Selma, Alabama, when they attempted to cross the Edmund Pettus Bridge in a march to Montgomery to lobby for voting rights. This time, several thousand gathered again in Selma to conduct a march to the State Capitol. They successfully completed their protest, which culminated with a rally on the steps of the State Capitol building. King began his address by paying tribute to the struggle that had launched his civil rights leadership a decade earlier: "Montgomery was the first city in the South in which the entire Negro community united and squarely faced its age-old oppressors. Out of its struggle more than bus integration was won. A new idea more powerful than guns or clubs was born. Negroes took it and carried it across the South in epic battles that electrified a nation and the world." As he neared his conclusion, King reflected: "In the glow of lamplight on my desk a few nights ago, I gazed again upon the wondrous signs of our time, full of hope and promise for the future and I smiled to see in the newspaper photographs of nearly a decade ago, the faces so bright, so solemn of our valiant heroes, the people of Montgomery." Just a few hundred yards from Dexter Avenue Baptist Church, King paid homage to the people of Montgomery whose sacrifices and courage had catapulted him to the forefront of the national civil rights struggle.[8]

E. D. Nixon remained in Montgomery until his death, convinced that King's prominence was directly tied to his participation in a local struggle in the 1950s. Nixon claimed that "King was not the same man when he left here as when he took over the boycott." He changed because Nixon, Parks, Robinson, Burks, and countless working-class blacks "pushed him a whole lot. Right now people don't like to hear me say this . . . but it isn't what Reverend King did for Montgomery, it's what the people of Montgomery did for Reverend King." King agreed to a point, crediting his time in the Alabama capital for sharpening his approach to social change: "The experience in Montgomery did more to clarify my thinking than all the books that I had read. As the days unfolded, I became more and more convinced of the power of nonviolence. Nonviolence became more than a method to which I gave intellectual assent; it became a commitment to a way of life." Perhaps the author James Baldwin best captured the significant influence of Montgomery on King: "It is true that it was *they* who had begun the struggle of which he was now the symbol and the leader; it is true that it had taken all of *their* insistence to overcome in him a grave reluctance to stand where he now stood. But it is also true, and it does not happen often, that once he had accepted the place they had prepared for him, their struggle became absolutely indistinguishable from his own, and took over and controlled his life. He suffered with them and, thus, he helped them to suffer." Baldwin's 1961 essay accurately conveys the deep and abiding influence Montgomery's local struggle had on Martin Luther King Jr. It also recognizes the very real contributions King made to both the local and national struggle. Baldwin's reflections accent the seminal role the people of Montgomery played in King's emergence and effectiveness as a civil rights leader. The Martin Luther King Jr. remembered and celebrated around the world was born in Montgomery.[9]

Notes

Prologue

1. Among works that have explored the impact of Montgomery on the broader civil rights movement, see Morris, *The Origins of the Civil Rights Movement;* Branch, *Parting the Waters;* Fairclough, *To Redeem the Soul of America;* Garrow, *Bearing the Cross;* and D. Williams, with Greenhaw, *The Thunder of Angels.* Several recent works have elevated the roles played by Jo Ann Robinson, Mary Fair Burks, Rosa Parks, and E. D. Nixon in laying the groundwork for the bus boycott. See, for instance, Garrow, ed., *The Montgomery Bus Boycott and the Women Who Started It;* Dyson, *I May Not Get There with You,* 202–4; Burns, *To The Mountaintop,* 19–25; and D. Williams, with Greenhaw, *The Thunder of Angels.*

2. Over the past few decades, several historians have examined the significant role people in local communities played in preparing the way for and leading the civil rights movement. Others have also helpfully examined the connections of labor to the civil rights movement. See, for example, Payne, *I've Got the Light of Freedom;* Dittmer, *Local People;* Fairclough, *Race and Democracy;* Eick, *Dissent in Wichita;* Whitaker, *Race Work;* Theoharis and Woodard, eds., *Groundwork;* Honey, *Southern Labor and Black Civil Rights;* Korstad, *Civil Rights Unionism;* and Minchin, *The Color of Work.*

3. Payne, *I've Got the Light of Freedom,* 417–18.

4. *Pittsburgh Courier,* December 7, 1957.

5. Eskew, *But for Birmingham.* Over the last few years of King's life, he began to participate more directly in efforts to bring about economic justice, as evidenced in his support for the striking Memphis sanitation workers and in his organization of the interracial Poor People's Campaign.

6. Branch, *Parting the Waters,* 558.

7. Garrow, ed., *The Montgomery Bus Boycott and the Women Who Started It;* Crawford, Rouse, and Woods, eds., *Women in the Civil Rights Movement.* For more on the contributions of women to the struggle, see Collier-Thomas and Franklin, *Sisters in the Struggle.* For a detailed study of the life and contributions of Ella Baker, see Ransby, *Ella Baker and the Black Freedom*

Movement. Gender analysis of the civil rights era is beginning to consider the construction of masculinity (see Estes, *I Am a Man!*).

8. Johnny E. Williams, *African American Religion and the Civil Rights Movement in Arkansas;* Chappell, *A Stone of Hope;* and Marsh, *The Beloved Community.*

9. *The Papers of Martin Luther King, Jr.,* vol. 6.

10. Branch, *Parting the Waters,* 225; Branch, *Pillar of Fire,* 24.

11. MIA mass meeting at Holt Street Baptist Church, December 5, 1955, in *The Papers of Martin Luther King, Jr.,* 3: 71.

12. Rosa Parks to Mrs. Henry F. Shepherd, July 6, 1955, Mss 265, Folder 22, Box 22, Highlander Research and Education Center.

1. "The Stirring of the Water"

1. *Montgomery Advertiser,* April 14, 1952: "The new section of seats in the bowl will be reserved for Negroes"; "Just three minutes before the annual Easter Sunrise Service was to begin in Cramton Bowl yesterday, the rain, which had been falling steadily, stopped." Portia Trenholm, "Memoirs," April 17, 1958, Portia Trenholm Papers. This twelve-page document, composed during the bus boycott, includes a cover letter from the Alabama State College professor L. D. Reddick to Portia Trenholm dated April 17, 1958. While the *Montgomery Advertiser* stories regarding the service indicate blacks attended in 1952, articles about the 1953 event do not mention African American attendees or the availability of bus services for the event (*Montgomery Advertiser,* April 14, 1952, April 3, 6, 1953).

2. While many historians have examined the Montgomery bus boycott in great detail, few have given serious attention to the climate in the city in the years prior to King's arrival in 1954. Those who do consider this period tend to consider only particular aspects of the situation. For instance, Taylor Branch focuses primarily on the tenure of Vernon Johns at Dexter (*Parting the Waters,* 1–26). *Dividing Lines,* J. Mills Thornton's recent work on Montgomery, Selma, and Birmingham, does an excellent job chronicling the political and demographic shifts facing Montgomery following World War II. Thornton recognizes the major African American voices that set the scene for the civil rights movement, yet his attention remains fixed on the political ramifications of the city's demographic shifts. Montgomery's white citizens who worked against white supremacy escape Thornton's notice. Willy Leventhal has highlighted many of the white participants who had an impact on Montgomery, including Clifford and Virginia Durr, Aubrey Williams, Juliette Morgan, and Clara Rutledge. His narrative does not extend back to

the early 1950s, however, when these white activists were finding their voices (Leventhal, "The White Folks," in Gray, Leventhal, Sikora, and Thornton, *The Children Coming On,* 195–223). Most other significant contributors to the historiography of the Montgomery movement deal sparingly with events prior to King's arrival in 1954.

3. Rogers, *Confederate Home Front,* 5, 52. Rogers notes that in 1860, workers in Montgomery handled more than 1 million cotton bales. In 1958, Ralph David Abernathy described Montgomery as "a non-industrial city. Montgomery is just a shopping center for what we call the Black-Belt areas" (Abernathy, "The Natural History of a Social Movement: The Montgomery Improvement Association," master's thesis, Department of Sociology, Atlanta University, August 1958, in Garrow, ed., *The Walking City*).

4. For a detailed history of Maxwell Air Force Base, see Ennels and Newton, *The Wisdom of Eagles.* Taylor Branch asserts that Maxwell and nearby Gunter Air Force bases contributed almost $50 million a year to the local economy (Branch, *Parting the Waters,* 13).

5. Thornton, *Dividing Lines,* 23. For a thorough exploration of the significant political shifts in Montgomery during the decade prior to the boycott, including the election of Dave Birmingham, see ibid., 20–40.

6. Abernathy, "The Natural History of a Social Movement," in Garrow, ed., *The Walking City,* 109; Preston Valien, "The Montgomery Bus Protest as a Social Movement," ibid., 94; Steven Milner, "The Montgomery Bus Boycott: A Case Study in the Emergence of a Social Movement," ibid., 433.

7. Kathy Dunn Jackson, "You Can Go Home Again," in Westhauser, Smith, and Fremlin, eds., *Creating Community,* 19–20.

8. *Alabama Tribune,* September 19, 1952; Thornton, *Dividing Lines,* 38.

9. Thornton, *Dividing Lines,* 33–35.

10. Garrow, *The Montgomery Bus Boycott and the Women Who Started It,* 21; Thornton, *Dividing Lines,* 35.

11. For a thorough discussion regarding the founding and history of Tuskegee Institute, see Norrell, *Reaping the Whirlwind;* and Harlan, *Booker T. Washington.* Portia Trenholm, "Memoirs," 2. Trenholm claims that during the 1930s, "the buying power of Tuskegee instructors was higher than" that of teachers at Alabama State Teachers College in Montgomery.

12. Rogers, Ward, Atkins, and Flynt, *Alabama: The History of a Deep South State,* 329; Juan Williams and Ashley, *I'll Find a Way or Make One,* 312–13; Jo Ann Robinson to H. Councill Trenholm, August 3, 1950, H. Councill Trenholm Papers.

13. Roberson, *Fighting the Good Fight*, 21, 56; Virginia Durr to Clark and Mairi Foreman, February 26, 1953, in Sullivan, ed., *Freedom Writer*, 47. Montgomery's NAACP chapter was not alone in its middle-class orientation. According to Manford Berg in his recent study of the NAACP, the years immediately following World War II saw a vast increase in working-class memberships, a period that corresponds with when E. D. Nixon was president of his local and state chapters. Despite this surge, Berg admits that "the local leaders continued to be male and middle-class." The spike in membership nationally was short-lived, with a 1946 high-water mark of roughly 540,000 members decreasing to 350,000 in 1948, and falling to 150,000 in 1950 (Berg, *"The Ticket to Freedom,"* 109–11).

14. E. D. Nixon to Walter White, December 14, 1944, Group II, Box C-4, Montgomery Branch, National Association for the Advancement of Colored People (NAACP) Papers, 1940–1954, Library of Congress, Washington, D.C. Hereafter cited as Montgomery NAACP Papers.

15. Rosa Parks to Ella Baker, May 2, 1945, Donald Jones to Ella Baker, 1945, Montgomery NAACP Papers.

16. E. D. Nixon to W. G. Porter, 1945, W. G. Porter to Ella Baker, December 1945, Montgomery NAACP Papers; Parks, with Haskins, *Rosa Parks, My Story*, 80–95.

17. Brinkley, *Rosa Parks*, 48, 71.

18. The Citizens Overall Committee letterhead used in 1944 lists most major African American organizations in Montgomery as members. The presidents and leaders of the NAACP, the Negro Civic League, and the City Federation of Colored Women's Clubs were joined by President Trenholm of Alabama State Teachers College, several prominent businessmen, teachers, and ministers, as well as local newspaper editors in serving as members of the Citizens Overall Committee. The particular correspondence concerned the need to upgrade "the condition of the Ladies rest room in the Colored Waiting Room in the Union Station." Nixon also drew attention to the filth of the wash basin and the unsanitary state of the drinking water provided (E. D. Nixon to the President of the Louisville and Nashville Railroad, February 7, 1944, Box 27, Nixon Collection; Nixon, interview by Lumpkin).

19. Garrow, ed., *The Montgomery Bus Boycott and the Women Who Started It*, 27; *Alabama Tribune*, December 5, 1952.

20. Nixon, interview by Lumpkin; Warlick, "'Man of the Year' for '54," 27; Donald Jones to Ella Baker, 1945, Ella Baker to E. D. Nixon, January 21, 1946, Montgomery NAACP Papers; Gray, Leventhal, Sikora, and Thornton, *The Children Coming On*, 225.

21. Charles G. Gomillion was the dean of students and a sociology pro-

fessor at Tuskegee Institute. He was involved in the leadership of the local NAACP chapter and in the Tuskegee Civic Association. In 1957, the Alabama state senator Sam Englehardt Jr. sponsored a successful bill before the state legislature that redrew the boundaries of Tuskegee in an attempt to nullify the black vote in the community. In response, Gomillion led a boycott of Tuskegee's white merchants. With Fred Gray as their attorney, they filed suit against the Alabama legislature's ruling. In 1961, the U.S. Supreme Court found for the plaintiffs in a case known as *Gomillion vs. Lightfoot* (Robert E. Hughes, Alabama Council on Human Relations newsletter [January 1958], Fellowship of Reconciliation Papers; Gray, *Bus Ride to Justice,* 112–24). The 1946 election was the first Alabama Democratic primary in the twentieth century in which blacks could legally vote. In 1944, the U.S. Supreme Court had ruled white primaries unconstitutional (Thornton, *Dividing Lines,* 27). Turnipseed, interview by Durr.

22. Egerton, *Speak Now against the Day,* 101, 321, 464.

23. Gould Beech and Mary Beech, interview by Durr.

24. Virginia Durr to Otto Nathan, August 29, 1951, in Sullivan, ed., *Freedom Writer,* 35–36.

25. Durr, *Outside the Magic Circle,* 241–47.

26. *Montgomery Advertiser,* June 9, 1952.

27. The Southern Conference Education Fund (SCEF) grew out of the Southern Conference for Human Welfare (SCHW), an organization formed during the New Deal era in an effort to mobilize a liberal coalition in the South. Founded in 1946, when the SCHW began to focus on political lobbying, the SCEF was a tax-exempt organization focused primarily on challenging racial discrimination in the South through the dissemination of information (Egerton, *Speak Now against the Day,* 441, 529–30). Dombrowski to Morgan, June 19, 1952, Morgan to Dombrowski, July 8, 1952, Morgan Papers; Clifford and Virginia Durr, interview by Lumpkin.

28. Andrews, interview by Durr.

29. Ibid.

30. Clifford and Virginia Durr, interview by Lumpkin; Nixon, interview by Lumpkin.

31. For a thorough description of the founding of both Columbus Avenue Baptist Church (First Baptist Church) and Dexter Avenue Baptist Church, see Roberson, *Fighting the Good Fight,* 1–23.

32. Branch, *Parting the Waters,* 1–5, 107.

33. Roberson, *Fighting the Good Fight,* 23–50.

34. Vaughn and Wills, eds., *Reflections on Our Pastor,* 6.

35. Pierce, interview by Lumpkin.

36. Ibid. Pierce characterized Johns as a "rough, knock-down, drag-out" type of person who was "a very militant guy." While Pierce admitted that "Johns pulverized the soil and planted the seed" for the Montgomery movement, he characterized him as "too brusque," which prevented him from galvanizing the people of Dexter and the broader community. Zelia Evans and J. T. Alexander, in their history of Dexter, add: "One sermon preached during his pastorate was entitled, 'It's safe to Murder Negroes in Alabama.' Its announcement on the bulletin board landed him before a grand jury which tried to prevent him from preaching it. Neither the grand jury nor the Klu [*sic*] Klux Klan cross that was burned the day of the sermon kept him from delivering his planned discourse" (Evans and Alexander, eds., *The Dexter Avenue Baptist Church*, 64).

37. Pierce, interview by Lumpkin; Lewis and Ligon, interview by Lumpkin; Evans and Alexander, eds., *The Dexter Avenue Baptist Church 1877–1977*, 64. Lewis Baldwin credits Johns for paving the way, noting King's "success in bringing the Dexter Avenue Church to the forefront of the struggle owed much to the contributions and inspiration of persons who preceded him in Montgomery. One such person was Vernon Johns, the imposing, scholarly, and controversial figure who was King's immediate predecessor at the Dexter Avenue Church" (Baldwin, *There Is a Balm in Gilead*, 183).

38. Gray, interview by Lumpkin. These outside perspectives on Dexter may be a bit simplistic. According to the member Thelma Rice, the congregation "was a mixed church across the board. There were those who were domestics, there were those who were skilled workers, there were those who were in the educational field. There were the professionals, but there was a mixture." While Rice may be overstating her case, given the small percentage of middle-class blacks in the city, the congregation undoubtedly did include some from the working class (Rice, interview by Lumpkin).

39. Mary Fair Burks, "Trailblazers: Women in the Montgomery Bus Boycott," in Crawford, Rouse, and Woods, eds., *Women in the Civil Rights Movement*, 76, 78.

40. D. Williams, with Greenhaw, *The Thunder of Angels*, 81; Elaine M. Smith, "Living A Womanist Legacy," in Westhauser, Smith, and Fremlin, eds., *Creating Community*, 74–75.

41. While Burks and Jo Ann Robinson claim the organization was founded in 1946 and that Robinson became president in 1950, both dates are incorrect. Burks's contention that she was inspired by a Vernon Johns sermon eliminates the possibility that the group was founded in 1946, as Johns did not become Dexter's pastor until 1947. Additionally, in 1953 Mary Fair Burks composed a letter to the editor of the *Montgomery Advertiser* that

she signed, "Mary Fair Burks, President, Negro Women's Political Council" (*Montgomery Advertiser*, April 21, 1953). J. Mills Thornton claims the WPC emerged after local black women were excluded from the newly formed Montgomery League of Women Voters, which began in December 1947. When national leaders of the League of Women Voters refused to charter a black chapter in the city, the WPC was born (see Thornton, *Dividing Lines*, 32, 78, 590n23). While this broader consideration explains the need for an independent organization, Burks's story fleshes out the specific events that sparked the timing of the WPC, which started closer to 1949 than 1946.

42. Thelma Glass notes the scope of the organization's vision: "We had two very strong chapters going, but the whole idea was to have a political council in each area of Montgomery. Four, I think, was in the original plan: east, west, north and south, with its own membership and what not" (Gray, Leventhal, Sikora, and Thornton, *The Children Coming On*, 131). Ibid., 229.

43. Garrow, ed., *The Montgomery Bus Boycott and the Women Who Started It*, 15–16.

44. Crawford, Rouse, and Woods, eds., *Women in the Civil Rights Movement*, 75; Garrow, ed., *The Montgomery Bus Boycott and the Women Who Started It*, 22.

45. Burns, ed., *Daybreak of Freedom*, 59–61; Thornton, *Dividing Lines*, 46.

46. Gray, Leventhal, Sikora, and Thornton, *The Children Coming On*, 130, 228–29; Garrow, ed., *The Montgomery Bus Boycott and the Women Who Started It*, 28.

47. Vaughn and Wills, eds., *Reflections on Our Pastor*, 14–16.

48. Rice, interview by Lumpkin; Evans and Alexander, eds., *The Dexter Avenue Baptist Church 1877–1977*, 64. See also Roberson, *Fighting the Good Fight*, 100–101.

49. Vaughn and Wills, eds., *Reflections on Our Pastor*, 6, 45.

50. Branch, *Parting the Waters*, 11; Roberson, *Fighting the Good Fight*, 105–6.

51. *Montgomery Advertiser*, November 11, 1952. The front-page story claimed Reeves confessed to robbing and assaulting Prescott, but he denied raping her, and the chief deputy sheriff, George Mosley, said that medical examiners concluded "the woman definitely was not raped." Authorities eventually charged Reeves with assaulting six white women over the previous sixteen months. Prescott later claimed that Reeves had tried to rape her. A story by Joe Azbell noted "some 150 Negroes were quizzed by policemen in the 16 month investigation" (*Montgomery Advertiser*, November 13, 1952).

When Reeves took the stand in his trial, he "repudiated six confessions alleg-edly made to investigating officers" (*Montgomery Advertiser,* November 29, 1952). The jury reached a guilty verdict in thirty-eight minutes, and Reeves was sentenced to death (*Montgomery Advertiser,* November 30, 1952; De-cember 4, 5, 1952). Burns, *To the Mountaintop,* 1.

52. Vaughn and Wills, eds., *Reflections on Our Pastor,* 25.

2. "The Gospel I Will Preach"

1. King to Coretta Scott, July 18, 1952, in *The Papers of Martin Luther King, Jr.,* 6: 123–26.

2. The change of names from Michael to Martin for both father and son appears to have taken place gradually during the mid-1930s. See *The Papers of Martin Luther King, Jr.,* 1: 31; and King Sr., with Riley, *Daddy King: An Autobiography,* 26. Martin Luther King, "An Autobiography of Religious Development," in *Papers of Martin Luther King, Jr.,* 1: 361. Much of the historiography of the past few decades has corrected earlier works that overemphasized the white liberal theological roots of King's intellec-tual development. Lewis Baldwin's *There Is a Balm in Gilead* highlights the black southern roots of King's thought: "The black experience and the black Christian tradition were the most important sources in the shaping of King's life, thought, vision, and efforts to translate the ethical ideal of the beloved community into practical reality" (2). Baldwin notes that previous works, such as Kenneth Smith and Ira Zepp's *The Search for the Beloved Commu-nity* and John Ansbro's *Martin Luther King, Jr.,* represent "a narrow, elit-ist, and racist approach that assumes that the black church and the larger black community are not healthy and vital contexts for the origin of intel-lectual ideas regarding theology and social change. The consequence of that approach has been to abstract King's intellectual development from his social and religious roots—family, church, and the larger black com-munity—and to treat it primarily as a product of white Western philosophy and theology" (3). Other scholars have made similar arguments regarding the primacy of Atlanta, King's family, and Ebenezer in King's development, including Cone, *Martin and Malcolm and America;* Miller, *Voice of Deliver-ance;* Lischer, *The Preacher King;* and Dyson, *I May Not Get There with You: The True Martin Luther King, Jr.*

3. For a detailed account of the 1906 riot, see Mixon, *The Atlanta Riot.* For a thorough study of Atlanta in the 1930s and 1940s, see Ferguson, *Black Politics in New Deal Atlanta.*

4. Introduction to vol. 1 of *Papers of Martin Luther King, Jr.,* 1: 6, 15,

33. For a discussion of Williams's influence on Martin Luther King Sr., see ibid., 1: 24–28.

5. Martin Luther King Sr., moderator's address, Atlanta Missionary Baptist Association, October 17, 1940, as quoted ibid., 1: 34; King Jr., "Acceptance Address at Dexter Avenue Baptist Church," May 2, 1954, ibid., 6: 154–57. While King referred to his father's church as part of the "fundamentalist line," Daddy King's faith was more nuanced than rigid (King Jr., "An Autobiography of Religious Development," November 22, 1950, ibid., 1: 361). Although Daddy King's theological views on salvation, Scripture, and the nature of Jesus were more conservative, these did not lead to division with those holding more modern views on God, the Bible, and theology. Despite King Jr.'s more liberal theological leanings, his father heartily supported his ordination to the ministry. Keith Miller helpfully notes: "What separates white fundamentalists from liberal white Protestants is the issue of the literal truth of scripture. But, despite the clash between J. H. Jackson and Gardner Taylor, black Protestants have never found the issue of Biblical literalism to be paramount or divisive. In fact, Biblical literalism is essentially a non-issue among black Protestants. Throughout his public career King never publicly stated whether he believed the Bible to be literally true. Nor in hundreds of interviews and press conferences was he ever asked to do so. The entire question did not matter to him, his followers, or other blacks" (Miller, *Voice of Deliverance*, 222–23n56). Although Miller's analysis is a bit simplistic, his framework is helpful for understanding the cohesion of black pastors around social issues even though they differed theologically.

6. King Jr., "An Autobiography of Religious Development," November 22, 1950, in *Papers of Martin Luther King, Jr.*, 1: 359–60: "I was much too young to remember the beginning of this depression, but I do recall how I questioned my parent about the numerous people standing in bread lines when I was about five years of age. I can see the effects of this early childhood experience on my present anti capitalistic feelings." See also King Jr., *Stride toward Freedom*, 90; and Baldwin, *There Is a Balm in Gilead*, 122. Baldwin demonstrates the influence of the plight of the poor and working class on King in his analysis of King's summer jobs: "The fact that he chose the work of a common laborer is indeed remarkable, especially since, being the son of a prominent pastor and civic leader, he could have easily gotten less demanding jobs" (27).

7. King Jr., "An Autobiography of Religious Development," November 22, 1950, in *Papers of Martin Luther King, Jr.*, 1: 361; Warren, *King Came Preaching*, 15. Most of the recent scholarship on King has made this point as well, including Baldwin's *There Is a Balm in Gilead*, Lischer's *Preacher King*,

and Cone's *Malcolm and Martin and America*. Lischer also elevates the significance of the African American preaching tradition, noting King "learned more from the Negro preacher's methods of sustaining a people and readying it for action than from any of his courses in graduate school; he absorbed more from his own church's identification with the Suffering Servant than from anything he read in Gandhi. What came earliest to him remained the longest and enabled him to put a distinctively Christian seal on the struggle for civil rights in the United States" (Lischer, *The Preacher King*, 6). Lischer also emphasizes that King experienced the potential transforming power of God's Word from his childhood at Ebenezer: "He believed that the preached Word performs a sustaining function for all who are oppressed and a corrective function for all who know the truth but lead disordered lives. He also believed that the Word of God possesses the power to change hearts of stone. This was not an abstract theology but an empirical experience. He had seen it happen in his father's church." Lischer specifically cites William Holmes Borders, Sandy Ray, and Gardner Taylor, three learned and influential black preachers of the day, and family friends all, as having an influence on young King (48). Borders was also a rival of Daddy King, as his Wheat Street Baptist Church sat a mere block west of Ebenezer on Auburn Avenue. As a teen, King would often sneak out of Ebenezer so he could slip into the balcony at Wheat Street to catch Borders's Sunday morning sermon.

8. King Jr., "An Autobiography of Religious Development," November 22, 1950, in *Papers of Martin Luther King, Jr.*, 1: 263.

9. King Jr., "My Call to the Ministry," August 7, 1959, ibid., 6: 367–68.

10. Benjamin Elijah Mays (1894–1984) served as the dean of Howard University's School of Religion from 1934 to 1940, at which time he became the president of Morehouse College, a position he held until 1967. Mays received his Ph.D. from the University of Chicago and was the author of several books, including *The Negro's God* (1938). For more on Mays, see his autobiography, *Born to Rebel*, esp. 191, 265; and Carter, ed., *Walking Integrity*, xi. Years later, in his essay "Pilgrimage to Nonviolence," King downplayed the influence of Morehouse, reducing the school's influence on his adoption of nonviolence to his exposure to Thoreau's *Essay on Civil Disobedience*. Throughout, King stressed the influence of predominantly white theologians, philosophers, and social thinkers, while downplaying many of the significant African American influences on his life and thought, including Mays (King Jr., *Stride toward Freedom*, 90–107). King sought input from George Kelsey, Stanley Levison, and Bayard Rustin in composing the essay (see King to Kelsey, March 31, 1958; Kelsey to King, April 4, 1958, in *Papers*

of Martin Luther King, Jr., 4: 391–92, 394–95; and Levison to King, April 1, 1958, Box 29A, King Papers, Boston University).

11. King Jr., "Preaching Ministry," November 24, 1948, in *Papers of Martin Luther King, Jr.* 6: 69–77.

12. *Pittsburgh Courier*, June 15, 1946. In a later article, Mays made a similar case for the type of commitment necessary to experience liberty: "Freedom is an achievement and not a gift. Whether it is freedom from external circumstances or freedom from an internally cramped spirit or soul, it must be achieved. It is seldom, if ever, given freely and it is never inwardly achieved without struggle and years of discipline. This is true of nations. It is true of races and it is equally true of individuals" (Mays, "Nehru," *Pittsburgh Courier*, December 7, 1946).

13. Mays, "Signs of Hope," *Pittsburgh Courier*, June 29, 1946; Mays, "Justice for All," *Pittsburgh Courier*, February 22, 1947. In a later article, Mays sounded a similar note: "The faith of faiths is the deep-seated conviction that wrong cannot ultimately triumph over right, that that which is essentially evil will not survive, and that the universe itself sustains the good and fights on the side of right. If this is not so, there is little to hope for in this life" (Mays, "Ray of Hope," *Pittsburgh Courier*, January 17, 1948). King Jr., "Will Capitalism Survive?" February 15, 1950, in *Papers of Martin Luther King, Jr.*, 6: 104–5; "The Death of Evil upon the Seashore," July 24, 1955, Folder 110, Sermon File; King Jr., "Going Forward by Going Backward," April 4, 1954, in *Papers of Martin Luther King, Jr.*, 6: 159–63. These quotes closely correspond to a selection from Harry Emerson Fosdick's sermon "Why We Believe in a Good God," found in his book *On Being Fit to Live With: Sermons on Post-war Christianity*. While King's language more closely corresponds to Fosdick's, King's attraction to these quotes was undoubtedly influenced by his exposure to the moral underpinnings that informed the chapel sermons of Mays.

14. Mays, "Law Is Weapon," *Pittsburgh Courier*, August 10, 1946; Mays, "Inferiority among Negroes," *Pittsburgh Courier*, May 10, 1947; King Jr., "Overcoming an Inferiority Complex," July 14, 1957, in *Papers of Martin Luther King, Jr.*, 6: 303–16.

15. Mays, "Man's Greatest Enemy," *Pittsburgh Courier*, February 8, 1947; King Jr., "Mastering Our Fears," July 21, 1957, in *Papers of Martin Luther King, Jr.*, 6: 319–21.

16. Mays, "Advice to Graduates," *Pittsburgh Courier*, June 7, 1947.

17. King Jr., "Transformed Nonconformist," November 1954, in *Papers of Martin Luther King, Jr.*, 6: 195–98.

18. Mays, "Two Fears," *Pittsburgh Courier*, July 20, 1946.

19. Mays, "Non-Violence," *Pittsburgh Courier,* February 28, 1948. Mays met Gandhi on December 31, 1946, while visiting India. Mays's article highlighted the courage, faith, and forgiveness Gandhian nonviolence demonstrates: "The nonviolent man must be absolutely fearless. . . . Non-violence is the essence of faith. He knows the method of non-violence will win. Nothing else can. This one can readily see, is faith in the moral and spiritual nature of the universe." Finally Mays noted: "He died practicing what he preached. The press said that when falling he gave a sign which meant 'forgive'" (Mays, "Power of Spirit," *Pittsburgh Courier,* December 21, 1946).

20. King Jr., "Six Talks in Outline," November 23, 1949, in *Papers of Martin Luther King, Jr.,* 1: 249. In his essay "Pilgrimage to Nonviolence," King credits a lecture by the Howard University president Mordecai Johnson as the launching point for his exploration of Gandhi. Delivered while King was attending Crozer, Johnson's words may have served as a catalyst for King, not because they were new, but rather because they resonated with a message he had heard years earlier while a student at Morehouse (King Jr., *Stride toward Freedom,* 96).

21. Mays, "The Church amidst Ethnic and Racial Tensions," speech delivered at the Second Assembly of the World Council of Churches, Northwestern University, Evanston, Ill., August 1954, transcribed as appendix B in Mays, *Born to Rebel,* 354.

22. Mays, "Another Victory," *Pittsburgh Courier,* January 31, 1948; King Jr., "Loving Your Enemies," August 31, 1952, in *Papers of Martin Luther King, Jr.,* 6: 126–28; King Jr., "Meaning of Forgiveness," ibid., 6: 580–81.

23. W. Thomas McGann, "Statement on Behalf of Ernest Nichols, *State of New Jersey vs. Ernest Nichols,*" July 1950, in King Jr., *Papers of Martin Luther King, Jr.,* 1: 327–29; King Jr., introduction to vol. 1 of *Papers of Martin Luther King, Jr.,* 1: 53.

24. For more on personalism, see Deats and Robb, eds., *The Boston Personalist Tradition in Philosophy, Social Ethics, and Theology;* and Borrow, *Personalism: A Critical Introduction.* Keith Miller, in assessing King's affinity for personalism, argues King "appreciated Personalist ideas because they were reassuringly familiar. His gravitation to Personalism is unsurprising inasmuch as the Personalists emphasized the same fatherly, personal God he heard praised in every sermon, hymn, and prayer offered at Ebenezer Church during his childhood and adolescence" (Miller, *Voice of Deliverance,* 62). Lewis Baldwin echoes Miller, noting King's "conviction about the reality of the personal God was cultivated by the black church and black religion long before he entered a seminary and a university" (Baldwin, *There Is a Balm in Gilead,* 170).

25. Lischer, for instance, deemphasizes the influence of theologians on King's thinking: "Profound changes in the graduate student's thinking cannot be attributed to Niebuhr despite the mature King's need to make it appear that Niebuhr had once made a decisive difference. Such was the dominance of Niebuhr: one was virtually obligated to retroject Niebuhr into one's intellectual formation and stake out a position in relation to his, which is precisely what King did in his brief 1958 sketch, 'Pilgrimage to Nonviolence,' in which he credits Niebuhr for dampening his 'superficial optimism,' concerning human nature" (Lischer, *The Preacher King,* 61). Keith Miller comes to a similar conclusion: "Despite what he wrote in 'Pilgrimage,' King arrived at seminary with his most important ideas already intact. Although the African-American church does not appear in 'Pilgrimage,' it provided him with the foundation for virtually all the ideas of the essay." Miller goes on to write: "King did not need the prodding of Niebuhr to awaken from a state of fatuous optimism because he never suffered from such a state. Under segregation blacks in the South confronted collective evil every single day. They did not enjoy the luxury of naïve optimism" (Miller, *Voice of Deliverance,* 54–55, 59). James Cone also challenges King's assertions in "Pilgrimage," noting, "In regard to deepening King's optimism about the elimination of racism, the political philosophy of integrationism and the faith of the black church were much more important than Hegel or any other white thinker" (Cone, *Martin and Malcolm and America,* 30). King Jr., *Stride toward Freedom,* 90–107. King borrowed portions of "Pilgrimage to Nonviolence" regarding his commitment to the social gospel from Harry Emerson Fosdick's *Hope of the World* and Robert McCracken's *Questions People Ask.* King Jr., "The Weaknesses of Liberal Theology I," 1948, in *Papers of Martin Luther King, Jr.,* 6: 78–80.

26. King Jr., "Sermon Introductions," November 30, 1948–February 16, 1949, in *Papers of Martin Luther King, Jr.,* 6: 83–84. In the case of "Sermon Introductions," King's use of Sheen constitutes academic plagiarism. The editors of the Martin Luther King, Jr. Papers Project have identified many egregious examples of plagiarism in King's academic work at Crozer and Boston, including portions of his doctoral dissertation. When King's plagiarism came to light, the *Journal of American History* devoted an issue to the topic (78 [June 1991]). King Jr., "The False God of Science," July 5, 1953, in *Papers of Martin Luther King, Jr.,* 6: 130–32. King began his sermon with, "Dr. William Ernest Hecking has said that all life is divided into work and worship; that which we do for ourselves and that which we let the higher than ourselves do." Fosdick's sermon begins, "Professor Hocking is right in saying that all man's life can be reduced to two aspects, work and worship—that which we

do ourselves, and what we let the higher than ourselves do to us" (Fosdick, *Successful Christian Living*, 173–74). King kept an annotated copy of *Successful Christian Living* in his home study, along with many other collections of sermons by Fosdick and other prominent preachers. For further examination of this topic, see Dyson, *I May Not Get There with You*, 137–54; Miller, *Voice of Deliverance*, 132–48, 193–97; and Lischer, *The Preacher King*, 93–118. King Jr., "The False God of Nationalism," July 12, 1953, in *Papers of Martin Luther King, Jr.*, 6: 132–33. King leans on Fosdick's "Christianity's Supreme Rival" in developing this sermon. King notes, "If time permitted, I would trace the history of this new religion, unravel the strands that, woven together, have produced it. In its present form it is a modern phenomenon developing from the eighteenth century on, but that it is now dominant in the world is clear." By comparison, Fosdick wrote, "Were there time, one might trace the history of this dogma, unravel the strands that, woven together, have produced it. In its present form it is a modern phenomenon developing from the eighteenth century on, but that it is now dominant in the world is clear" (Fosdick, *Hope of the World*, 159). King had a copy of *Hope of the World* in his home study. King Jr., "First Things First," August 2, 1953, in *Papers of Martin Luther King, Jr.*, 6: 143–46; King Jr., "Communism's Challenge to Christianity," August 9, 1953, ibid., 6: 146–50. King used three paragraph-long sections of Fosdick's "Righteousness First" (Fosdick, *A Great Time to Be Alive*, 21–30). For his message on communism, King used several sections of McCracken's "The Christian Attitude to Communism" (McCracken, *Questions People Ask*, 164–69). For further consideration of King's homiletic plagiarism, see Miller, *Voice of Deliverance*; Lischer, *Preacher King*; Dyson, *I May Not Get There with You*; and Warren, *King Came Preaching*.

27. Introduction to vol. 2 of *Papers of Martin Luther King, Jr.*, 2: 12–13.

28. Bellamy, *Looking Backward: 2000–1887*; Scott to King, April 7, 1952, in *Papers of Martin Luther King, Jr.*, 6: 124; King to Coretta Scott, July 18, 1952, ibid., 6: 123–26. See also King Jr., "Civilization's Great Need," 1949, ibid., 6: 86–88.

29. King Jr., "Mastering Our Evil Selves," June 5, 1949, in *Papers of Martin Luther King, Jr.*, 6: 94–97; King Jr., "Splinters and Planks," July 24, 1949, ibid., *Papers*, 6: 97–99.

30. King Jr., "Loving Your Enemies," August 31, 1952, in *Papers of Martin Luther King, Jr.*, 6: 126–28. King continued to challenge racism and call for social change during the summer of 1953. In a sermon on the influence of nationalism, King noted, "In America it is preached by the McCarthys and the Jenners, the advocators of white supremacy, and the America first move-

ments" (King Jr., "The False God of Nationalism," July 12, 1953, ibid., 6: 132–33). In a later sermon, King declared his allegiance to a socially engaged Christianity: "I happen to be a firm believer in what is called the 'social gospel.' Indeed, no one can intelligently care for personal life without caring about genetics and social reform" (King Jr., "Accepting Responsibility for Your Actions," July 26, 1953, ibid., 6: 139–42). In a sermon assessing communism, King acknowledged their "strong attempt to eliminate racial prejudice. Communism seeks to transcend the superficialities of race and color, and you are able to join the Communist party whatever the color of your skin or the quality of blood in your veins." Later in the sermon, King lamented: "Slavery could not have existed in America for more than two hundred fifty years if the Church had not sanctioned it. Segregation and discrimination could not exist in America today without the sanction of the Church. I am ashamed and appalled at the fact that Eleven O'Clock on Sunday morning is the most segregated hour in Christian America" (King Jr., "Communism's Challenge to Christianity," August 9, 1953, ibid., 6: 146–50).

31. Jo Ann Robinson, "Negroes Eat Too," *Montgomery Advertiser,* October 13, 1952.

32. In addition to Vernon Johns, the tenure of Alfred Charles Livingston Arbouin as the pastor of Dexter was cut short when his wife struck up a friendship with a Maxwell Air Force Base soldier while Arbouin attended the 1946 National Baptist Convention. The deacons ended up forcing Arbouin out through the courts, although the whole matter was done in secret (Roberson, *Fighting the Good Fight,* 75–79; Branch, *Parting the Waters,* 5–6). Vaughn and Wills, eds., *Reflections on our Pastor,* 3–4. The Dexter deacon Joseph T. Brooks wrote King's parents in mid-November in an effort to find out when King Jr. would be home from Boston so that the church could arrange to have him preach as a candidate for their vacant pulpit. Brooks commented, "I have heard so many fine things about him and his ability and possibility, that I am intensely interested in having him down." King Jr. responded to the letter the next week, noting he would be able to preach at Dexter on the second or third Sunday in January (J. T. Brooks to Martin Luther King Sr., and Alberta Williams King, November 16, 1953; King to J. T. Brooks, November 24, 1953 in *The Papers of Martin Luther King, Jr.,* 2: 211, 221).

3. "Making a Contribution"

1. For a description of King's job opportunities, his interest in Dexter, and the history of the congregation, see the introduction to vol. 2 of *Papers of*

Martin Luther King, Jr., 2: 28–31. Lischer explains why King elected to serve as a pastor rather than pursue a job as a professor: "Ebenezer had taught King that the basic unit of Christianity in the world is the congregation. Although he had absorbed the universal principle of liberalism, when the time came for him to embark upon a career, he turned again to the congregation as the only vehicle of redemption he knew. Perhaps he understood that Christianity was never meant to work in the lecture hall or at the level of abstract principles but, rather, among a community that is joined by race, family, neighborhood, and economics, but whose truest identity transcends all of these" (Lischer, *The Preacher King,* 74). Branch, *Parting the Waters,* 105–8.

2. *Montgomery Advertiser,* January 24, 1954.

3. Coretta Scott King claims "Three Dimensions" was the first sermon she heard King preach (Coretta Scott King, *My Life with Martin Luther King, Jr.,* 59). King also delivered a sermon with this title in September 1953 while serving at Ebenezer ("King Jr. to End Series of Summer Sermons; Ebenezer," *Atlanta Daily World,* September 5, 1953). King borrowed the primary outline of "Three Dimensions" from Phillips Brooks's sermon "The Symmetry of Life," found in Brooks, *Selected Sermons,* 195–206. King Jr., *Stride toward Freedom,* 17; King Jr., "The Dimensions of a Complete Life," January 24, 1954, in *Papers of Martin Luther King, Jr.,* 6: 150–56.

4. Nesbitt and Randall to King, March 7, 1954, and King to Pulpit Committee, Dexter Avenue Baptist Church, March 10, 1954, in *Papers of Martin Luther King, Jr.,* 2: 256, 258. James Dombrowski recorded this incident in his diary on February 8, 1954 (Mss 566, Folder 4, Box 15, Dombrowski Papers). Virginia Durr to Marge Frantz, February 1954, in Sullivan, ed., *Freedom Writer,* 64.

5. *Alabama Tribune,* April 2, 1954.

6. Jo Ann Robinson to Mayor Gayle, May 21, 1954, in Garrow, ed., *The Montgomery Bus Boycott and the Women Who Started It,* viii.

7. King Jr., "Going Forward by Going Backward," April 4, 1954, in *Papers of Martin Luther King, Jr.,* 6: 159–63. The sermon's content parallels the body of a sermon he delivered five weeks earlier in Detroit (King Jr., "Rediscovering Lost Values," ibid., 2: 248–56). King also delivered a version of this sermon on August 16, 1953, at Ebenezer Baptist Church.

8. King Jr., "Accepting Responsibility for Your Actions," July 26, 1953, ibid., 6: 139–42. On the inside of the folder containing this sermon, King wrote: "ΑΡΥΛ: Preached at Dexter May 2, 1954."

9. King Jr., "Acceptance Address at Dexter Avenue Baptist Church," May 2, 1954, ibid., 6: 164–67.

10. E. D. Nixon, "It Took Guts to Do These Things," in Wigginton, ed., *Refuse to Stand Silently By,* 221.

11. *Alabama Tribune,* December 18, 1953.

12. *Montgomery Advertiser,* April 15, 1954, April 17, 1954, May 2, 1954. The four male officers were Lee E. Jarrett, Walter L. Jarrett, Willie C. Miller, and Arthur G. Worthy. The editorial board of the *Alabama Tribune,* in its October 1, 1954, issue, praised the City of Montgomery for "taking the lead in Alabama in the area of sound civic progress. It recently placed three Negro women on its police force to bring its number of Negro law enforcement officers up to seven. It is the first Alabama city to employ Negro women for school traffic purposes."

13. King Jr., "Mental and Spiritual Slavery," May 1954, in *Papers of Martin Luther King, Jr.,* 6: 167–70.

14. King Jr., "A Religion of Doing," July 4, 1954, in *Papers of Martin Luther King, Jr.,* 6: 170–74. King adapted this quotation from Fosdick's sermon "There Is No Death," in which Fosdick wrote: "I plead instead for a church that will be a fountainhead of a better social order. Any church that pretends to care for the souls of people but is not interested in the slums that damn them, the city government that corrupts them, the economic order that cripples them, and international relations that, leading to peace or war, determine the spiritual destiny of innumerable souls—that kind of church, I think, would hear again the Master's withering words: 'Scribes and Pharisees, hypocrites!'" (Harry Emerson Fosdick, *The Hope of the World,* 25). King, "What Is Man?" July 11, 1954, in *Papers of Martin Luther King, Jr.,* 6: 174–79.

15. Wigginton, ed., *Refuse to Stand Silently By,* 221. See also Gray, Leventhal, Sikora, and Thornton, *The Children Coming On,* 13–14. Virginia Durr to Mairi and Clark Foreman, September 8, 1954, in Sullivan, ed., *Freedom Writer,* 75; *Alabama Tribune,* September 10, 1954.

16. King Jr., "God's Love," December 23, 1962, ET-40, Martin Luther King Estate Collection. King may have gotten this illustration from Howard Thurman's *Jesus and the Disinherited,* 50. King, "God's Love," September 5, 1954, in *Papers of Martin Luther King, Jr.,* 6: 179–81.

17. King Jr., "Vision of a World Made New," September 9, 1954, in *Papers of Martin Luther King, Jr.,* 6: 181–84.

18. Warlick, "'Man of the Year' for '54," 27; *Alabama Tribune,* July 30, 1954; *Montgomery Advertiser,* "Colored Section," November 23, 1954.

19. Garrow, ed., *The Montgomery Bus Boycott and the Women Who Started It,* 37.

20. King Jr., *Stride toward Freedom,* 27, 34.

21. King Jr., "Recommendations to the Dexter Avenue Baptist Church for the Fiscal Year 1954–1955," September 5, 1955, in *Papers of Martin Luther King, Jr.*, 2: 287.

22. For a critique of King's model of leadership that draws on his acceptance address at Dexter, see Ransby, *Ella Baker and the Black Freedom Movement*, 170–95.

23. Baldwin, *There Is a Balm in Gilead*, 312; Lischer, *The Preacher King*, 78.

24. King Jr., "Recommendations to the Dexter Avenue Baptist Church for the Fiscal Year 1954–1955," September 5, 1955, in *Papers of Martin Luther King, Jr.*, 2: 290. King Jr., *Stride toward Freedom*, 30.

25. Coretta Scott King, "Answers, Voter Registration Questionnaire of the Dexter Avenue Baptist Church Social and Political Action Committee," October 17, 1954, Folder 15, Box 77, King Papers, 1954–1968, Boston University; Mary Fair Burks, "Social and Political Action Committee, Report 3," October 31, 1954, Folder 15, Box 77, ibid.

26. King Jr., *Stride toward Freedom*, 26–27. Lewis Baldwin argues that "some of King's most profound and inspiring sermons were delivered at the Dexter Avenue Baptist Church in the year prior to the Rosa Parks incident. He went to Dexter with the notion that sermonizing involved the proclamation of God's word in relationship to a myriad of human concerns, and with the idea that every sermon should have as its purpose the head-on constructive meeting of some spiritual, social, cultural, or personal problem that puzzles the mind, bears upon the conscience, and interferes with the complete flow of life" (Baldwin, *There Is a Balm in Gilead*, 288). Likewise, Lischer notes: "King came to his first congregation with a cache of sermon manuscripts he had developed in his college and graduate school days. During his first year he worked very hard at producing and memorizing new manuscripts, which he pointedly left on his chair when he rose to enter the pulpit. He also brought with him a repertoire of poetic verses and longer set pieces already committed to memory and distributed throughout his body of sermons" (Lischer, *The Preacher King*, 80–81).

27. Rice, interview by Lumpkin; Underwood, interview by Lumpkin; Gray, Leventhal, Sikora, and Thornton, *The Children Coming On*, 133.

28. King Jr., "Propagandizing Christianity," September 12, 1954, in *Papers of Martin Luther King, Jr.*, 6: 184–87.

29. King Jr., "New Wine in New Bottles," October 17, 1954, in *Papers of Martin Luther King, Jr.*, 6: 192–94.

30. The glowing memories of King before the boycott by Nixon, Carr, and other Montgomery residents may not have been as pronounced at the

time. Although King undoubtedly impressed them, they would always view King through the lens of his civil rights leadership, coloring their earliest recollections. Rosa Parks, minutes, Montgomery branch meeting, January 9, 1955, Montgomery NAACP Papers (NN-Sc). Nixon, interview by Lumpkin. In this interview, Nixon claimed he heard King speak on the second Sunday in August 1955. While King was unanimously elected to the branch's executive committee at that meeting, there is no indication in the very thorough minutes of the event that King offered any remarks, suggesting Nixon was recalling his response to this January speech (Rosa Parks, minutes, Montgomery branch executive committee meeting, August 14, 1955, Montgomery NAACP Papers, [NN-Sc]). Johnnie Carr, interview by Steven M. Millner, July 17, 1977, in Garrow, ed. *The Walking City,* 529. Carr also claims she first heard King in August 1955, but credits the Dexter deacon R. D. Nesbitt with introducing King. In this January meeting, however, King was introduced by Ralph Abernathy. Carr may have remembered King's June address to the NAACP, when he was introduced by Nesbitt (Rosa Parks, minutes, mass meeting at First CME Church, June 19, 1955, Montgomery NAACP Papers [NN-Sc]).

31. *Montgomery Advertiser,* January 12, 1955.

32. Dexter Avenue Baptist Church, "Social and Political Action Committee Digest, Number 2," January 1955, Folder 15, Box 77, King Papers, Boston University; King Jr., *Stride toward Freedom,* 34–35.

33. *Alabama Tribune,* January 28, 1955.

34. Virginia Durr to Corliss Lamont, February 9, 1955, in Sullivan, ed., *Freedom Writer,* 81.

35. "Negroes' Most Urgent Needs," LPR 127, Baskin Papers.

36. Thornton, *Dividing Lines,* 49.

37. The *Montgomery Advertiser* city editor Joe Azbell devoted a significant portion of his March 1, 1955, editorial to the housing dilemma faced by the city's African American residents. Noting that some believed "the Negro housing situation will become so critical this year some move will have to be started to open new subdivisions," Azbell referenced James Holt, the president of the First Federal Savings and Loan Association, who called the housing crisis for blacks in Montgomery the largest housing problem the city faced." The editor suggested no possible solutions to the problem (Joe Azbell, "City Limits," *Montgomery Advertiser,* March 1, 1955). *Montgomery Advertiser,* March 20, 1955; J. Mills Thornton, "Challenge and Response in the Montgomery Bus Boycott of 1955–1956," in Garrow, ed., *The Walking City,* 336. Thornton examines the demographic and political shifts that occurred in Montgomery in the 1950s. He notes that the "Demographic

exploitation of racial tensions promised to counter Birmingham's exploitation of class tensions and thus to capture support in the eastern wards" where
many working-class whites were moving in (335–36). Parks, an ally of Birmingham, defeated the incumbent Cleere, while Gayle returned as mayor.
Thornton adds: "The lesson of Parks's victory appeared to be that, given
the new social realities produced by the city's rapid postwar growth, an East
Montgomerian would always defeat a South Montgomerian when the issues
remained class oriented. The lesson of Sellers's victory appeared to be that a
vigorous exploitation of racial antipathies could give a South Montgomerian
at least a fighting chance of defeating an East Montgomerian. Gayle was, of
course, a South Montgomerian. But Gayle's dilemma was much more complicated than this analysis would imply. First, he was unlikely to abandon a set
of beliefs that he had held sincerely for many decades merely because political
strategy seemed to dictate this course. Second, developments within the business community rendered it less than certain that a sound strategy actually
dictated this course" (337–38).

38. West, interview by Lee; Virginia Durr to Jessica Mitford, March 1955,
in Sullivan, ed., *Freedom Writer*, 84–85. See also Rosa Parks, minutes, Montgomery branch executive committee meeting, March 22, 1955, Montgomery NAACP Papers (NN-Sc).

39. Virginia Durr to Jessica Mitford, March 1955, April 8, 1955, May
5, 1955, and May 6, 1955, in Sullivan, ed., *Freedom Writer*, 84–87. At an
NAACP meeting in July, the attorney Fred Gray indicated he "paid 47.50
for the Claudette Colvin case transcript. Since the violation of the segregation of transportation law charge was dismissed against her, the NAACP
has no case but to have her exonerated of the assault and battery charge."
Noting Colvin was on probation and a ward of the state, Gray informed
the executive committee that he had filed a motion for a new trial, hoping
she would be exonerated due to false arrest. The branch agreed to appeal
the Colvin case on these grounds (Rosa Parks, minutes, Montgomery branch
executive committee meeting, July 13, 1955, Montgomery NAACP Papers
[NN-Sc]).

40. Abernathy, "The Natural History of a Social Movement," in Garrow,
ed., *The Walking City*, 109–10.

41. King Jr., "Other Mountains," May 15, 1955, in *Papers of Martin
Luther King, Jr.*, 6: 214. See also Trenholm to King, May 2, 1955, ibid., 2:
556–57.

42. Rosa Parks, minutes, mass meeting at First CME Church, June 19,
1955, Montgomery NAACP Papers (NN-Sc); King, "The Peril of Superficial
Optimism in the Area of Race Relations," June 19, 1955, in *Papers of Mar-*

tin Luther King, Jr., 6: 214–15; King Jr., "Discerning the Signs of History," June 26, 1955, ibid., 6: 216–19.

43. King Jr., "The Death of Evil upon the Seashore," July 24, 1955, Folder 101, Sermon File.

44. Graetz, *A White Preacher's Memoir: The Montgomery Bus Boycott* (Montgomery: Black Belt Press, 1998), 35–37.

45. Ibid., 50.

46. Juliette Morgan to William A. Gayle, July 13, 1955, Box 4, Morgan Papers.

47. Rosa Parks, minutes, Montgomery branch executive committee meeting, July 13, 1955, Montgomery NAACP Papers (NN-Sc). Founded in 1932, the Highlander Folk School served as a critical southern training center for labor and civil rights activists.

48. Rosa Parks to Mrs. Henry F. Shepherd, July 6, 1955, Mss 265, Folder 22, Box 22, Highlander Research and Education Center; Parks, with Haskins, *Rosa Parks: My Story*, 102–7.

49. Rosa Parks, minutes, Montgomery branch executive committee meeting, August 14, 1955, Montgomery NAACP Papers (NN-Sc).

50. Virginia Durr to Jessica Mitford, May 6, 1955, in Sullivan, ed., *Freedom Writer*, 87–88; Yeakey, "The Montgomery Alabama Bus Boycott, 1955–56," 9–13, 16–18.

51. Yeakey, "The Montgomery Alabama Bus Boycott, 1955–1956," 22–23. Lamont Yeakey, in his dissertation on the bus boycott, claims that Montgomery's black clubs and social organizations "crisscrossed class, geographic, and occupational lines." His only support for this assertion is based on an anecdote of a time when a club reached out to help a poor family who had lost their home to a fire when they heard about the family's plight. While such charitable contributions did provide some connection between the classes, they were predicated on a paternalistic model of racial uplift. For the most part, the clubs and social circles reinforced rather than broke down class distinctions (ibid., 50–53).

52. King Jr., "Worship," August 7, 1955, in *Papers of Martin Luther King, Jr.*, 6: 222–25. In *Stride toward Freedom*, King used similar language to describe his earliest impressions of Dexter: "I was anxious to change the impression in the community that Dexter was a sort of silk-stocking church catering only to a certain class. Often it was referred to as the 'big folks church.' Revolting against this idea, I was convinced that worship at its best is a social experience with people of all levels of life coming together to realize their oneness and unity under God. Whenever the church, consciously or unconsciously, caters to one class it loses the spiritual force of the 'whosoever

will, let them come' doctrine, and is in danger of becoming little more than a social club with a thin veneer of religiosity" (25).

53. King Jr., "Looking Beyond Your Circumstances," September 18, 1955, in *Papers of Martin Luther King, Jr.*, 6: 225–30.

54. For more on the death of Emmett Till and its significance, see Whitfield, *A Death in the Delta*. King, "Pride versus Humility," September 25, 1955, in *Papers of Martin Luther King, Jr.*, 6: 230–34.

55. King Jr., "The Impassable Gulf (The Parable of Dives and Lazarus)," October 2, 1955, in *Papers of Martin Luther King, Jr.*, 6: 235–39. In developing this sermon, King relied on George Buttrick's insights on the parable (see Buttrick, *The Parables of Jesus*, 87–91).

56. J. Mills Thornton III, "Challenge and Response in the Montgomery Bus Boycott of 1955–1956," in Garrow, ed., *The Walking City*, 338–39.

57. "Annual of the Alabama Baptist State Convention, 1955," "Special Session," September 15, 1955; "Regular Session," November 15, 16, 17, 1955, Birmingham, Ala., p. 125, LPR 135, Folder 7, Box 7, Alabama State Archives.

58. Alabama Council on Human Relations newsletter, no. 4 (October 1955), Folder 5, Box 4, Baskin Papers.

59. King Jr., "The One-Sided Approach of the Good Samaritan," November 20, 1955, in *Papers of Martin Luther King, Jr.*, 6: 239–40.

60. Largely unaware of the content of many of King's early Dexter sermons, Richard Lischer erroneously concluded: "During the summer and fall of 1955 Pastor King reverted to a more philosophical style of preaching. He delivered well-rounded statements on the meaning of life, such as 'Discerning the Signs of History,' 'The Death of Evil upon the Seashore,' and 'The One-Sided Approach of the Good Samaritan.' During the first year he rarely attacked the problem of racism in Montgomery, though he did encourage and finally require NAACP membership and voter registration. When the bus crisis broke in December of that year, he suddenly found a focus and a climax for his sermons. The abstractions give way to the demands of the struggle. The sign of history par excellence is liberation. The evil that must die upon the seashore is segregation. The Good Samaritan now teaches not merely love but a dangerous love between the races. Everything has changed." He also mistakenly concludes that "In King's early speeches, the viciousness of racism is minimized" (Lischer, *The Preacher King*, 83–84, 87). King later described his first eighteen months in Montgomery as a time when "there was a ground swell of discontent. Such men as Vernon Johns and E. D. Nixon had never tired of keeping the problem before the conscience of the community. When others had feared to speak, they had spoken with courage. When oth-

ers had dared not take a stand, they had stood with valor and determination." He later added: "through the work of men like Johns and Nixon there had developed beneath the surface a slow fire of discontent, fed by the continuing indignities and inequities to which the Negroes were subjected. These were fearless men who created the atmosphere for the social revolution that was slowly developing in the Cradle of the Confederacy. But this discontent was still latent in 1954" (King Jr., *Stride toward Freedom*, 38–39).

4. "They Are Willing to Walk"

1. Gray, Leventhal, Sikora, and Thornton, *The Children Coming On*, 13.

2. Jo Ann Robinson, leaflet, *Another Negro woman has been arrested*, December 2, 1955, Montgomery County District Attorney's Files.

3. Gray, *Bus Ride to Justice*, 52. Steven M. Millner also stresses this point: "Nixon, and his political allies, Robinson and Burks, continued to move rapidly because they sensed they had to outflank the generally conservative local black clergy" (Millner, "The Montgomery Bus Boycott: A Case Study in the Emergence of a Social Movement," in Garrow, ed., *The Walking City*, 452). Garrow, ed., *The Montgomery Bus Boycott and the Women Who Started It*, 53. Regarding Robinson's critical role in the genesis of the boycott, her fellow WPC member Mary Fair Burks reflected: "nobody worked more diligently than she did as a member of the board of the Montgomery Improvement Association and as a representative of the Women's Political Council. Although others had contemplated a boycott, it was due in large part to Jo Ann's unswerving belief that it *could* be accomplished, and her never-failing optimism that it *would* be accomplished, and her selflessness and unbounded energy that it *was* accomplished" (Crawford, Rouse, and Woods, eds., *Women in the Civil Rights Movement*, 75). Rosa Parks, J. E. Pierce, Robert Graetz, "Montgomery Story," August 21, 1956, Highlander Folk School Papers.

4. *Southern Exposure* 9, no. 1 (Spring 1981): 14. According to David Garrow, Abernathy called King before Nixon's second call, and persuaded King to support the boycott (Garrow, *Bearing the Cross*, 18). Ibid., 53.

5. Garrow, ed., *The Montgomery Bus Boycott and the Women Who Started It*, 48–50. B. J. Simms, in an interview with Steven M. Millner, discussed the Alabama State College president's response to the boycott: "Trenholm just understood. He did not give any orders. He did not mention it. Did not try to curtail anybody. He was all for it. But officially he would never acknowledge it. He just didn't know, so to speak. He could be hypocritical just like white folks were" (Simms, interview by Millner, January 9, 1979, 584).

6. Garrow, ed., *The Montgomery Bus Boycott and the Women Who Started It*, 55; Ralph Abernathy, Martin Luther King Jr., and Jo Ann Robinson, leaflet, *Don't Ride the Bus*, December 2, 1955, in *Papers of Martin Luther King, Jr.*, 3: 67. Abernathy, "The Natural History of a Social Movement," in Garrow, ed., *The Walking City*, 118. In his thesis, Abernathy often referred to his own observations in the third person, as in his telling of this encounter between him and King, which he credits to "a distinguished Baptist preacher and perhaps the most effective leader of the movement in respect to strategies and operational tactics." Participants in the meeting at Dexter have remembered the gathering differently. King asserted that Bennett was so excited about the boycott, and so eager to direct the efforts, that he charged, "This is no time to talk; it is time to act." Only after nearly an hour of protests from the forty plus at the meeting did Bennett yield the floor, at which point plans for the boycott developed (King Jr., *Stride toward Freedom*, 46–48). Robinson remembered more than a hundred turning out for the meeting, highlighting the positive outcomes of the meeting rather than emphasizing any of its tension (Garrow, ed., *The Montgomery Bus Boycott and the Women Who Started It*, 55–56). Rosa Parks recalled a more divided meeting: "Some of the ministers wanted to talk about how to support the protest, but others wanted to talk about whether or not to have a protest. Many of them left the meeting before any decisions were made" (Parks, Haskins, *Rosa Parks: My Story*, 129). Uriah Fields asserts that Bennett opposed the boycott, which may have added to the aggravation of those gathered (Fields, *Inside the Montgomery Bus Boycott*, 36). Ralph Abernathy elevated his role in the meeting, saying Nixon had left it to him to make sure things went well in Nixon's absence. Believing he had arranged for Reverend Hubbard to lead the meeting, Abernathy was shocked when Hubbard announced Bennett would be presiding. After Bennett rambled on for some time, and with only around twenty people remaining, Abernathy claims he interrupted and took the chair for the rest of the meeting (Abernathy, *And the Walls Came Tumbling Down*, 138–39).

7. Crawford, Rouse, and Woods, eds., *Women in the Civil Rights Movement*, 82–83; Edgar N. French, "The Beginning of a New Age," 1962, in Garrow, ed., *The Walking City*, 177.

8. Crawford, Rouse, and Woods, eds., *Women in the Civil Rights Movement*, 83.

9. Ibid., 72–74.

10. King, "Why Does God Hide Himself?" December 4, 1955, in *Papers of Martin Luther King, Jr.*, 6: 241–42. King borrowed the title and theme of his sermon from Robert McCracken, "Why Does God Hide Himself?"

Radio Sermon, April 27, 1947. King kept a copy of McCracken's sermon in his homiletic files (King Jr., Folder 165, Sermon File).

11. Abernathy, "The Natural History of a Social Movement," in Garrow, ed., *The Walking City*, 119.

12. Warrant, *City of Montgomery vs. Rosa Parks,* December 5, 1955; Transcript of Record and Proceedings, *City of Montgomery vs. Rosa Parks,* December 5, 1955; Appeal Bond, *City of Montgomery vs. Rosa Parks,* December 5, 1955 (File 4559, Circuit Court, Montgomery County Records, Montgomery County Court House). Fred Gray mistakenly claimed Parks was found guilty of disorderly conduct (Gray, *Bus Ride to Justice,* 55–56). See also Thornton, *Dividing Lines,* 596–97n71. Nixon, interview by Millner, 547. Nixon also claimed regarding Parks's court case: "But you know, King, he wasn't there." According to Fred Gray, Ralph Abernathy, and personal recollections in his memoir of the boycott, King was in fact at the courthouse that morning (Gray, *Bus Ride to Justice,* 55–57; Abernathy, *And the Walls Came Tumbling Down,* 142; King Jr., *Stride toward Freedom,* 55).

13. Fields, *Inside the Montgomery Bus Boycott,* 41; Abernathy, "The Natural History of a Social Movement," in Garrow, ed., *The Walking City*, 129–30.

14. King Jr., *Stride toward Freedom,* 56–57.

15. Ibid., 56–58.

16. Fields, interview by Millner, 534.

17. Garrow, *Bearing the Cross,* 21–22. Steven M. Millner suggests the demand for black bus drivers was included to placate E. D. Nixon, "whose grass-roots organizing had put him in contact with hundreds of black men who had hopes that they could hold dignified and clean jobs. Many of these, who were called the 'forgotten fellows' by Nixon, had been ignored by their government and many local 'tie and collar' blacks, these individuals were appealed to by this request, and in other ways by leaders like E. D. Nixon" (Garrow, ed., *The Walking City*, 468). J. Mills Thornton also speculates that the demand to hire black bus drivers reflected the influence of Nixon in his meeting with French and Abernathy. He argues that Nixon was far more passionate about this demand than the clergy involved in the boycott (Thornton, "Challenge and Response in the Montgomery Bus Boycott of 1955–1956," in Garrow, ed., *The Walking City*, 599); Edgar N. French, "The Beginning of a New Age," 1962, ibid., 179.

18. Robinson, interview by Lee; *Alabama Tribune,* December 16, 1955.

19. King Jr., *Stride toward Freedom,* 59, 101.

20. MIA mass meeting at Holt Street Baptist Church, December 5, 1955, in *Papers of Martin Luther King, Jr.,* 3: 71–74; King Jr., *Stride toward Freedom,* 63.

21. Lewis and Ligon, interview by Lumpkin.

22. Gray, Leventhal, Sikora, and Thornton, *The Children Coming On,* 137; *American Socialist* 3, no. 4 (April 1956): 10.

23. Norman Walton, "The Walking City: A History of the Montgomery Bus Boycott," in Garrow, ed., *The Walking City,* 30. Walton's article was originally published in five installments in the *Negro History Bulletin,* beginning in October 1956 and ending in January 1958. Walton was a professor of history at Alabama State College. For more on the significance of early cab and carpool rides, see Millner, "The Montgomery Bus Boycott," in Garrow, ed., *The Walking City,* 474.

24. James Cone incorrectly assumes King did not develop his love ethic until later, stressing the central role of justice as his grounding principle early in the boycott: "No interpreter of King has identified justice as the primary focus of his thinking at the start of the Montgomery bus boycott. Most are so eager to stress love as the center of his thought and actions (as King himself did when he reflected on the event) that they (like King) fail to note that this was a later development in his thinking" (Cone, *Martin and Malcolm and America,* 63). While King did focus more of his Holt Street address on justice than love, his sermons prior to the bus protest reveal that the centrality of love was a core principle King brought to the movement, rather than one he gained through the struggle. Cone is right to emphasize the centrality of justice in King's pre-boycott preaching as well. In King's view, the love ethic of Jesus demanded a commitment to justice. For evidence of King's emphasis on love prior to the boycott, see King, "Loving Your Enemies," August 31,1952, in *Papers of Martin Luther King, Jr.,* 6: 126–28; and "God's Love," September 5, 1954, in *Papers of Martin Luther King, Jr.,* 6: 179–81. In his study of King's preaching, Richard Lischer also argues a transformation occurred during the boycott. Although unaware of the gradual sharpening of King's preaching in the months prior to his Holt Street address, Lischer captures the essence of the growth King experienced during this season: "After the Boycott had commenced, King's Sunday morning sermons found a new purpose and vitality. The specificity of *race,* which he had assiduously avoided in his graduate education, now sharpened the point of his biblical interpretation and preaching. No one sermon captured the transformation that was taking place within him, but his first major rhetorical triumph, the address to the massed protesters at the Holt Street Baptist Church in Montgomery, left him changed utterly" (Lischer, *The Preacher King,* 85).

25. Robinson, interview by Garrow. King included the story of Mother Pollard in his published sermon collection (King Jr., "Antidotes for Fear," in *Strength to Love,* 125).

26. Minutes, Alabama Council on Human Relations, December 7, 1955, in Burns, ed., *Daybreak of Freedom,* 97; Friedland, *Lift up Your Voice Like a Trumpet,* 27–28.

27. King Jr., *Stride toward Freedom,* 109–12; Tom Johnson, "4-Hour Huddle: Bus Boycott Conference Fails to Find Solution," *Montgomery Advertiser,* December 9, 1955, in Burns, ed., *Daybreak of Freedom,* 98–99; King to the National City Lines, Inc., December 8, 1955, in *Papers of Martin Luther King, Jr.* 3: 80–81; King, "Statement of Negro Citizens on Bus Situation," December 10, 1955, in *Papers of Martin Luther King, Jr.,* 3: 81–83.

28. Friedland, *Lift up Your Voice Like a Trumpet,* 28.

29. Juliette Morgan, "Lesson from Gandhi," *Montgomery Advertiser,* December 12, 1955.

30. Robert Graetz, letter to editor, *Time,* December 22, 1955, Folder 30, Box 107, King Papers, Boston University.

31. Vaughn and Wills, eds., *Reflections on Our Pastor,* 5–6, 16–17, 28.

32. Rosa Parks, minutes, Montgomery branch executive committee special meeting, December 13, 1955, Montgomery NAACP Papers (NN-Sc).

33. Garrow, ed., *The Montgomery Bus Boycott and the Women Who Started It,* 67. Michael Eric Dyson highlights the significant contributions of grassroots leaders in Montgomery whose efforts were minimized in *Stride toward Freedom:* "Without WPC's ingenious tactical maneuvers, quick response, and organizational efficiency, the Montgomery bus boycott may have never occurred. But beyond a token nod to their efforts and those of Rosa Parks, King barely recognized WPC's achievements in his account of the year-long boycott, *Stride toward Freedom.* Moreover, without the spur of grass-roots leaders like E. D. Nixon, the ministers who seized the helm of leadership, or were forced to take up the reins of the boycott—might never have acted bravely to exploit Parks's act of social rebellion for the black community" (Dyson, *I May Not Get There with You,* 203).

34. King, "Our God Is Able," January 1, 1956, in *Papers of Martin Luther King, Jr.,* 6: 243–46.

35. Richard Lischer argues King's sermons functioned similarly in 1968: "Although he is preaching to others the value of rising above the forces that threaten to destroy 'our personalities,' it is clear that the preacher, beleaguered by criticism of his anti-war activities and his plans for the Poor People's Campaign, is ministering to his own spirit. . . . As King desperately exhorts his congregation to choose life over death, it is himself he is urging to persevere" (Lischer, *The Preacher King,* 167–68). Cone, *Malcolm and Martin and America,* 124.

36. Parks, Horton, and Nixon, interview by Terkel.

37. Allen, interview by Millner, 522–23.

38. Burns, ed., *Daybreak of Freedom,* 139; King Jr., *Stride toward Freedom,* 78.

39. Uriah J. Fields, "Negroes Cannot Compromise," *Montgomery Advertiser,* January 5, 1956, in Burns, ed., *Daybreak of Freedom,* 113–14; Erna Dungee, MIA Executive Board minutes, January 23, 1956, ibid., 121–24.

40. "To the Commissioners of the City of Montgomery," January 9, 1956, in *Papers of Martin Luther King, Jr.,* 3: 97–98. *Montgomery Advertiser,* January 10, 1956.

41. *Alabama Tribune,* January 13, 1956.

42. King Jr., "How to Believe in a Good God in the Midst of Glaring Evil," January 15, 1956, in *Papers of Martin Luther King, Jr.,* 6: 247–49.

43. Hughes, interview by Holden.

44. Anna Holden, "Notes from ACHR meeting," January 20, 1956, Montgomery, Ala., Valien Collection.

45. King Jr., *Stride toward Freedom,* 125–26. The historian Steven M. Millner argues the response of the people to the settlement announcement was "a pointed warning to the MIA's leaders that they too had no room for shabby backroom deals that might be perceived as the proverbial sellout. The protest's leaders were thus put on notice that a firm refusal to back down was their sole leadership alternative. This strengthened the faction of militants with whom King increasingly aligned in backroom debates" (Millner, "The Montgomery Bus Boycott," in Garrow, ed., *The Walking City,* 478). MIA press release, "The Bus Protest Is Still On," January 22, 1956, in *Papers of Martin Luther King, Jr.,* 3: 100–101.

46. King Jr., "Redirecting Our Missionary Zeal," January 22, 1956, in *Papers of Martin Luther King, Jr.,* 6: 249–50.

47. Thrasher, interview by Holden. J. Mills Thornton claims Thrasher was at the meeting on January 21 with the three black ministers who agreed to the settlement. Thrasher and Hughes probably met with white ministers the previous week, came up with a proposed compromise solution, and presented it to the city commissioners and bus officials. Then, without Thrasher or Hughes present, these commissioners presented the plan to three hand-selected African American ministers, who accepted the plan without communication with the MIA. See Thornton, *Dividing Lines,* 72.

48. T. T. Allen to Ella Baker, March 29, 1942, Group II, Box C-4, Montgomery NAACP Papers; West, interview by Lee; King Jr., *Stride toward Freedom,* 78.

49. "Notes on MIA Executive Board Meeting, by Donald T. Ferron," January 23, 1956, in *Papers of Martin Luther King, Jr.,* 3: 101–5. Uriah

Fields claims King was in favor of dropping the demand for black bus drivers (Fields, *Inside the Montgomery Bus Boycott*, 79). King Jr., *Stride toward Freedom*, 114; Hughes, interview by Holden, January 18, 1956.

50. Thornton, *Dividing Lines*, 73.

51. Whatley, interview by Holden; Hughes, interview by Holden, March 27, 1956; Parks, Pierce, and Graetz, "Montgomery Story."

52. King Jr., *Stride toward Freedom*, 134–35.

53. Miller, *Voice of Deliverance*, 138; Cone, *Martin and Malcolm and America*, 124; Warren, *King Came Preaching*, 40; Baldwin, *There Is a Balm in Gilead*, 189n87.

54. "'Montgomery Dangerous' Negro Warns after Weekend of Violence," *New York Post*, January 28, 1957.

55. Burns, ed., *Daybreak of Freedom*, 128–29; Donald T. Ferron, "Notes on MIA Executive Board Meeting," January 30, 1956, in *Papers of Martin Luther King, Jr.*, 3: 109–12.

56. Willie Mae Lee, "Notes on MIA Mass Meeting at First Baptist Church," January 30, 1956, in *Papers of Martin Luther King, Jr.*, 3: 113–14.

57. Joe Azbell, "Blast Rocks Residence of Bus Boycott Leader," *Montgomery Advertiser*, January 31, 1956, in *Papers of Martin Luther King, Jr.*, 3: 114–15. For other accounts of the bombing and King's response, see Willie Mae Lee, "The Bombing Episode," January 31, 1956, Valien Collection; and King Jr., *Stride toward Freedom*, 136–38.

58. Miller, *Voice of Deliverance*, 87.

59. Burns, *Daybreak of Freedom*, 76–77. Burns cites transcript of *Browder v. Gayle* federal court testimony, Montgomery, Ala., May 11, 1956, p. 23 (Burns, ed., *Daybreak of Freedom*, 266); Lewis and Ligon, interview by Lumpkin.

5. "Living under the Tension"

1. King Jr., "It's Hard to Be a Christian," February 5, 1956, in *Papers of Martin Luther King, Jr.*, 6: 251–52.

2. Thornton, *Dividing Lines*, 78. Thornton argues the primary focus of the boycott was not integrating the buses, but rather challenging white supremacy. He asserts that the protesters "sought not the right to sit with whites, but rather the right not to be unseated in favor of whites, as well as at least a degree of protection from public humiliation at the hands of white bus drivers." While this may have been true for some in the boycott, Nixon and others in his camp always saw the legal side of the Parks case as the critical portion, with a trajectory that began four days before the decision was made

to extend the bus boycott indefinitely. While satisfying the conditions may have ended the boycott, it would not necessarily have ended the legal battle. Thornton more accurately describes the perspective of the white leadership in writing: "Segregation on the initiative of blacks and under black control was unacceptable because authorities' genuine motive, whether consciously or unconsciously, was not the separation of the races but the subordination of blacks to whites."

3. Donald T. Ferron, "Notes on MIA Executive Board Meeting," February 2, 1956, in *Papers of Martin Luther King, Jr.,* 3: 120.

4. Gray, *Bus Ride to Justice,* 70; Nixon, interview by Lumpkin, 2–3. See also Newton, *Montgomery in the Good War,* 137–38. According to J. Mills Thornton, Arthur Madison was persuaded by one of his brothers to return to the South to help the family gain the requisite number of registered voters to gain a municipal charter for Madison Park as an all-black town (Thornton, *Dividing Lines,* 28).

5. Donald T. Ferron, "Notes on MIA Executive Board Meeting," February 2, 1956, in *Papers of Martin Luther King, Jr.,* 3: 120, 122. See also Gray, *Bus Ride to Justice,* 78.

6. *Papers of Martin Luther King, Jr.,* 3: 121; Glasco, interview by Ferron; Wilson, interview by Ferron.

7. King, interview by Ferron. For further information on King's meeting with Folsom, see Cliff Mackay, "Ala. Bus Boycotters Sing 'My Country 'Tis of Thee,'" *Baltimore Afro-American,* February 11, 1956.

8. Donald T. Ferron, "Notes on MIA Executive Board Meeting," February 2, 1956, in *Papers of Martin Luther King, Jr.,* 3: 120. King later claimed that, after the bombing, friends and church leaders encouraged him to hire a bodyguard, which he resisted, claiming, "I had no fears now, and consequently needed no protection." He eventually acquiesced, however, and "also went down to the sheriff's office and applied for a license to carry a gun in the car; but this was refused" (King Jr., *Stride toward Freedom,* 140). King Jr., interview by Ferron.

9. Burns, ed., *Daybreak of Freedom,* 159. See also Garrow, *Bearing the Cross,* 66–67. Rustin, "Montgomery Diary," in *Liberation,* April 1956, 7.

10. Rustin, "Montgomery Diary," in *Liberation,* April 1956, 8.

11. Garrow, *Bearing the Cross,* 68.

12. John M. Swomley Jr. to Glenn Smiley, February 29, 1956, Fellowship of Reconciliation Papers; Garrow, *Bearing the Cross,* 70.

13. Burns, ed., *Daybreak of Freedom,* 153–54; Draper, *Conflict of Interests,* 22–24; Clifford Durr, interview by Holden. See also *Montgomery Advertiser,* February 11, 1956. Draper, *Conflict of Interests,* 31–32.

14. Frazier, interview by Holden.

15. Burns, ed., *Daybreak of Freedom*, 181; *Southern Exposure* 9, no. 1 (spring 1981): 18.

16. Lawrence Reddick, report on Fred D. Gray, July 17, 1956, Folder 7, Box 2, Reddick Papers.

17. Birmingham, interview by Holden.

18. Azbell, interview by Holden.

19. Box 3, Morgan Papers; Clifford Durr and Virginia Durr, interview by Lumpkin, 14–16; Morgan, interviews by Holden, February 7, 1956, March 26, 1956.

20. "Fellowship of the Concerned: The Supreme Court Decision—Building Community Understanding, Meeting Minutes," Folder 1, Andrews Collection; *The Children Coming On*, 203.

21. Parks, Pierce, and Graetz, "Montgomery Story."

22. King Jr., *Stride toward Freedom*, 121–22; Matthews, interview by Holden.

23. Ralph Abernathy, Memo to the Men of Montgomery, February 20, 1956, Garrow Collection; Matthews, interview by Holden; King Jr., *Stride toward Freedom*, 122.

24. *State of Alabama v. M.L. King, Jr.*, March 22, 1956, in *Papers of Martin Luther King, Jr.*, 3: 186–87; Lawrence D. Reddick, "The Bus Boycott in Montgomery," March 15, 1956, in Garrow, ed., *The Walking City*, 80; Abernathy, Memo to the Men of Montgomery, February 20, 1956.

25. Indictment, *State of Alabama v. M.L. King, Jr., et al.*, in *Papers of Martin Luther King, Jr.*, 3: 132–33; Bayard Rustin, "Montgomery Diary," *Liberation*, April 1956, 8.

26. King Jr., *Stride toward Freedom*, 143–46; Wayne Phillips, "Negroes Pledge to Keep Boycott," *New York Times*, February 24, 1956.

27. King Jr., "Faith in Man," February 26, 1956, in *Papers of Martin Luther King, Jr.*, 6: 253–55. See also Wayne Phillips, "Negro Pastors Press Bus Boycott by Preaching Passive Resistance," *New York Times*, February 27, 1956.

28. King's growing awareness of security issues led him to cancel a scheduled speaking engagement in Tuscaloosa, Alabama, noting "my present position of leadership in Montgomery demands that I take all precaution possible. The letter was sent a day after riots in Tuscaloosa had led to the temporary dismissal of Autherine Lucy from the University of Alabama. The invitation for King to speak in Tuscaloosa had come on January 10 and was subsequently accepted. Clearly, the climate in both Montgomery and Tuscaloosa changed significantly within a short month (King to Fred Drake,

February 7, 1956, in *Papers of Martin Luther King, Jr.*, 3: 127–28). Donald Ferron, "Report on MIA Mass Meeting," February 27, 1956, in Burns, ed., *Daybreak of Freedom*, 174.

29. In February, nearby Tuscaloosa played host to a showdown over the court-ordered integration of the University of Alabama. Autherine Lucy, in a case argued by the NAACP attorney Thurgood Marshall, had won admission to the school leading the university to admit her as the school's first black student on February 3. Peaceful protests soon gave way to rioting in the city. A few days later, the board of trustees decided Lucy could no longer attend classes out of concern for her own safety, and eventually the school suspended her. Montgomery residents committed to resisting racial change were undoubtedly emboldened by this reactionary course of action by University of Alabama officials (Burns, ed., *Daybreak of Freedom*, 43). An editorial in the February 7, 1956, *Tuscaloosa News* concluded: "Yes, there's peace on the University campus this morning. But what a price has been paid for it!" King, "When Peace Becomes Obnoxious," March 18, 1956, in *Papers of Martin Luther King, Jr.*, 6: 257–59.

30. King, "When Peace Becomes Obnoxious," March 18, 1956, in *Papers of Martin Luther King, Jr.*, 6: 257–59. King repeated the story of his encounter with a white Montgomery resident in *Stride toward Freedom*, 40.

31. "Testimony in *State of Alabama v. M.L. King, Jr.*," March 22, 1956, in *Papers of Martin Luther King, Jr.*, 3: 183–97. For further testimony from the trial, see Burns, ed., *Daybreak of Freedom*, 59–73.

32. King Jr., "Reactions to Conviction," March 22, 1956, in *Papers of Martin Luther King, Jr.*, 3: 198–99; King Jr., "Address to MIA Mass Meeting at Holt Street Baptist Church," March 22, 1956, ibid., 3: 199–201.

33. King Jr., interview by Azbell.

34. Reverend Thomas R. Thrasher, "Alabama's Boycott," March 1956, in Garrow, ed., *The Walking City*, 59–67.

35. Introduction to vol. 3 of *Papers of Martin Luther King, Jr.*, 3: 46; King Jr., "Address to MIA Mass Meeting at Day Street Baptist Church," April 26, 1956, ibid., 3: 230–32; King Jr., "Fleeing from God," April 29, 1956, ibid., 6: 259–61. See also Art Carter, "Rev. King is 'King' in Montg'ry," *Baltimore Afro-American*, May 12, 1956.

36. Almena Lomax, "Mother's Day in Montgomery," *Los Angeles Tribune*, May 18, 1956, in *Papers of Martin Luther King, Jr.*, 3: 263–67.

37. "Recommendations to MIA Executive Board," May 1956, ibid., 3: 271–73.

38. On April 25, 1956, National City Lines informed the MIA that they would be unable to guarantee the hiring of African American bus drivers due

to union contracts (*Papers of Martin Luther King, Jr.,* 3: 45). Burns, ed., *Daybreak of Freedom,* 138, 245. See also Lewis, interview by Ferron.

39. Garrow, ed., *The Montgomery Bus Boycott and the Women Who Started It,* 113–14; Robinson, interview by Lee.

40. King Jr., *Stride toward Freedom,* 73. For more on Solomon Seay's contributions, see Yeakey, "The Montgomery Alabama Bus Boycott," 83–93; Gray, Leventhal, Sikora, and Thornton, *The Children Coming On,* 226.

41. Gray, Leventhal, Sikora, and Thornton, *The Children Coming On,* 134; King Jr., *Stride toward Freedom,* 86.

42. Parks, Pierce, and Graetz, "Montgomery Story."

43. Ibid.; Lawrence D. Reddick, "The Bus Boycott in Montgomery," March 15, 1956, in Garrow, ed., *The Walking City,* 81.

44. Azbell, interview by Holden.

45. Underwood, interview by Lumpkin.

46. Thomas, interview by Lee.

47. *Race Relations Law Reporter* (August 1956): 669–78, in Burns, ed., *Daybreak of Freedom,* 272–73.

48. *American Socialist,* April 1956, 11.

49. Gray, Leventhal, Sikora, and Thornton, *The Children Coming On,* 13. Palmer, interview by Ferron.

50. MIA Nominating Committee to MIA President and Executive Board, May 24, 1956, Montgomery Improvement Association Collection. In the meeting, held on May 16, Fields was officially replaced by Reverend W. J. Powell as recording secretary. Nominating committee members included Reverend A. W. Wilson (chairman), Dr. Moses Jones, Mrs. Jo Ann Robinson, Reverend A. W. Murphy, Reverend B. J. Simms, Reverend R. J. Glasco, and Mrs. Erna A Dungee (secretary).

51. MIA newsletter, vol. 1, no. 2 (June 23, 1956), Montgomery Improvement Association Collection.

52. Nixon, interview by Millner, 550; Graetz, *A White Preacher's Memoir,* 107–8.

53. Carr, interview by Millner, 530; Simms, interview by Millner, 579; Fields, interview by Millner, 536; Nixon, interview by Millner, 548.

54. Allen, interview by Millner, 524–25.

55. King Jr., *Stride toward Freedom,* 157–58, 186. Following the bombing, Graetz sent a letter to the U.S. Justice Department seeking an investigation of all racially motivated violence in the city. In the letter to U.S. Attorney General Herbert Brownell, Graetz reported rumors that Commissioner Sellers may have had foreknowledge of the bombings of King's and Nixon's homes the previous winter. Regarding the bombing of his own home, Graetz

claimed he was most concerned about Mayor Gayle's assertion that blacks had done it for publicity: "And apparently the police have been ordered to find the colored people who did it, or at least someone that it can conveniently be blamed on. At least four colored men have been arrested with the bombing" (Graetz to Brownell, September 4, 1956, Graetz Papers).

56. William J. Powell, Montgomery Improvement Association, Special Committee Meeting minutes, September 25, 1956, Folder 16, Box 30, King Papers, Boston University.

57. King Jr., "Living under the Tension of Modern Life," September 1956, in *Papers of Martin Luther King, Jr.*, 6: 262–70.

58. King Jr., "The Fellow Who Stayed at Home," October 1956, ibid., 6: 272–75.

59. King penned these words in the margin of J. Wallace Hamilton's "The Fellow Who Stayed at Home," a sermon published in his book *Horns and Halos in Human Nature*, 172–73.

60. King Jr., *Stride toward Freedom*, 158–60; Garrow, *Bearing the Cross*, 80.

61. "Annual of the Alabama Baptist State Convention," One Hundred Thirty-Fourth Annual Session, November 13–16, 1956, 134–35, Alabama State Archives.

62. King Jr., *Stride toward Freedom*, 170–72.

63. Ibid., 69.

64. King Jr., "Conquering Self-Centeredness," August 11, 1957, in *Papers of Martin Luther King, Jr.*, 4: 255. Lerone Bennett later recalled his impressions of King during the boycott, remembering he had "a tremendous rapport with people from a platform. He had this—and even later—no matter how much it might have cost him personally—this ability to swing with people in the streets. People that he'd never seen. They'd say, 'Hey, Reverend,' and you know, he could deal with them" (Gray, Leventhal, Sikora, and Thornton, *The Children Coming On*, 238). *Dexter Echo* 1, no. 8, October 17, 1956, Folder 3, Box 2, Reddick Papers.

65. The historian Stewart Burns aptly notes how much King learned from the people of Montgomery: "King's responsiveness to ordinary people, his determination to learn from them and to absorb their varying perspectives, represented a distinguishing mark of his leadership from Montgomery until the end of his life." He continues: "Subleaders and foot soldiers not only strengthened his commitment but also emboldened him to take further risks and to rise above his comfort zone and socialization" (Burns, ed., *Daybreak of Freedom*, 15).

66. King Jr., "We Are Still Walking," *Liberation*, December 1956. The

articles listed six initiatives that would shape the MIA's future direction: to establish the black-owned bank in Montgomery; to organize a credit union that would mobilize resources for cooperative economic programs; to expand the number of registered African American voters in the city; to establish institutions to train people in nonviolent direct action; to shoulder some of the load of black leadership in Alabama after the outlawing of the NAACP; and "to give aid to those who have sacrificed in our cause." In Robert Graetz's memoir of the boycott, he recalls division within the MIA leadership regarding the optimal direction the organization should take. While a group comprised largely of clergy wanted to focus on "largely ceremonial goals" such as integrating the airport facilities, the larger group, composed of nonclergy and Graetz, wanted a program that would connect with the needs of the masses. "Though the clergy, the natural leaders in this church movement, attracted most of the spotlight, the lay participants included some of the most courageous and hard-working people in the Negro community" (Graetz, *A White Preacher's Memoir*, 109). Burns, ed., *Daybreak of Freedom*, 331–32.

6. "Bigger Than Montgomery"

1. King Jr., *Stride toward Freedom*, 175–76. For a detailed account of the agenda for the gathering in Atlanta, see "Montgomery Improvement Association Press Release, Bus Protestors Call Southern Negro Leaders Conference on Transportation and Nonviolent Integration," January 7, 1957, in *Papers of Martin Luther King, Jr.*, 4: 94–95.

2. King Jr., *Stride toward Freedom*, 176–77, 179–80.

3. King Jr., "The Ways of God in the Midst of Glaring Evil," January 13, 1957, in *Papers of Martin Luther King, Jr.*, 4: 107–9. King Jr., "Outline, Address to MIA Mass Meeting," January 14, 1957, ibid., 4: 109–10.

4. King Jr., *Stride toward Freedom*, 178; "King Says Vision Told Him to Lead Integration Forces," *Montgomery Advertiser*, January 28, 1957, in *Papers of Martin Luther King, Jr.*, 4: 114–15.

5. King Jr., interview by Richard Heffner, *The Open Mind*, February 10, 1957, in *Papers of Martin Luther King, Jr.*, 4: 126–31; Kwame Nkrumah to King, January 22, 1957, ibid., 4: 112–13; Vaughn and Wills, eds., *Reflections on Our Pastor*, 32. Fosdick published a book titled *A Great Time to Be Alive*.

6. MIA Future Planning Committee, meeting minutes, March 14, 1957, Folder 10, Box 2, King Papers, Boston University.

7. MIA Future Planning Committee, report, April 18, 1957, Folder 30, Box 16, King Papers, Boston University.

8. King Jr., "The Birth of a New Nation," April 7, 1957, in *Papers of Martin Luther King, Jr.,* 4: 155–67.

9. King Jr., "Questions Easter Answers," April 21, 1957, ibid., 6: 283–93.

10. King to Samuel McCrea Cavert, November 27, 1959, Folder 32, Box 33A, King Papers, Boston University; A. Philip Randolph, Martin Luther King, Jr., and Roy Wilkins, "Call to a Prayer Pilgrimage for Freedom," April 5, 1957, in *Papers of Martin Luther King, Jr.,* 4: 151–53; William Holmes Borders to King, April 6, 1957, ibid., 4: 153–54.

11. Bayard Rustin to King, May 10, 1957, in *Papers of Martin Luther King, Jr.,* 4: 199–201; King Jr., "Give Us the Ballot," May 17, 1957, ibid., 4: 208–15. King's reticence to draw strong connections between labor and the civil rights movement may be connected in part to the significant opposition he had faced from white unions in Montgomery during the bus boycott.

12. E. D. Nixon to King, June 3, 1957, ibid., 4: 217–18; King Jr., "Statement on Meeting with Richard M. Nixon," June 13, 1957, ibid., 4: 222–23; King Jr., "Remarks in Acceptance of the Forty-second Spingarn Medal at the Forty-eighth Annual NAACP Convention," June 28, 1957, ibid., 4: 228–32.

13. Clifford and Virginia Durr, interview by Lumpkin, 15–16.

14. King Jr., *Stride toward Freedom,* 85.

15. King Jr., "Conquering Self-Centeredness," August 11, 1957, in *Papers of Martin Luther King, Jr.,* 4: 248–59.

16. Durr to Horton, February 18, 1956, November 5, 1956, in Burns, ed., *Daybreak of Freedom,* 155, 298; Durr to Clark and Mairi Foreman, December 17, 1956, Durr Papers. The historian Steven M. Millner notes regarding the MIA's leadership at the end of 1956: "By the boycott's final days, the 'tie and collar' crowd and local ministers had become the dominant forces in the MIA. Grass roots leaders such as E. D. Nixon and Reverend Cherry became increasingly bitter about being pushed aside and left the MIA's leadership circle. Though King and his successors tried, no major effort paralleling the bus protest emerged in Montgomery. Lacking local issues to organize around and faced with a growing usurpation of organizational positions by status seekers, the MIA became further removed from the local black masses. This process escalated after King's permanent departure for Atlanta in early 1960" (Millner, "The Montgomery Bus Boycott," in Garrow, ed., *The Walking City,* 516).

17. King to Ralph Abernathy, February 26, 1957, in *Papers of Martin Luther King, Jr.,* 4: 143–44.

18. Parks, interview by Millner, 564; Rosa Parks to King, August 23,

1957, in *Papers of Martin Luther King, Jr.*, 4: 261. King Jr., "A Look to the Future," September 2, 1957, ibid., 4: 269–76; Nixon, interview by Lumpkin. See also Highlander Folk School, Program, "The South Thinking Ahead," September 2, 1957, Dexter Avenue King Memorial Baptist Church Collection.

19. King Jr., "Annual Report, Dexter Avenue Baptist Church," October 23, 1957, in *Papers of Martin Luther King, Jr.*, 4: 287–90.

20. King Jr., "Loving Your Enemies," November 17, 1957, ibid., 4: 315–24.

21. MIA newsletter, vol. 1, no. 7 (November 18, 1957), Montgomery Improvement Association Collection.

22. King Jr., "Some Things We Must Do," December 5, 1957, in *Papers of Martin Luther King, Jr.*, 4: 328–43.

23. Trezzvant W. Anderson, "How Has Dramatic Bus Boycott Affected Montgomery Negroes?" *Pittsburgh Courier*, November 9, 1957.

24. Ibid. See also John Henrik Clarke to King, December 20, 1957, in *Papers of Martin Luther King, Jr.*, 4: 344–45.

25. *Pittsburgh Courier*, November 16, 1957.

26. Ibid., November 23, 30, 1957.

27. "Anderson Criticized for 'Boycott' Article," *Pittsburgh Courier*, December 7, 1957.

28. Anderson, "How Has Dramatic Bus Boycott Affected Montgomery Negroes?" *Pittsburgh Courier*, December 14, 28, 1957.

29. King Jr., press release, "Announcement of the Crusade for Citizenship," November 5, 1957, in *Papers of Martin Luther King, Jr.*, 4: 307–8; King to the Southern Christian Leadership Conference, February 4, 1958, ibid., 4: 358–60; King Jr., "Address Delivered at a Meeting Launching the SCLC Crusade for Citizenship at Greater Bethel AME Church," February 12, 1958, ibid., 4: 367–71.

30. E. D. Nixon to King, November 4, 1957, Folder 15, Box 106, King Papers, Boston University; King to E. D. Nixon, March 6, 1958, in *Papers of Martin Luther King, Jr.*, 4: 376–77; Vaughn and Wills, eds., *Reflections on Our Pastor*, 8.

31. Burns, *To the Mountaintop*, 1; King Jr., "Statement Delivered at the Prayer Pilgrimage Protesting the Electrocution of Jeremiah Reeves," April 6, 1958, in *Papers of Martin Luther King, Jr.*, 4: 396–98. See also King Jr., *Stride toward Freedom*, 31–32; "Ministerial Group Scores Easter Negro Mass Meet" and "King's Group Accepts Invitation to Talks," *Montgomery Advertiser*, April 13, 1958.

32. For examples of the types of questions King fielded, and his responses,

see King Jr., "Advice for Living," from September 1957 to December 1958, in vol. 4 of *Papers of Martin Luther King, Jr.* A. Philip Randolph, Lester B. Granger, Martin Luther King, and Roy Wilkins, "A Statement to the President of the United States," June 23, 1958, ibid., 4: 426–29.

33. Davis accused Abernathy of having an extramarital affair with his wife, who was a member of Abernathy's First Baptist Church. Davis threatened Abernathy with a gun and a hatchet. A few months later, the jury dismissed assault charges against Davis ("Negro Jailed after Attack on Leader of Bus Boycott," *Montgomery Advertiser* August 30 1958; "Jury Rejects Abernathy Charges," *Montgomery Advertiser*, November 22, 1958); "King Charges Police Brutal after Arrest," *Montgomery Advertiser*, September 4, 1958; King Jr., "Statement to Eugene Loe," in *Papers of Martin Luther King, Jr.*, 4: 487–90.

34. E. D. Nixon to King, September 9, 1958, in *Papers of Martin Luther King, Jr.*, 4: 492. Nixon refers to Rustin's 1947 conviction for breaking North Carolina's segregation laws, following which Rustin spent twenty-two days on a chain gang to complete his sentence. For Rustin's journal entries during his incarceration, see Carbado and Weise, eds., *Time on Two Crosses*, 31–57. King to E. D. Nixon, September 16, 1958, in *Papers of Martin Luther King, Jr.*, 4: 494–95.

35. King, "Some Things We Must Do," December 5, 1957, in *Papers of Martin Luther King, Jr.*, 4: 328–43; *Pittsburgh Courier*, December 7, 1957.

36. Friedland, *Lift up Your Voice Like a Trumpet*, 30. See also Durr, *Outside the Magic Circle*, 309. Andrews, interview by Durr.

37. Andrews, interview by Durr.

38. King Jr., "A Knock at Midnight," September 14, 1958, in *Papers of Martin Luther King, Jr.*, 6: 347–50. King borrowed portions of this sermon from Niles, "Summons at Midnight."

39. King Jr., "Statement upon Return to Montgomery," October 24, 1958, in *Papers of Martin Luther King, Jr.*, 4: 513–14.

40. Vaughn and Wills, *Reflections on Our Pastor*, 31.

41. King, annual report, Dexter Avenue Baptist Church, November 18, 1958, in *Papers of Martin Luther King, Jr.*, 4: 537–39.

42. Kenneth L. Buford, William C. Patton, and King to Dwight D. Eisenhower, January 25, 1959, ibid., 5: 111–12; King to G. Mennen Williams, January 28, 1959, ibid., 5: 112–13.

43. "Account by Lawrence Dunbar Reddick of Press Conference in New Delhi on 10 February 1959," ibid., 5: 125–29; James E. Bristol to Corinne B. Johnson, March 10, 1959, ibid., 5: 137–42.

44. King, "A Walk through the Holy Land," March 29, 1959, ibid., 5: 164–75.

45. MIA newsletter, vol. 1, no. 12 (April 30, 1959), Montgomery Improvement Association Collection; *Montgomery Advertiser,* March 21, 1959.

46. Session of Trinity Presbyterian Church to Mrs. Arnold Smith, April 13, 1959, Folder 1, Andrews Collection; Fred L. Shuttlesworth to King, April 24, 1959, in *Papers of Martin Luther King, Jr.,* 5: 189–90. In the mid-1940s, Horace G. Bell had been one of Nixon's greatest critics, denouncing him in several letters to the NAACP national office in New York. See, for instance, Horace G. Bell to Ella Baker, November 25, 1945, Group II, Box C-4, Montgomery NAACP Papers; King to John Malcolm Patterson, May 28, 1959, in *Papers of Martin Luther King, Jr.,* 5: 216–17.

47. King, "A Tough Mind and a Tender Heart," August 30, 1959, in *Papers of Martin Luther King, Jr.,* 6: 372–78. King borrowed portions of this sermon from Gerald Kennedy, "The Mind and Heart," in Kennedy's *The Lion and the Lamb.*

48. Ibid. A number of Alabama State College professors lost their jobs in the spring of 1960 for supporting thirty-five ASC students who were arrested for staging a sit-in at the Montgomery County Court House snack bar. Among those losing their jobs were Lawrence Reddick, Jo Ann Robinson, and Mary Fair Burks (MIA newsletter, vol. 2, no. 3 [September 21, 1960], Gregory Papers, 1955–1965).

49. King to Simeon Booker, October 20, 1959, in *Papers of Martin Luther King, Jr.,* 5: 313–15.

50. King, "Draft, Resignation from Dexter Avenue Baptist Church," November 29, 1959, ibid., 5: 328-29. Based on his own experience and having explored the symbolic role Gandhi played in the Indian independence movement, King believed a successful freedom movement was enhanced by the presence of a symbolic leader. During the summer of 1959, King replied to a letter from an Angolan student who sought some assistance and advice for her nation's independence movement. Significantly, King suggested a good starting place would be to find an individual who would "stand as a symbol for your independence movement. As soon as your symbol is set up it is not difficult to get people to follow, and the more the oppressor seeks to stop and defeat the symbol, the more it solidifies the movement" (King to Deolinda Rodrigues, July 21, 1959, ibid., 5: 250–51). T. H. Randall to King, December 1, 1959, ibid., 5: 332.

51. King, "Address at the Fourth Annual Institute on Nonviolence and Social Change," December 3, 1959, ibid., 5: 333–43.

52. King to the Montgomery County Board of Education, August 28, 1959, ibid., 5: 270–72.

53. King, "Address at the Fourth Annual Institute on Nonviolence and Social Change," December 3, 1959, ibid., 5: 333–43.

54. Gray, Leventhal, Sikora, and Thornton, *The Children Coming On,* 131.

55. Underwood, interview by Lumpkin; Vaughn and Wills, eds., *Reflections on Our Pastor,* 12, 51. Richard Lischer believes a large part of the reason for King's departure was the difficulty sustaining growth at the church, given King's frequent absences: "Despite the fame of its pastor, the church was not thriving. In response to King's absenteeism and his delegation of his duties to others, the power of the deacons reasserted itself, and the pastor found himself 'under fire.' King was encouraged either to cut back on his outside commitments or to leave Dexter. When his responsibilities in the Movement led him back to Atlanta and his father's church, he left a congregation both saddened and relieved by his departure" (Lischer, *The Preacher King,* 79).

56. Vaughn and Wills, eds., *Reflections on Our Pastor,* 62, 80–81, 100.

57. "Dexter Honors Dr. & Mrs. King!!" *Dexter Echo,* February 3, 1960, MS 22 #722, Coretta Scott King Collection.

58. King, "Address Delivered during 'A Salute to Dr. and Mrs. Martin Luther King' at Dexter Avenue Baptist Church," January 31, 1960, ET-56, Martin Luther King Estate Collection.

59. King, "Address Delivered at the Montgomery Improvement Association's 'Testimonial of Love and Loyalty,'" February 1, 1960, ET-53, ET-54, Martin Luther King Estate Collection.

60. SCLC press release, "Dr King Leaves Montgomery for Atlanta," December 1, 1959, Folder 40, Box 35, King Papers, Boston University.

61. Lewis and Ligon, interview by Lumpkin.

Epilogue

1. Lawrence Dunbar Reddick, "The Montgomery Situation," April 1960, Folder 5, Box 2, Reddick Papers; H. Councill Trenholm to James McFadden, March 4, 1960, Folder 15, Box 2, ibid.

2. Virginia Durr to Clark Foreman, March 1960, in Sullivan, ed., *Freedom Writer,* 198–99.

3. Garrow, ed., *The Montgomery Bus Boycott and the Women Who Started It,* 168; Mary Fair Burks to King, March 31, 1960, Box 20, King Papers, Boston University; King to Mary Fair Burks, April 5, 1960, in *Papers of Martin Luther King, Jr.,* 5: 406–8; Mary Fair Burks, "Trailblazers: Women in the Montgomery Bus Boycott," in Crawford, Rouse, and Woods, eds., *Women in the Civil Rights Movement,* 76.

4. Friedland, *Lift up Your Voice Like a Trumpet,* 30. See also Durr, *Outside the Magic Circle,* 309.

5. King, "Statement at Mass Meeting Supporting Freedom Riders," May 21, 1961, Montgomery to Memphis Film Research Files; Montgomery Improvement Association Bulletin, November 25, 1961, box 4, White House Staff Files, Harris Wofford Files.

6. Thornton, *Dividing Lines,* 599n76.

7. Millner, "The Montgomery Bus Boycott," in Garrow, ed., *The Walking City,* 517.

8. King, "Address at the Steps of the State Capitol at the conclusion of the Selma to Montgomery March," March 25, 1965, Coretta Scott King Collection.

9. Nixon, interview by Millner, 551; King Jr., *Strength to Love,* 151–52; James Baldwin, "The Dangerous Road before Martin Luther King," *Harper's Magazine,* February 1961.

Bibliography

Primary Sources

Abernathy, Ralph David. *And the Walls Came Tumbling Down.* New York: Harper and Row, 1989.

Alabama Religious Organizations Publications. Alabama Department of Archives and History, Montgomery.

Allen, Erna Dungee. Interview by Steven M. Millner. August 6, 1977. In Garrow, *The Walking City,* 521–25.

Andrews, Olive. Collection. Alabama Department of Archives and History, Montgomery.

———. Interview by Virginia Durr. February 3, 1988. Transcript. Virginia Durr Oral History Collection, Alabama Department of Archives and History, Montgomery.

Azbell, Joe. Interview by Anna Holden. February 7, 1956. Transcript. Preston Valien Collection, Amistad Research Center, Tulane University, New Orleans.

Baskin, Inez Jesse Turner. Papers. Alabama Department of Archives and History, Montgomery.

Beech, Gould, and Mary Gould. Interview by Virginia Durr. 1988. Tape recording. Virginia Durr Oral History Collection, Alabama Department of Archives and History, Montgomery.

Birmingham, Dave. Interview by Anna Holden. February 1, 1956. Transcript. Preston Valien Collection, Amistad Research Center, Tulane University, New Orleans.

Brooks, Phillips. *Selected Sermons.* New York: Dutton, 1949.

Burns, Stewart, ed. *Daybreak of Freedom: The Montgomery Bus Boycott.* Chapel Hill: University of North Carolina Press, 1997.

Buttrick, George. *The Parables of Jesus.* New York: Harper and Brothers, 1928.

Carbado, Devon W., and Donald Weise, eds. *Time on Two Crosses: The Collected Writings of Bayard Rustin.* San Francisco: Cleis Press, 2003.

Carr, Johnnie. Interview by Steven M. Millner. July 17, 1977. In Garrow, ed., *The Walking City,* 527–32.

Crawford, Vicki L., Jacqueline Anne Rouse, and Barbara Woods, eds. *Women in the Civil Rights Movement: Trailblazers and Torchbearers, 1941–1965.* Brooklyn, N.Y.: Carlson, 1990.

Dexter Avenue King Memorial Baptist Church Collection. Montgomery, Ala.

Dombrowski, James. Papers, 1918–1980. University of Wisconsin Archives, Madison.

Durr, Clifford, and Virginia Durr. Interview by Norman Lumpkin. April 5, 1973. In *Statewide Oral History Project,* vol. 3, Alabama Center of Higher Education, 1974. Alabama State University Archives, Montgomery.

Durr, Virginia Foster. Papers. Schlesinger Library of the History of Women in America, Radcliffe College, Cambridge, Mass.

Fellowship of Reconciliation Papers. 1943–1973. Swarthmore College Peace Collection, Swarthmore, Pa.

Fields, Uriah J. *Inside the Montgomery Bus Boycott—My Personal Story.* Baltimore: AmErica House, 2002.

———. Interview by Steven M. Millner. November 25, 1977. In Garrow, ed., *The Walking City,* 533–36.

———. *The Montgomery Story: The Unhappy Effects of the Montgomery Bus Boycott.* New York: Exposition Press, 1959.

Fosdick, Harry Emerson. *A Great Time to Be Alive.* New York: Harper and Brothers, 1944.

———. *Hope of the World.* New York: Harper and Brothers, 1933.

———. *On Being Fit to Live With: Sermons on Post-war Christianity.* New York: Harper and Brothers, 1946.

———. *Successful Christian Living.* New York: Harper and Brothers, 1937.

Frazier, G. Stanley. Interview by Anna Holden. February 3, 1956. Transcript. Preston Valien Collection, Amistad Research Center, Tulane University, New Orleans.

Garrow, David. Collection. Emory University, Atlanta.

———, ed. *The Montgomery Bus Boycott and the Women Who Started It: The Memoir of Jo Ann Gibson Robinson.* Knoxville: University of Tennessee Press, 1987.

———, ed. *The Walking City: The Montgomery Bus Boycott, 1955–1956.* Brooklyn, N.Y.: Carlson, 1986.

Glasco, R. J. Interview by Donald T. Ferron. January 27, 1956. Transcript. Preston Valien Collection, Amistad Research Center, Tulane University, New Orleans.

Graetz, Robert S. *A White Preacher's Memoir: The Montgomery Bus Boycott.* Montgomery: Black Belt Press, 1998.

————. Papers. Privately held.

Gray, Frank D., Willy S. Leventhal, Frank Sikora, and J. Mills Thornton. *The Children Coming On . . . A Retrospective of the Montgomery Bus Boycott.* Montgomery: Black Belt Press, 1998.

Gray, Fred D. *Bus Ride to Justice: Changing the System by the System, the Life and Work of Fred D. Gray.* Montgomery, Ala.: Black Belt Communications Group, 1995.

————. Interview by Norman Lumpkin. September 1, 1973. In *Statewide Oral History Project,* vol. 4, Alabama Center of Higher Education, 1974. Alabama State University Archives, Montgomery.

Gregory, Hazel. Papers, 1955–1965. Center for Nonviolent Social Change, Atlanta.

Hamilton, J. Wallace. *Horns and Halos in Human Nature.* New York: Fleming H. Revell, 1954.

Hampton, Henry, and Steve Fayer, eds. *Voices of Freedom: An Oral History of the Civil Rights Movement from the 1950s through the 1980s.* New York: Bantam Books, 1990.

Highlander Folk School Papers. Tennessee State Archives, Nashville.

Highlander Research and Education Center Papers. Wisconsin Historical Society, Madison.

Hughes, Robert. Interviews by Anna Holden. January 18, 1956, March 27, 1956. Transcript. Preston Valien Collection, Amistad Research Center, Tulane University, New Orleans.

Kennedy, Gerald. *The Lion and the Lamb.* New York: Abingdon-Cokesbury, 1950.

King, Coretta Scott. Collection. Privately held.

————. *My Life with Martin Luther King, Jr.* New York: Holt, Rinehart, and Winston, 1969.

King, Martin Luther. Estate Collection. Privately held.

————. Interview by Joe Azbell. March 23, 1956. In *Papers of Martin Luther King, Jr.,* 3: 202–3.

————. Interview by Donald Ferron. February 4, 1956. In *Papers of Martin Luther King, Jr.,* 3: 125.

————. Papers. 1954–1968. Boston University, Boston.

————. *The Papers of Martin Luther King, Jr.* Vol. 1, *Called to Serve, January 1929–June 1951,* edited by Clayborne Carson, Ralph E. Luker, and Penny A. Russell. Berkeley and Los Angeles: University of California Press, 1992.

————. *The Papers of Martin Luther King, Jr.* Vol. 2, *Rediscovering Precious Values, July 1951–November 1955,* edited by Clayborne Carson, Ralph E.

Luker, Penny A. Russell, and Peter Holloran, Berkeley and Los Angeles: University of California Press, 1994.

———. *The Papers of Martin Luther King, Jr.* Vol. 3, *Birth of a New Age, December 1955–December 1956,* edited by Clayborne Carson, Stewart Burns, Susan Carson, Peter Holloran, and Dana L. H. Powell. Berkeley and Los Angeles: University of California Press, 1997.

———. *The Papers of Martin Luther King, Jr.* Vol. 4, *Symbol of the Movement, January 1957–December 1958,* edited by Clayborne Carson, Susan Carson, Adrienne Clay, Virginia Shradron, and Kieren Taylor. Berkeley and Los Angeles: University of California Press, 2001.

———. *The Papers of Martin Luther King, Jr.* Vol. 5, *Threshold of a New Decade, January 1959–December 1960,* edited by Clayborne Carson, Tenisha Armstrong, Susan Carson, Adrienne Clay, and Kieran Taylor. Berkeley and Los Angeles: University of California Press, 2005.

———. *The Papers of Martin Luther King, Jr.* Vol. 6, *Advocate of the Social Gospel, September 1948–March 1963,* edited by Clayborne Carson, Susan Carson, Susan Englander, Troy Jackson, and Gerald Smith. Berkeley and Los Angeles: University of California Press, 2007.

———. "Sermon File." Coretta Scott King Collection, privately held.

———. *Strength to Love.* New York: Harper and Row, 1963.

———. *Stride toward Freedom: The Montgomery Story.* New York: Harper, 1958.

———. "We Are Still Walking." *Liberation,* December 1956.

King, Martin Luther, Sr., with Clayton Riley. *Daddy King: An Autobiography.* New York: William Morrow, 1980.

Lewis, Rufus A. Interview by Donald T. Ferron. January 20, 1956. Transcript. Preston Valien Collection, Amistad Research Center, Tulane University, New Orleans.

Lewis, Rufus, and Eugene Ligon. Interview by Norman Lumpkin. June 25, 1973. In *Statewide Oral History Project,* vol. 3, Alabama Center of Higher Education, 1974. Alabama State University Archives, Montgomery.

Matthews, G. T. Interview by Anna Holden. March 27, 1956. Transcript. Preston Valien Collection, Amistad Research Center, Tulane University, New Orleans.

McCracken, Robert J. *Questions People Ask.* New York: Harper and Brothers, 1951.

Montgomery Branch, National Association for the Advancement of Colored People. Papers. 1940–1954. Library of Congress, Washington, D.C.

———. Papers. Minutes, 1954–1955. Schomburg Center for Research in

Black Culture, New York Public Library, New York. Cited in the notes as NN-Sc.

Montgomery County District Attorney's Files. Montgomery County Court House, Montgomery.

Montgomery Improvement Association Collection, Alabama State University Archives, Montgomery.

Montgomery to Memphis Film Research Files. Privately held.

Morehouse College Collection. Robert W. Woodruff Library Archives, Clark Atlanta University, Atlanta.

Morgan, Juliette. Interviews by Anna Holden. February 7, 1956, March 26, 1956. Transcript. Preston Valien Collection, Amistad Research Center, Tulane University, New Orleans.

Morgan, Lili Bess Olin. Papers. Alabama Department of Archives and History, Montgomery.

Niles, D. T. "Summons at Midnight." *Christian Century* 71 (1954): 1037–39.

Nixon, E. D. Collection. Alabama State University Archives, Montgomery.

———. Interview by Norman Lumpkin. April 11, 1973. In *Statewide Oral History Project,* vol. 3, Alabama Center of Higher Education, 1974. Alabama State University Archives, Montgomery.

———. Interview by Steven M. Millner. July 27, 1977. In Garrow, ed., *The Walking City,* 545–51.

Palmer, H. J. Interview by Donald T. Ferron. February 2, 1956. Transcript. Preston Valien Collection, Amistad Research Center, Tulane University, New Orleans.

Parks, Rosa. Interview by Steven M. Millner. January 20, 1980. In Garrow, ed., *The Walking City,* 553–67.

———, with Jim Haskins. *Rosa Parks: My Story.* New York: Puffin Books, 1992.

Parks, Rosa, Myles Horton, and E. D. Nixon. Interview by Studs Terkel. June 8, 1973. Highlander Research and Education Center Records, Wisconsin Historical Society, Madison.

Pierce, James. Interview by Norman Lumpkin. April 23, 1973. In *Statewide Oral History Project,* vol. 3, Alabama Center of Higher Education, 1974. Alabama State University Archives, Montgomery.

Reddick, Lawrence Dunbar. Papers. Schomburg Center for Research in Black Culture, New York Public Library, New York.

Rice, Thelma. Interview by Norman Lumpkin. August 22, 1973. In *Statewide Oral History Project,* vol. 3, Alabama Center of Higher Education, 1974. Alabama State University Archives, Montgomery.

Robinson, Jo Ann. Interview by David Garrow. April 5, 1984. Privately held.
———. Interview by Willie M. Lee. February 7, 1956. Transcript. Preston Valien Collection, Amistad Research Center, Tulane University, New Orleans.
———. Interview by Steven M. Millner. August 10, 1977. In Garrow, ed., *The Walking City*, 569–73.
Rustin, Bayard. "Montgomery Diary." *Liberation*, April 1956.
Simms, B. J. Interviews by Steven M. Millner. July 16, 1977, January 9, 1979. In Garrow, ed., *The Walking City*, 575–80 and 581–84, respectively.
Sullivan, Patricia, ed. *Freedom Writer: Virginia Foster Durr, Letters from the Civil Rights Years*. New York: Routledge, 2003.
Thomas, Althea Thompson. Interview by Willie Mae Lee. January 23, 1956. Transcript. Preston Valien Collection, Amistad Research Center, Tulane University, New Orleans.
Thrasher, Thomas. Interview by Anna Holden. January 23, 1956. Transcript. Preston Valien Collection, Amistad Research Center, Tulane University, New Orleans.
Thurman, Howard. *Jesus and the Disinherited*. New York: Abingdon Press, 1949.
Trenholm, H. Councill. Papers. Alabama State University Archives, Montgomery.
Trenholm, Portia. Papers. Alabama State University Archives, Montgomery.
Turnipseed, Andrew. Interview by Virginia Durr. 1988. Virginia Durr Oral History Collection, Alabama Department of Archives and History, Montgomery.
Underwood, O. B. Interview by Norman Lumpkin. August 17, 1973. In *Statewide Oral History Project*, vol. 4, Alabama Center of Higher Education, 1974. Alabama Department of Archives and History, Montgomery.
Valien, Preston. Collection, Amistad Research Center, Tulane University, New Orleans.
Vaughn, Wally G., and Richard W. Wills, eds. *Reflections on Our Pastor: Dr. Martin Luther King, Jr. at Dexter Avenue Baptist Church [1954–1960]*. Dover, Mass.: Majority Press, 1999.
"Walking Their Way to Freedom." *American Socialist* 3, no. 4 (April 1956).
Warlick, W. D. "'Man of the Year' for '54, Porter E. D. Nixon Is Montgomery's Choice." *Pullman News*, April 1955.
West, A. W. Interview by Willie Mae Lee. January 23, 1956. Transcript. Preston Valien Collection, Amistad Research Center, Tulane University, New Orleans.

Whatley, Raymond E. Interview by Anna Holden. January 26, 1956. Transcript. Preston Valien Collection, Amistad Research Center, Tulane University, New Orleans.
White House Staff Files. Harris Wofford Files. John F. Kennedy Library, Boston.
Wigginton, Eliot, ed. *Refuse to Stand Silently By: An Oral History of Grass Roots Social Activism in America, 1921–64.* New York: Doubleday, 1991.
Wilson, A. W. Interview by Donald T. Ferron. January 27, 1956. Transcript. Preston Valien Collection, Amistad Research Center, Tulane University, New Orleans.

Secondary Sources

Ansbro, John J. *Martin Luther King, Jr.: The Making of a Mind.* Maryknoll, N.Y.: Orbis Books, 1982.
Baldwin, Lewis. *There Is a Balm in Gilead: The Cultural Roots of Martin Luther King, Jr.* Minneapolis: Fortress Press, 1991.
———. *To Make the Wounded Whole: The Cultural Legacy of Martin Luther King, Jr.* Minneapolis: Fortress Press, 1992.
Bellamy, Edward. *Looking Backward: 2000–1887.* Boston: Tickner, 1888.
Bennett, Lerone. *What Manner of Man: A Biography of Martin Luther King, Jr.* Chicago: Johnson, 1968.
Berg, Manfred. *"The Ticket to Freedom": The NAACP and the Struggle for Black Political Integration.* Gainesville: University Press of Florida, 2005.
Billingsley, Andrew. *Mighty Like a River: The Black Church and Social Reform.* New York: Oxford University Press, 1999.
Borrow, Rufus, Jr. *Personalism: A Critical Introduction.* St. Louis: Chalice Press, 1999.
Branch, Taylor. *Parting the Waters: America in the King Years, 1954–1963.* New York: Simon and Schuster, 1988.
———. *Pillar of Fire: America in the King Years, 1963–1965.* New York: Simon and Schuster, 1998.
Brinkley, Douglass. *Rosa Parks.* New York: Lipper/Viking Press, 2000.
Burns, Stewart. *To The Mountaintop: Martin Luther King Jr.'s Sacred Mission to Save America: 1955–1968.* New York: HarperCollins, 2004.
Burrow, Rufus, Jr. *Personalism: A Critical Introduction.* St. Louis: Chalice Press, 1999.
Buttrick, George. *The Parables of Jesus.* Garden City, N.Y.: Doubleday, Doran, 1928.

Calloway-Thomas, Carolyn, and John Louis Lucaites, eds. *Martin Luther King, Jr., and the Sermonic Power of Public Discourse.* Tuscaloosa: University of Alabama Press, 1993.

Carson, Clayborne. *In Struggle: SNCC and the Black Awakening of the 1960s.* Cambridge: Harvard University Press, 1981.

Carter, Lawrence Edward, Sr., ed. *Walking Integrity: Benjamin Elijah Mays, Mentor to Martin Luther King Jr.* Macon, Ga.: Mercer University Press, 1998.

Chappell, David L. *A Stone of Hope: Prophetic Religion and the Death of Jim Crow.* Chapel Hill: University of North Carolina Press, 2004.

Colaiaco, James A. *Martin Luther King, Jr.: Apostle of Militant Non-Violence.* New York: St. Martin's Press, 1997.

Collier-Thomas, Bettye, and V. P. Franklin. *Sisters in the Struggle: African-American Women in the Civil Rights–Black Power Movement.* New York: New York University Press, 2001.

Cone, James H. *Martin and Malcolm and America: A Dream or a Nightmare.* Maryknoll, N.Y.: 1991.

Deats, Paul, and Carol Robb, eds. *The Boston Personalist Tradition in Philosophy, Social Ethics, and Theology.* Macon, Ga.: Mercer University Press, 1986.

Dittmer, John. *Local People: The Struggle for Civil Rights in Mississippi.* Urbana: University of Illinois Press, 1995.

Draper, Alan. *Conflict of Interests: Organized Labor and the Civil Rights Movement, 1954–1968.* Ithaca, N.Y.: ILR Press, 1994.

Durr, Virginia Foster. *Outside the Magic Circle.* Tuscaloosa: University of Alabama Press, 1985.

Dyson, Michael Eric. *I May Not Get There with You: The True Martin Luther King, Jr.* New York: Free Press, 2000.

Egerton, John. *Speak Now against the Day: The Generation before the Civil Rights Movement in the South.* Chapel Hill: University of North Carolina Press, 1994.

Eick, Gretchen Cassel. *Dissent in Wichita: The Civil Rights Movement in the Midwest, 1954–1972.* Urbana: University of Illinois Press, 2001.

Ennels, Jerome A., and Wesley Phillips Newton. *The Wisdom of Eagles: A History of Maxwell Air Force Base.* Montgomery, Ala.: Black Belt Press, 1997.

Erskine, Noel Leo. *King among the Theologians.* Cleveland: Pilgrim Press, 1994.

Eskew, Glenn. *But for Birmingham.* Tuscaloosa: University of Alabama Press, 1997.

Estes, Steve. *I Am a Man!: Race, Manhood, and the Civil Rights Movement.* Chapel Hill: University of North Carolina Press, 2005.

Evans, Zelia, and J. T. Alexander, eds. *The Dexter Avenue Baptist Church.* Montgomery, Ala.: Dexter Avenue Baptist Church, 1978.

Fairclough, Adam. *Race and Democracy: The Civil Rights Struggle in Louisiana, 1915–1972.* Athens: University of Georgia Press, 1995.

———. *To Redeem the Soul of America: The Southern Christian Leadership Conference and Martin Luther King, Jr.* Athens: University of Georgia Press, 1987.

Ferguson, Karen. *Black Politics in New Deal Atlanta.* Chapel Hill: University of North Carolina Press, 2002.

Friedland, Michael. *Lift up Your Voice Like a Trumpet: White Clergy and the Civil Rights and Antiwar Movements, 1954–1973.* Chapel Hill: University of North Carolina Press, 1998.

Fulop, Timothy E., and Albert J. Raboteau, eds. *African-American Religion: Interpretive Essays in History and Culture.* New York: Routledge, 1997.

Garrow, David J. *Bearing the Cross: Martin Luther King, Jr. and the Southern Christian Leadership Conference.* New York: Random House, 1986.

Halberstam, David. *The Children.* New York: Random House, 1998.

Harlan, Louis R. *Booker T. Washington: The Wizard of Tuskegee.* New York: Oxford University Press, 1983.

Honey, Michael K. *Southern Labor and Black Civil Rights: Organizing Memphis Workers.* Urbana: University of Illinois Press, 1993.

Korstad, Robert Rodgers. *Civil Rights Unionism: Tobacco Workers and the Struggle for Democracy in the Mid-Twentieth-Century South.* Chapel Hill: University of North Carolina Press, 2003.

Lassiter, Valentino. *Martin Luther King in the African American Teaching Tradition.* Cleveland: Pilgrim Press, 2001.

Lentz, Richard. *Symbols, the News Magazines, and Martin Luther King.* Baton Rouge: Louisiana State University Press, 1990.

Lewis, David Levering. *King: A Critical Biography.* New York: Praeger, 1970.

Lincoln, C. Eric, ed. *Martin Luther King, Jr.: A Profile.* New York: Hill and Wang, 1970.

Lincoln, C. Eric, and Lawrence Mamiya. *The Black Church in the African-American Experience.* Durham, N.C.: Duke University Press, 1990.

Lischer, Richard, ed. *The Company of Preachers: Wisdom on Preaching Augustine to the Present.* Grand Rapids, Mich.: Eerdmans, 2002.

———. *The Preacher King: Martin Luther King Jr. and the Word That Moved America.* New York: Oxford University Press, 1995.

Lofton, Fred C., ed. *Our Help in Ages Past: Sermons from Morehouse*. Elgin, Ill.: Progressive National Baptist Convention, 1987.

Marsh, Charles. *The Beloved Community: How Faith Shapes Social Justice from the Civil Rights Movement to Today*. New York: Basic Books, 2005.

Martin Luther King, Jr. Papers Project. "The Student Papers of Martin Luther King, Jr.: A Summary Statement on Research." *Journal of American History* 78, no. 1 (June 1991).

Mays, Benjamin E. *Born to Rebel: An Autobiography*. Athens: University of Georgia Press, 1987.

———. *The Negro's God as Reflected in his Literature*. Boston: Chapman and Grimes, 1938.

Miller, Keith D. *Voice of Deliverance: The Language of Martin Luther King, Jr. and Its Sources*. New York: Free Press, 1992.

Minchin, Timothy J. *The Color of Work: The Struggle for Civil Rights in the Southern Paper Industry, 1945–1980*. Chapel Hill: University of North Carolina Press, 2001.

Mitchell, Henry H. *Black Preaching*. Philadelphia: Lippincott, 1970.

———. *The Recovery of Preaching*. San Francisco: Harper and Row, 1977.

Mixon, Gregory. *The Atlanta Riot: Race, Class and Violence in a New South City*. Gainesville: University Press of Florida, 2005.

"Montgomery Bus Boycott." *Southern Exposure* 9, no. 1 (Spring 1981).

Morris, Aldon. *Origins of the Civil Rights Movement: Black Communities Organizing for Change*. New York: Free Press, 1984.

Newton, Wesley. *Montgomery in the Good War: Portrait of a Southern City, 1939–1946*. Tuscaloosa: University of Alabama Press, 2000.

Norrell, Robert J. *Reaping the Whirlwind: The Civil Rights Movement in Tuskegee*. New York: Knopf, 1985.

Oates, Stephen B. *Let the Trumpet Sound: The Life of Martin Luther King, Jr.* New York: Harper and Row, 1982.

Payne, Charles M. *I've Got the Light of Freedom: The Organizing Tradition and the Mississippi Freedom Struggle*. Berkeley and Los Angeles: University of California Press, 1995.

Ransby, Barbara. *Ella Baker and the Black Freedom Movement: A Radical Democratic Vision*. Chapel Hill: University of North Carolina Press, 2003.

Roberson, Houston Bryan. *Fighting the Good Fight: The Story of Dexter Avenue King Memorial Baptist Church, 1865–1977*. New York: Routledge, 2005.

Rogers, William Warren, Jr. *Confederate Home Front: Montgomery during the Civil War*. Tuscaloosa: University of Alabama Press, 1999.

Rogers, William Warren, Robert David Ward, Leah Rawls Atkins, and Wayne Flynt. *Alabama: The History of a Deep South State*. Tuscaloosa: University of Alabama Press, 1994.

Smith, Kenneth L., and Ira G. Zepp. *Search for the Beloved Community: The Thinking of Martin Luther King, Jr.* Valley Forge, Pa.: Judson Press, 1974.

Theoharis, Jeanne, and Komozi Woodard, eds. *Groundwork: Local Black Freedom Movements in America*. New York: New York University Press, 2005.

Thornton, J. Mills. *Dividing Lines: Municipal Politics and the Struggle for Civil Rights in Montgomery, Birmingham, and Selma*. Tuscaloosa: University of Alabama Press, 2002.

Warren, Mervyn A. *King Came Preaching: The Pulpit-Power of Dr. Martin Luther King Jr.* Downers Grove, Ill.: Inter-Varsity Press, 2001.

Weisbrot, Robert. *Freedom Bound: A History of America's Civil Rights Movement*. New York: Norton, 1990.

Westhauser, Karl E., Elaine M. Smith, and Jennifer A. Fremlin, eds. *Creating Community: Life and Learning at Montgomery's Black University*. Tuscaloosa: University of Alabama Press, 2005.

Whitaker, Matthew C. *Race Work: The Rise of Civil Rights in the Urban West*. Lincoln: University of Nebraska Press, 2005.

Whitfield, Stephen J. *A Death in the Delta: The Story of Emmett Till*. Baltimore: Johns Hopkins University Press, 1988.

Williams, Donnie, with Wayne Greenhaw. *The Thunder of Angels: The Montgomery Bus Boycott and the People Who Broke the Back of Jim Crow*. Chicago: Lawrence Hill Books, 2006.

Williams, John A. *The King God Didn't Save: Reflections on the Life and Death of Martin Luther King, Jr.* New York: Coward-McCann, 1970.

Williams, Johnny E. *African American Religion and the Civil Rights Movement in Arkansas*. Oxford: University Press of Mississippi, 2003.

Williams, Juan, and Dwayne Ashley. *I'll Find a Way or Make One: A Tribute to Historically Black Colleges and Universities*. New York: Amistad, 2004.

Wilmore, Gayraud. *Black Religion and Black Radicalism*. Garden City, N.Y.: Doubleday, 1972.

Yeakey, Lamont Henry. "The Montgomery Alabama Bus Boycott, 1955–56." Ph.D. diss., Columbia University, 1979.

Young, Andrew. *An Easy Burden: The Civil Rights Movement and the Transformation of America*. New York: HarperCollins, 1996.

Index